Therapist Self-Disclosure

Therapist Self-Disclosure gives clinicians professional and practical guidance on how and when to self-disclose in therapy. Chapters weave together theory, research, case studies, and applications to examine types of self-disclosure, timing, factors and dynamics of the therapeutic relationship, ethics in practice, and cultural, demographic, and vulnerability factors. Chapter authors then examine self-disclosure with specific client populations, including clients who are LGBTQ, Christian, multicultural, suffering from eating disorders, or trauma, in forensic settings, at risk for suicide, with intellectual disability, or are in recovery for substance abuse. This book will be very helpful to graduate students, early career practitioners, and more seasoned professionals who have wrestled with decisions about whether to self-disclose under various clinical circumstances.

Graham S. Danzer, PsyD is a graduate-affiliate of Alliant International University California School for Professional Psychology (CSPP). He is the author/ coauthor of 18 peer-reviewed articles, four full-length textbooks, and a textbook chapter in *The Encyclopedia of Individual and Personality Differences*. Dr. Danzer has also received 15 merit-based awards and commendations.

Therapist Self-Disclosure

*An Evidence-Based Guide
for Practitioners*

Graham S. Danzer, PsyD

Routledge
Taylor & Francis Group

NEW YORK AND LONDON

First published 2019
by Routledge
711 Third Avenue, New York, NY 10017

and by Routledge
2 Park Square, Milton Park, Abingdon, Oxon, OX14 4RN

Routledge is an imprint of the Taylor & Francis Group, an informa business

Library of Congress Cataloging-in-Publication Data
Names: Danzer, Graham, author.
Title: Therapist self-disclosure : an evidence-based guide for practitioners /
    Graham S. Danzer.
Description: New York, NY : Routledge, 2018. | Includes bibliographical
    references.
Identifiers: LCCN 2018019682| ISBN 9781138302235 (hbk : alk. paper) |
    ISBN 9781138302242 (pbk : alk. paper) | ISBN 9780203730713 (ebk)
Subjects: | MESH: Self Disclosure | Psychotherapy | Professional-Patient
    Relations | Counseling | Evidence-Based Practice
Classification: LCC RC480 | NLM WM 62 | DDC 616.89/14—dc23
LC record available at https://lccn.loc.gov/2018019682

ISBN: 978-1-138-30223-5 (hbk)
ISBN: 978-1-138-30224-2 (pbk)
ISBN: 978-0-203-73071-3 (ebk)

Typeset in Minion
by Swales & Willis Ltd, Exeter, Devon, UK

Contents

Contributors

Dr. Apryl Alexander is a Clinical Assistant Professor in the Graduate School of Professional Psychology at the University of Denver. She also serves at the Director of the Outpatient Competency Restoration Program at the Denver Forensic Institute for Research, Service, and Training (Denver FIRST). She received her Psy.D. in Clinical Psychology from the Florida Institute of Technology with concentrations in forensic psychology and child and family therapy. Her research broadly focuses on violence and victimization, forensic assessment, and trauma- and culturally-informed practice. Her work has been published in leading journals including *Journal of Forensic Psychology Practice, Child Maltreatment, Journal of Child Sexual Abuse*, and *Sexual Abuse: A Research and Treatment Journal*. Dr. Alexander is recipient of the 2017 American Psychological Association's (APA) Early Career Achievement Award and the 2017 APA Section on Child Maltreatment Early Career Award for Outstanding Contributions to Research.

Kevin Andresen is in pursuit of his PsyD. He has a special interest in working with adults with anxiety, specifically OCD. He enjoys sports, music, and socializing with friends.

Cristelle Audet, PhD, is a registered psychotherapist and Associate Professor in Counseling Psychology at the University of Ottawa. She is interested in promoting counseling and psychotherapy practices informed by constructivist and social justice values. Her research interests are in the area of client experiences of psychotherapy, particularly forefronting under-represented voices in counseling. She also co-edited the book *Social and Counseling: Discourse in Practice* (Routledge, 2018) with David Paré.

Dr. Tyson Bailey is a clinical and forensic psychologist in Lynnwood, Washington who primarily works with individuals who have experienced attachment-related trauma. He is a partner in a trauma informed group practice and an associate editor for Psychological Trauma: Theory, Research, Practice, and Policy. Dr. Bailey has held leadership roles in Division 56 (Trauma Psychology) and American Psychological Association governance.

Dr. Ryan Barbeau is a licensed psychologist in Florida. He is an associate professor of psychology at Santa Fe College where he teaches and an adjunct clinical assistant professor at the University of Florida where he provides clinical services and supervises doctoral trainees. Previously Dr. Barbeau has taught masters and doctoral courses such as Multicultural Counseling for Diverse Populations and Issues in the Assessment and Treatment of Diverse Populations. Clinically he has provided services and supervision in a range of settings including a correctional facility, veterans' hospital, community mental health center, school district, and university counseling center.

Andrea Che, PhD is a bilingual English and Mandarin speaking licensed clinical psychologist in the San Francisco Bay Area with specialized clinical training, professional work and research experience with severe mental illness (SMI), neuropsychology and behavioral medicine. She earned her doctorate at the Pacific Graduate School of Psychology (PGSP) at Palo Alto University and completed her postdoctoral fellowship at the UC Davis Medical Center.

Barry A. Farber received his PhD from Yale University in 1978. The following year he became a member of the clinical psychology faculty at Teachers College, Columbia University, where he's been ever since. He served as Director of Clinical Training there for 24 years. He has varied interests within the area of psychotherapy research, including the nature and consequences of therapists' provision of positive regard, and the extent to which patients, therapists, supervisors and supervisees do and don't disclose to each other. With coauthors Matt Blanchard and Melanie Love, his book, *Secrets and Lies in Psychotherapy* (essentially a follow-up to his 2006 book, *Self-disclosure in Psychotherapy)* will be published in 2019 by APA Publications. He is also the coauthor of *The Psychotherapy of Carl Rogers: Cases and commentary,* as well as a book called *Rock 'n Roll Wisdom: What psychologically astute lyrics can teach about life and love.* He maintains a small private practice of psychotherapy and currently serves as editor *of Journal of Clinical Psychology: In Session.*

Dr. Jen Henretty earned her MS and PhD in clinical psychology from the University of Memphis, where she studied psychotherapy processes, including therapist self-disclosure, and was awarded the prestigious S. Howard Bartley Scholar and the Society of Psychotherapy Research's Enrico E. Jones Memorial Awards. Dr. Henretty has published her research, including oft-cited qualitative and quantitative therapist self-disclosure meta-analyses, in such journals as Clinical Psychology Review, Psychotherapy Research, and the Journal of Counseling Psychology. After graduating, she began working with clients with eating disorders and has functioned as an eating disorder subject matter expert for CBS radio and the LA Times newspaper. She currently is the Executive Director of Quality Management & Clinical Outcomes for Discovery Behavioral Health, is an outpatient family therapist in greater Los Angeles and Orange County, and recently completed a journal manuscript on therapist self-disclosure of eating disorder recovery status.

Devlin Jackson is an advanced clinical psychology doctoral student at Teachers College, Columbia University. She received her M.A. in Clinical Psychology from Teachers College and an Ed.M. in Higher Education from the Harvard Graduate School of Education. Her research in the area of psychotherapy has focused on honesty and disclosure among supervisees in clinical supervision, among patients in psychotherapy, and most recently, among clinicians themselves.

Dr. Reena Kapoor is an Associate Professor of Psychiatry in the Law and Psychiatry Division at the Yale School of Medicine, where her clinical work and scholarship focus on the intersection between serious mental illness and the criminal justice system. She serves as Associate Program Director for the Yale forensic psychiatry fellowship, teaching and supervising fellows in the largest training program for forensic psychiatrists in the United States. Dr. Kapoor has lectured widely on forensic psychiatry and holds leadership positions in several professional organizations. She is President of the International Association for Forensic Psychotherapy (IAFP), a member of the Executive Council of the American Academy of Psychiatry and the Law (AAPL), and a corresponding member of the American Psychiatric Association's Council on Psychiatry and Law. Dr. Kapoor completed her residency training in psychiatry at Harvard Medical School and a forensic psychiatry fellowship at Yale. She is a graduate Northwestern University's Feinberg School of Medicine.

Dr. Gerald E. Nissley, Jr. is a licensed clinical psychologist in private practice in Marshall, Texas. He continues to hold faculty appointments at several universities and is active in research and writing. His research interests include teaching of psychology and integration of faith into counseling.

Dr. Daniel Papapietro is a clinical and forensic psychologist, with 30 years of experience as a psychoanalytic psychotherapist. His clinical and research interests include the psychoanalytic/psychodynamic understanding of mentally ill individuals who have killed or nearly killed a close family member. He is the Chief of the Psychotherapy Service at Whiting Forensic Hospital, where he supervises, trains, and teaches psychologists and psychiatrists the theory and practice of psychoanalytic and psychodynamic psychotherapy. Dr. Papapietro is also an Assistant Clinical Professor of Psychiatry in the Yale Medical School's division of Law & Psychiatry.

David Sugarbaker, Psy, M.P.H. is a graduate of the PGSP-Stanford Psy.D. Consortium in Palo Alto, California. During his doctoral studies, he worked as a Research Associate at SRI International, a nationally recognized leader in sleep and neuroscience research in Stanford, California. In addition, he served as Director of the Clinical Psychology Research Program at John George Psychiatric Hospital, located in San Leandro, California. Later, he completed his internship at Albany Psychology Internship Consortium. Next year, he will begin a post-doctoral fellowship at Edith Nourse Rogers Memorial VA Hospital in Bedford, Massachusetts, where he will split his time between clinical psychotherapy and program development and evaluation activities. His primary research interests include psychotherapy and suicide prevention.

Dr. Tobias Wasser obtained his undergraduate degree in psychology at Wesleyan University and then completed medical school at the University of Connecticut School of Medicine. He completed all of his psychiatry training at Yale, first the psychiatry residency program, before completing fellowships in forensic psychiatry and then in public psychiatry. He is currently an Assistant Professor of Psychiatry in the department and on faculty in both the Public Psychiatry and Law and Psychiatry Divisions. He is also the Associate Program Director of the Yale Fellowship in Public Psychiatry and works clinically as the Chief Medical Officer of the Whiting Forensic Hospital.

Dr. Asha Wilkus-Stone earned her Masters and Doctorate in clinical psychology from California School of Professional Psychology at Alliant International University in San Francisco, and holds a Bachelor of Fine Arts from California Institute of the Arts. She chose Psychology as a second career after working a decade in apparel manufacturing, and almost five years as a volunteer with hospice. In her practice of psychology, she values service, empathy, self-examination, and social justice to do the difficult work of reducing suffering. The client populations and diagnostic issues with which she works include trauma recovery, new families and perinatal mood and anxiety disorders, emerging adults in adolescence and the college years, and adults exploring professional and existential issues in their therapy. She currently works in private practice in Santa Barbara, California.

Part I

Overview

CHAPTER 1

Introduction

Graham S. Danzer, PsyD

Therapist self-disclosure (TSD) has long frequented the counseling and psychotherapy literature (LaPorte, Sweifach, & Linzer, 2010). Over the past decade, the topic has received increased attention in theoretical debates (Audet & Everall, 2003), empirical research (Bitar, Kimball, Bermúdez, & Drew, 2014; Kelly & Rodriguez, 2007), and across many mental health disciplines (D'Aniello & Nguyen, 2017). There has been an expansion of ideas about what makes a TSD ethically appropriate (Audet, 2011) and how relevant ethical principles should guide therapist decisions to or not to disclose in different clinical scenarios (Bottrill, Pistrang, Barker, & Worrell, 2010; LaPorte et al., 2010).

Controversy about what TSD is and is not has complicated theoretical conceptualization, research efforts, and clinical discussions on the topic (Farber, 2006). Depending on the extent to which it is discouraged or encouraged, disclosure has been regarded in the literature as a therapist behavior (Bottrill et al., 2010), boundary crossing or violation (Audet, 2011), or as an intervention, clinical skill, and/or an expression of authenticity and genuineness (Bitar et al., 2014). A therapist's general position on TSD is informative about his or her sense of role, profession, and personal preferences for the nature and intensity of interpersonal interactions (Bottrill et al., 2010). While a therapist may no longer be able to remain a truly anonymous professional, there may also be a fine line between one who reveals too little and one who reveals too much (LaPorte et al., 2010; Rasmussen & Mishna, 2008; Thomas, 2008). Whereas disclosing too much may raise client questions about boundaries, disclosing too little may lead clients to perceive the therapist as an aloof and distant professional (Thomas, 2008).

The first step in a process of more deeply exploring this issue is to first acknowledge the reality that therapists generally *do disclose*. Moreover, TSD happens more frequently than a researcher or therapist might assume. Research suggests at least some extent of intentional self-disclosure is relatively common among most clinical practitioners (Aron, 1991; Audet, 2011; Greenberg, 1995). Across multiple studies, 65–90% of surveyed therapists acknowledged intentionally disclosing to clients *at least some of the time* (Audet, 2011; Audet

& Everall, 2003; Henretty & Levitt, 2010; Kelly & Rodriguez, 2007; LaPorte et al., 2010). Offering further specification, surveyed therapists in other studies reported disclosures made up between 1–13% of all of their interventions, with an average of 3.5% (Henretty & Levitt, 2010; Kelly & Rodriguez, 2007).

Therapeutic relationship factors offer at least a partial explanation for what may seem to be a relatively high level of disclosure. Commonly, TSD becomes more implicit and conversational as therapeutic relationships grow stronger (Russell, 2006). In research studies, therapists who had been in personal therapy with a disclosing therapist and reflected on the TSD as being positive were more likely to disclose with their own clients (Simon, 1990; Simone, McCarthy, & Skay, 1998). It is also likely that most of the aforementioned disclosures were/are not of the higher intimacy, historical content nature that raises Cain among conservative ethicists and practitioners.

From the research it is inferred that TSD not only *does* happen, but that it may be a preferred alternative to full neutrality and non-disclosure in many circumstances. The seemingly one-sided nature of clients necessarily disclosing far more than the therapist is a unique interpersonal pattern that deviates from established social norms and may therefore be difficult for clients in need of human connection to tolerate (D'Aniello & Nguyen, 2017). Thus, clients may perceive non-disclosing therapists as inaccessible (Goldstein, 1994) or even hostile (Henretty & Levitt, 2010). Surveyed clients have described therapists perceived as erring on the side of non-disclosure as overly formal, rigid, and authoritative (Audet, 2011). In response to non-disclosure, clients may become reluctant to disclose (Henretty & Levitt, 2010) and therapeutic impasses may occur (Wachtel, 1993). Whereas perfect neutrality intends to encourage and not interfere with client introspection and processing, the prior positions suggest that non-disclosure can have the opposite effect.

Even under strict ethical frameworks, TSD may still be appropriate. Conservative ethicists may support disclosure in cases where a therapist's undisclosed personal circumstances might otherwise negatively affect the course of treatment (Audet, 2011). The American Psychological Association's (APA) Code of Ethics offers no clear and explicit guidance, though several of its codes apply and suggest that therapists can no longer choose non-disclosure without having first considered both sides of the issue carefully (Henretty & Levitt, 2010). Going a step further, an APA task force included TSD under the category of "promising and probably effective" therapeutic interventions (Ackerman et al., 2001, p. 495).

From this review of literature it is inferred that the ethics of self-disclosure have moved at least incrementally in a progressive direction reminiscent of what is increasingly recognized as a two-person therapeutic relationship with a neutral, reserved, and professional component, as well as what is described by Gelso and Carter (1994) as an authentic and non-transferential component. Further scholarly discussion on this subject matter is necessary because the disclosing therapist invites an uncharted level of intimacy into a professional relationship historically built upon secrecy and subtlety (Bottrill et al., 2010).

Overview and Outline of the Text

Given recent advances in theory and research, the larger purpose of this text will be to go beyond the more conservative subject of whether or not to disclose, into a more critical discussion of what can or even should be disclosed to which clients by which therapists under what clinical and vulnerability circumstances and contexts. Although such decision-making is necessarily clinical and cannot be fully prescriptive, reflections upon the research are likely to be informative and, at times, reconciling. Scenarios in which self-disclosure may be a possibility are often of a higher intensity nature that can end up being the most clinically fruitful and/or hazardous. Conceptualizing such a scenario, in part, through the relevant scholarly literature may help practicing therapists to maintain an optimal balance between individualized and empirical care. In so doing, complex clinical decisions may be made with maximal likelihood of both helping clients and reducing likelihood of harm.

Outline of This Text

Parts I and II contain essential TSD background information as well as reviews of general research, theoretical, clinical, and ethical considerations. Part III will include summaries of scholarly writings and research on different populations or clinical contexts mentioned frequently in the literature. This will include different forms of trauma, as well as LGBTQ identity, physical illness, mortality, eating disorders, serious mental illness, religion and spirituality, forensic settings, and children and adolescents.

Whereas the vulnerability chapters flowed directly from the literature, the next set of 'responding to direct client inquiry' and 'clinical challenge' chapters in Parts IV and V will cover areas of practice that have been less researched, relatively under-attended to in clinical discussions, and/or expanded from the vulnerability chapters to cover some of the major nuances in practice. These chapters are written by invited guest researcher-practitioners with considerable expertise in their areas of authorship. They will offer a professional commentary on TSD within their area of current focus and identify some of the ways in which their perspectives align with or are informed by the research. Thus, this text contains not only a comprehensive and compartmentalized review of TSD research for ease of reading and referencing, but also expands from the literature based on clinical perspectives of a more consultative nature and with attention to elusive concepts and considerations unlikely to be fully captured through research methodology.

The final four discussant and concluding chapters in Part VI will consolidate prior positions and suggest to the reader the main take-aways from the TSD research, with advised applications to practice. More specifically, concluding chapters are intended to inform the reader about what key points should be at least momentarily considered before, during, and/or after scenarios wherein self-disclosure felt/feels like a possibility. As mentioned, these scenarios are among the most controversial and difficult to navigate even for seasoned and highly competent practitioners. In such circumstances, it is often helpful to reflect upon the scholarly research as a source of guidance or point of reference for clinical thinking and decision-making.

Rationale and Approach of the Text

Throughout the text, qualitative and quantitative research studies on client and therapist perspectives will be reviewed and compared. Whereas qualitative disclosure research informs an understanding of client and therapist experiences, quantitative research helps to explore objective differences in quantifiable outcomes (D'Aniello & Nguyen, 2017). Qualitative studies are difficult to generalize given typically small sample sizes, broad and diverse research questions, and interpretations necessarily being subjective and inferential (Harris, 2015). In turn, quantitative studies may be difficult to apply unilaterally to individual cases, because as noted by Rahman (2017), they offer more of a snap shot representation of a particular phenomenon, without as thorough and complete of a representation of individual perspectives and experiences. In addition, a limitation of all research is the perspective *of the researcher* may impact their results, as well as interpretation and presentation of those results (Moore & Jenkins, 2012).

The current text will attempt to compensate for each of these limitations by including all relevant and scholarly sources, organizing them in chapter subjects that flowed from the research, and noting where qualitative and quantitative research findings converge and diverge. Areas of consistency and difference will suggest to the reader how clients and therapists generally *experience or perceive* important aspects of TSD similarly or differently, with equal attention to each of the recurring perspectives on major clinical and contextual factors. In addition, areas of consistency and difference in the literature will be among the major points of discussion within the concluding section of chapters. Major, recurring, opposing, and unconventional positions will be presented. Doing so is intended to present to the research-informed practitioner a maximally thorough, organized, diverse, and reliable summary of findings. Flowing from areas of convergence and divergence in the literature, implications for practice will be presented throughout the text and highlighted in relevant concluding sections.

Recent research studies will be emphasized and prioritized in accordance with the contemporary research focus of this text, changing clinical and practice trends on the whole, and specific indications that TSD has only more recently grown in its general acceptability. With changing clinical trends in mind (including but not limited to TSD), unpublished and recent dissertations will be included in this text, in an effort to better incorporate the perspective of the next generation of practitioners and researchers. Key points in the first two sections of chapters will have multiple citations in order to show recurrent support in the literature. Key points will then be referenced in the vulnerability, clinical challenge, direct client inquiry, and implications for practice chapters in order to demonstrate applicability in other contexts.

Implications and recommendations will be general and advisory. Greater specificity would risk suggesting a more scripted and formulaic approach to TSD. In turn, this would risk de-prioritizing the client's individual needs and the therapist's intuitive understanding of those needs. For this reason, the need to individualize treatment and base conceptualizations *in part* through a reflection on the scholarly literature will be emphasized and referenced repeatedly. Thus, the following presentation is intended to inform though not dictate the research-informed practitioner's clinical thinking.

References

Ackerman, S., Benjamin, L., Beutler, L., Gelso, C., Goldfried, M., & Hill, C. (2001). Empirically supported therapy relationships: Conclusions and recommendations of the Division 29 Task Force. *Psychotherapy: Theory, Research, Practice, Training, 38*, 495–7.

Aron, L. (1991). The patient's experience of the analyst's subjectivity. *Psychoanalytic Dialogues, 1*(1), 29–51.

Audet, C. (2011). Client perspectives of therapist self-disclosure: Violating boundaries or removing boundaries? *Counselling Psychology Quarterly, 24*(2), 85–100.

Audet, C., & Everall, R. (2003). Counsellor self-disclosure: Client-informed implications for practice. *Counselling and Psychotherapy Research, 3*(3), 223–31.

Bitar, G., Kimball, T., Bermúdez, J., & Drew, C. (2014). Therapist self-disclosure and culturally competent case with Mexican-American court mandated clients: A phenomenological study. *Contemporary Family Therapy, 36*(3), 417–25.

Bottrill, S., Pistrang, N., Barker, C., & Worrell, M. (2010). The use of therapist self-disclosure: Clinical psychology trainees' experiences. *Psychotherapy Research, 20*(2), 165–80.

D'Aniello, C., & Nguyen, H. (2017). Considerations for intentional use of self-disclosure for family therapists. *Journal of Family Psychotherapy, 28*(1), 23–37.

Farber, B. (2006). *Self-disclosure in psychotherapy*. New York: Guilford Press.

Gelso, C., & Carter, J. (1994). Components of the psychotherapy relationship: Their interaction and unfolding during treatment. *Journal of Counseling Psychology, 41*(3), 296–306.

Goldstein, E. (1994). Self-disclosure in treatment: What therapists do and don't talk about. *Clinical Social Work Journal, 22*(4), 417–33.

Greenberg, J. (1995). Self-disclosure: Is it psychoanalytic? *Contemporary Psychoanalysis, 31*(2), 193–205.

Harris, A. (2015). To disclose or not to disclose? The LGBT therapist's question (Doctoral dissertation). Retrieved from ProQuest Dissertations and Theses database (No UMI No.).

Henretty, J., & Levitt, H. (2010). The role of therapist self-disclosure in psychotherapy: A qualitative review. *Clinical Psychology Review, 30*(1), 63–77.

Kelly, A., & Rodriguez, R. (2007). Do therapists self-disclose more to clients with greater symptomology? *Psychotherapy: Theory, Research, Practice, Training, 44*(4), 470–5.

LaPorte, H., Sweifach, J., & Linzer, N. (2010). Sharing the trauma: Guidelines for therapist self-disclosure following a catastrophic event. *Best Practices in Mental Health, 6*(2), 39–56.

Moore, J., & Jenkins, P. (2012). 'Coming out' in therapy? Perceived risks and benefits of self-disclosure of sexual orientation by gay and lesbian therapists to straight clients. *Counselling & Psychotherapy Research, 12*(4), 308–15.

Rahman, S. (2017). The advantages and disadvantages of using qualitative and quantitative approaches and methods in language 'testing and assessment' research: Literature review. *Journal of Education and Learning*, *6*(1), 102–12.

Rasmussen, B., & Mishna, F. (2008). A fine balance: Instructor self-disclosure in the classroom. *Journal of Teaching in Social Work*, *28*(1–2), 191–207.

Russell, G. (2006). Different ways of knowing: The complexities of therapist disclosure. *Journal of Gay & Lesbian Psychotherapy*, *10*(1), 79–94.

Simon, J. (1990). Criteria for therapist self-disclosure. In G. Stricker & M. Fisher (Eds.), *Self-disclosure in the therapeutic relationship* (pp. 207–25). New York: Plenum Press.

Simone, D., McCarthy, P., & Skay, C. (1998). An investigation of client and counselor variables that influence likelihood of counselor self-disclosure. *Journal of Counseling & Development*, *76*(2), 174–82.

Thomas, M. (2008). Shades of gray: Lesbian therapists explore the complexities of self disclosure to heterosexual clients (Doctoral dissertation). Retrieved from Smith College Theses, Dissertations, and Projects.

Wachtel, P. (1993). *Therapeutic communication: Principles and effective practice*. New York: Guilford Press.

CHAPTER 2

Ethics Applied in Practice

Graham S. Danzer, PsyD

The ethics of therapeutic self-disclosure (TSD) are an important starting point for the larger discussion that is this text. In general, professional ethics define the nature and boundaries of psychotherapy. Specific to the current subject matter, ethics are most frequently the underpinning of arguments erring toward supporting or discouraging TSD on the whole.

As noted in the introduction of this text, most therapists do disclose at least some of the time, while even conservative ethicists concede that disclosure can be appropriate at least under select circumstances. Thus, complete aversion to TSD may be a relative rarity. However, it is also likely that most therapists, researchers, academics, and theoreticians err generally and cautiously on the side of favor *or* disfavor to a disclosing therapist.

Major ethical arguments for and against disclosure, as well as the implications of those arguments for practice, are presented and discussed in this chapter. It is common for proponents to argue (in a language reminiscent of *beneficence*) that TSD frequently conveys the humanity of the therapist, helps to develop rapport with clients, and permits a level of authenticity that may contribute to the formation of a positive relationship, roundly understood to be central to therapeutic healing and growth. Opponents often counter (in a language reminiscent of *maleficence*) that TSD crosses professional boundaries, suggests the possibility of a dual relationship, and therefore should be substituted for any number of alternative interventions that competent therapists should be able to call upon in service of building professional and not personal relationships with clients. Neither perspective is mutually exclusive, as TSDs can be ethically appropriate and helpful to clients, unethical and unhelpful to clients, or both positive *and* negative. Major determinants of positive and negative outcome are each of the major clinical and contextual factors identified in separate chapters within the first two sections of chapters in this text.

Given that TSDs are a relatively normal occurrence in practice, and are at least passively supported in at least some circumstances in most clinical circles, there is less of a need and probably less clinical utility in debating self-disclosure in total. Thus, the question guiding this chapter is not the uncritical, should therapists disclose at all? But rather, when therapists are considering the possibility of TSD, what ethical factors and considerations should guide their decision-making? The latter half of this chapter, subsequent chapters within this section of chapters, and the following section of chapters (i.e., 'clinical factor' chapters) will progress into clear and practice-relevant discussions of clinical and contextual considerations that therapists should reflect upon *after* determining their decision *to disclose* is ethically appropriate.

Exercising Personal Restraint and Forethought

The starting point for TSD ethics is that therapists must first determine, prior to disclosing, that doing so is in the best interest of the client and is not self-indulgent (Hill & Knox, 2001; Zur, 2010). Therapists gaining personal enjoyment or reprieve from clients listening to their disclosures may also commit other more subtle forms of boundary *crossing* and be at greater risk for progressing into fuller, clearer, and more blatant boundary *violations* (D'Aniello & Nguyen, 2017). TSDs meeting the therapist's needs may portray the therapist as helpful, intelligent, or kind and friendly (Farber, 2006; Hill & Knox, 2002). Inappropriate TSDs necessarily call into question the therapist's judgment and decision-making regarding other interventions, fees, and their basis for whether or not to continue treatment (D'Aniello & Nguyen, 2017).

Prior to self-disclosing, therapists should momentarily reflect upon *how* and *in what ways* their disclosure may or may not benefit the client (D'Aniello & Nguyen, 2017), with this determination based in part on their understanding of the client's prior history of personal relationships and object relations (Ziv-Beiman & Shahar, 2016). Due to the inherently personal nature and at least 'boundary approaching' nature of TSD, it is reasonable for therapists to always question their motives or urges to disclose based on the potential of disclosures to complicate therapeutic relationships.

It is important to discuss self-disclosure considerations, possibilities, and motivations with a supervisor or peer (D'Aniello & Nguyen, 2017). From a psychodynamic perspective, a pull to self-disclose may suggest that the therapist's earlier life experiences are being triggered. In such moments, clinical thinking, restraint, and reflection are likely to be more beneficial to the client. Therapists feeling a sense of urgency to self-disclose may in fact need to urgently *disclose their urgency* to a peer or supervisor.

It is likely that many if not most if not all opportunities to self-disclose can be at least temporarily postponed and somehow revisited in somewhat comparable clinical circumstances in the future. It is reasonable to anticipate that TSDs first determined through supervision or consultation to be clinically appropriate may be even better timed, attuned, and potent when utilized in the future. Further, such exercises in professional restraint are likely to be beneficial to the individual client as well as other clients the therapist comes into contact with.

Specifically, benefits *from* exercising restraint are anticipated because therapists unusually or urgently pulled to disclose may be re-enacting their own interpersonal challenges and/or having a client's interpersonal pattern acted out upon them. In either case, it is likely that self-disclosing will be at least unhelpful to major treatment goals, harmful perhaps in both the short and long run of treatment, and thus making preliminary consultation essential. The following discussion provides an example of how making ethically appropriate decisions with regards to TSD is also what tends to be helpful to the client and of maximum clinical utility.

Factors Determining the Appropriateness of TSD

The scholarly literature offers additional ethical guidelines for therapists who have determined that TSD in a particular scenario is appropriate and have thus progressed into clinical thinking about how to disclose in a manner likely to be beneficial to the client. The client's personality traits and presenting symptomology must be considered (Dean, 2010). Therapists should be relatively clear in regards to the clinical aims of disclosure and utilize constructive wording (D'Aniello & Nguyen, 2017; LaPorte, Sweifach, & Linzer 2010; Sturges, 2012). While findings on frequency of TSD and outcomes are mixed (Dean, 2010), therapist writers and researchers consistently advise that disclosures should be infrequent, as well as brief and relevant to the client's experience (Audet & Everall, 2003; Bottrill, Pistrang, Barker, & Worrell, 2010; Henretty & Levitt, 2010; Kelly & Rodriguez, 2007; Sturges, 2012). As cautioned previously, excessive self-disclosure more clearly calls into the question the possibility of a self-interested/secondarily motivated therapist (D'Aniello & Nguyen, 2017).

Among the few ethical universals, sharing erotic feelings with a client is strongly discouraged (Fisher, 2004). It would be difficult to identify a scenario in which sharing erotic feelings lacked a personal/inappropriate motive *and* would be beneficial to the client. Rather, it is recommended that therapists refrain from such disclosures as recommended in the literature.

Alternatively, therapists are advised to instead acknowledge in consultation and supervision their erotic feelings and explore the possibility that sexualization may be brought about by a provocative client, represent the client and/or therapist's avoidance of deeper emotional intimacy, or may be reflected upon as a symbolic form of connection (Pope, Sonne, & Holroyd, 1995). Particularly in cases where clients have histories of sexual trauma, erotic transference and sexualization may occur as it is often their most comfortable, natural, and/or familiar method of connecting with potentially caring others, who may be expected to betray them by eventually if not immediately violating their boundaries. In essence, sexualization may protect the client from a potentially deeper form of intimacy, which if trusted and betrayed would likely be more traumatizing then a pre-emptive return to a more familiar pattern.

After considering ethical appropriateness and helpfulness, self-disclosure should also be considered as an issue related to therapist self-care. In their review of self-disclosure studies, Henretty and Levitt (2010) noted that the decision to self-disclose may at times have negative ramifications for the disclosing therapist. Depending in part on the client's reaction, therapists who self-disclose may then question their clinical decision-making, judgment, and competence. As a result, future interventional strategy may be tainted and perhaps to a degree that the effort to refrain from doing harm interferes with the simultaneous ethical responsibility to do good. Consistent with the latter idea, therapists must feel comfortable what they reveal in order to remain authentically connected to a client (Tantillo, 2004).

Bottrill et al. (2010) described a parallel process by which disclosing therapists and clients receiving therapist disclosure may experience similar feelings of vulnerability, discomfort, or internal conflict. TSD researchers also caution that, unlike therapists, clients are not responsible for maintaining the therapist's confidences and are free to pass on any information disclosed to them (Gibson, 2012; Sweezy, 2005). Accordingly, erring towards non-disclosure/less disclosure may offer therapists a comforting sense of safety and privacy (Henretty & Levitt, 2010).

Additionally, self-disclosure researchers make recommendations about how therapists should follow up on TSDs. After disclosing, the focus of the therapy should immediately be returned to the client (Sturges, 2012). Clinically, it may be advisable to do so by asking the client how he or she felt about the disclosure (Audet & Everall, 2003; Sturges, 2012). This approach reinforces appropriate therapeutic roles (Henretty & Levitt, 2010) and creates an opportunity for intense and productive in-vivo work (Vandenberghe & Silva Silvestre, 2014). During in-vivo work, it may be helpful to validate client responses reminiscent of healthy, reciprocal, and improved relational behavior (Tsai, Plummer, Kanter, Newring, & Kohlenberg, 2010). As clients may not immediately process the impact of the TSD, it may be necessary to revisit the occurrence at an appropriate time later in therapy (Henretty & Levitt, 2010).

Per Ziv-Beiman and Shahar (2016), when clients react negatively to TSDs, fully attending to and exploring their reactions is crucial. It is often advisable for therapists to attempt to repair these ruptures by empathically and directly acknowledging them, returning as quickly as possible to therapeutic patterns and processes previously shown to be helpful to the client, and either directly or indirectly conveying to the client an understanding of what may be a newly found or exacerbated ambivalence about the therapeutic relationship. Understanding does not necessarily have to be stated directly, as it may be conveyed purely through physical gestures or empathic tones of voice.

Therapists are further reminded that conservative ethical positions including but not limited to precautions against TSD are usually generated through well-seasoned clinical experiences with highly elusive clinical phenomena. It is not uncommon for conservative positions to advance in the aftermath of clinical mistakes, with subsequent intention to protect vulnerable clients in similar scenarios in the future. Applied to the current subject matter, precautions against TSD are likely to have flowed from boundary violations, clinical mistakes, and as a general and larger expression of what the field has learned therefrom. While these points should not be interpreted as indicating support for a fully non-disclosing therapist, they do suggest that a more cautionary approach to disclosing is ethically appropriate.

In the larger spirit of an ethical approach to self-disclosure decision-making, no research findings or perspectives presented henceforth in this text should be interpreted as suggesting a lack of appropriate caution. Rather, the following chapters are intended to be advisory in nature and in theory. Advisement from the literature is based on the presumption that due clinical diligence is being put forth in individually specific circumstances.

Conclusions

Although TSD decisions must be made based on the individual situation at hand, it is a basic principle of professional psychotherapy that general rules and principles must be reflected upon and applied in practice. As a result, clients are treated as individuals *in a professional relationship*. Indeed, it may not only be the case that professional ethics, boundaries, and parameters are what distinguishes a professional helping relationship from a peer-helping relationship or a social relationship, but also that these boundaries are an expression if not actualization of professional training, and intuitively among the major reasons why clients engender a level of trust and reverence in a professional psychotherapist in the first place.

For these reasons, the first major take-away for the research-informed practitioner seeking to make an ethically appropriate decision on whether or not to self-disclose is to first determine, and likely through consultation, that disclosure truly is in the best interest of the client and with thorough discussion and acknowledgement of potential ramifications. In many cases, ramifications and therapist motives may be subtle, elusive, and take time to understand, track, and appropriately channel or divert in the context of an inherently complicated and multi-layered therapeutic relationship. Whereas a therapist may easily recall and recount potential benefits of TSD related to rapport building, a highly aware, introspective, *and disclosing therapist* may not only reflect upon the frequency, content, and intimacy of TSDs, as discussed in prior and upcoming chapters of this text, but also identify their personal patterns with respect to disclosure, as an exercise in learning what he or she brings *into* the therapy. It is expected that such a reflective and fore-thinking therapist is likely to intuitively self-disclose in an ethically permissible manner, with TSD content and intimacy of content intuitively within the reasonable bounds of their comfort and self-care, and of appropriate brevity, relevance, and responsiveness to the client's needs from the relationship at a particular moment in treatment.

The same caution against over-disclosure also applies to the non-disclosing therapist. It is reasonable to suspect that a therapist erring in the direction of full non-disclosure may not only be perceived negatively by clients, as discussed in the introductory chapter of this text, but may be *rightly* perceived as an avoidant, disconnected, alienated, inattentive, or better-than personality. Whereas therapists pulled to disclose may do well to exercise restraint, therapists who give very little to their relationships are expected to have great difficulty retaining fragile, wounded, and suffering clients increasingly recognized as in need of a two-person connection. As discussed in more detail in the third section of (vulnerability) chapters in this text, an incrementally greater-than-usual level of authenticity, revelation, and 'emotional giving' is frequently discussed in the scholarly literature as beneficial to building, forging, and maintaining change-inspiring relationships with clients of diverse cultural, sexual, or religious identities, mental health and personality factors, and specialized treatment considerations such as histories of substance abuse or eating disorders.

Therefore, it is important for the research-informed practitioner *not to* conceptualize individualization of treatment or following rules and precepts in the TSD literature as competing priorities. Rather, it is paramount to recognize the need to optimize the balance between these goals within the ever-changing emotional landscape of psychotherapy. With such an aspiration in mind, it is hoped that the remainder of introductory, clinical factor, vulnerability, clinical challenge, direct client inquiry, and discussant chapters in this text sufficiently overview and discuss the major considerations of TSD and how they might apply or have merit in different scenarios in practice.

References

Audet, C., & Everall, R. (2003). Counsellor self-disclosure: Client-informed implications for practice. *Counselling and Psychotherapy Research, 3*(3), 223–31.

Bottrill, S., Pistrang, N., Barker, C., & Worrell, M. (2010). The use of therapist self-disclosure: Clinical psychology trainees' experiences. *Psychotherapy Research, 20*(2), 165–80.

D'Aniello, C., & Nguyen, H. (2017). Considerations for intentional use of self-disclosure for family therapists. *Journal of Family Psychotherapy, 28*(1), 23–37.

Dean, B. (2010). Therapist self-disclosure: Heterosexuals' perceptions of sexual minority therapists (Doctoral dissertation). Retrieved from the University Digital Conservancy database.

Farber, B. (2006). *Self-disclosure in psychotherapy.* New York: Guilford Press.

Fisher, C. (2004). Ethical issues in therapy: Therapist self-disclosure of sexual feelings. *Ethics & Behavior, 14*(2), 105–21.

Gibson, M. (2012). Opening up: Therapist self-disclosure in theory, research, and practice. *Clinical Social Work Journal, 40*(3), 287–96.

Henretty, J., & Levitt, H. (2010). The role of therapist self-disclosure in psychotherapy: A qualitative review. *Clinical Psychology Review, 30*(1), 63–77.

Hill, C., & Knox, S. (2001). Self-disclosure. *Psychotherapy: Theory, Research, Practice, Training, 38*(4), 413–17.

Hill, C., & Knox, S. (2002). Self-disclosure. In J. Norcross (Ed.), *Psychotherapy relationships that work: Therapist contributions and responsiveness to patients* (pp. 255–65). New York: Oxford University Press.

Kelly, A., & Rodriguez, R. (2007). Do therapists self-disclose more to clients with greater symptomology? *Psychotherapy: Theory, Research, Practice, Training, 44*(4), 470–5.

LaPorte, H., Sweifach, J., & Linzer, N. (2010). Sharing the trauma: Guidelines for therapist self-disclosure following a catastrophic event. *Best Practices in Mental Health, 6*(2), 39–56.

Pope, K., Sonne, J., & Holroyd, J. (1995). *Sexual feelings in psychotherapy: Explorations for therapists and therapists-in-training.* Washington, DC: American Psychological Association.

Sturges, J. (2012). Use of therapist self-disclosure and self-involving statements. *The Behavior Therapist, 35*(5), 90–3.

Sweezy, M. (2005). Not confidential. *Smith College Studies in Social Work, 75*(1), 81–91.

Tantillo, M. (2004). The therapist's use of self-disclosure in a relational therapy approach for eating disorders. *Eating Disorders, 12*(1), 51–73.

Tsai, M., Plummer, M., Kanter, J., Newring, R., & Kohlenberg, R. (2010). Therapist grief and functional analytic psychotherapy: Strategic self-disclosure of personal loss. *Journal of Contemporary Psychotherapy, 40*(1), 1–10.

Vandenberghe, L., & Silva Silvestre, R. (2014). Therapists' positive emotions in- session: Why they happen and what they are good for. *Counselling and Psychotherapy Research, 14*(2), 119–27.

Ziv-Beiman, S., & Shahar, G. (2016). Therapeutic self-disclosure in integrative psycho-therapy: When is this a clinical error? *Psychotherapy, 53*(3), 273–7.

Zur, O. (2010). Self-disclosure. In I. Weiner & W. Craighead (Eds.), *The Corsin encyclopedia of psychology* (4th ed., pp. 1532–4). Hoboken, NJ: John Wiley & Sons.

CHAPTER 3

Theoretical and Clinical Perspectives

Graham S. Danzer, PsyD and Kevin Andresen, MA

Clinical theories offer a multiplicity of perspectives on the subject of therapeutic self-disclosure (TSD). Although research does not identify any one particular model as significantly more predictive of positive outcomes, orientations are still important to discuss because they may influence the type and frequency of TSDs, which can in turn impact the extent to which they are helpful to clients (Ackerman & Hilsenroth, 2003; Audet & Everall, 2003). Additionally, theoretical guidance and grounding often helps therapists think through complex clinical scenarios in which TSD and other unconventional interventions may be up for consideration.

Prior to the late 1950s, traditional psychoanalytic models advanced by Sigmund Freud discouraged TSD in its entirety (Bitar, Kimball, Bermúdez, & Drew, 2014). The primary concern was that disclosure represented a departure from the neutrality necessary for the development of a truer form of transference (Henretty & Levitt, 2010). This view permeated Freud's followers in spite of Freud himself revealing many aspects of his personal life to his clients (Bottrill, Pistrang, Barker, & Worrell, 2010).

Around the time of the civil rights movement and increased egalitarianism, progressive therapies began to accept and even encourage moderated forms of TSD based on a newfound conceptualization of a two-person therapeutic relationship (Bitar et al., 2014; Tsai, Plummer, Kanter, Newring, & Kohlenberg, 2010). Humanistic therapist Sidney Jourard was first credited with using the term *self-disclosure* in 1958, and advanced the theory that TSD may encourage clients to reveal more about themselves and participate more authentically in therapy (Barrett & Berman, 2001; Henretty & Levitt, 2010). Consistent with Jourard's early conceptualization, though using somewhat different terminologies, the client-centered, humanistic, and existential schools advanced greater openness to TSD as an intervention in service of humanizing the therapeutic relationship, modeling appropriate transparency and authenticity, and encouraging reciprocity (Audet, 2011; Bottrill et al., 2010; Dean, 2010; Henretty & Levitt, 2010; Satterly, 2006). Further departing from early Freudian theories, self-psychology advanced the occasional and well-thought-out use of TSD for the purposes of expressing empathic attunement and validation, deepening the client's affective expressions, encouraging reciprocal client disclosure, helping clients access parts of their inner lives and experiences they may otherwise be disconnected from, and helping clients to re-experience their unmet earlier needs (i.e., facilitate a self-object transference [Tantillo, 2004]).

As compared to traditional psychoanalysts, modern analytic and psycho-dynamic schools are generally of a more progressive view of TSD. Within the field of relational psychoanalysis, self-disclosure is acknowledged as having the potential to encourage client disclosure, reciprocity, give-and-take in relationships, and in some cases, corrective experiences (Audet, 2011; Bottrill et al., 2010; Ziv-Beiman & Shahar, 2016). Contemporary analysts and psychodynamic practitioners usually concede that perfect neutrality is virtually impossible, though continue to err on the side of discouraging disclosure based on concern about contaminating the transference, countertransference, and inappropriate gratification of client curiosities (Audet, 2011; D'Aniello & Nguyen, 2017; Satterly, 2006). Similarly, early analytic cautions also influenced traditional and strategic family therapist's concerns about TSD and its potential to cause or represent boundary violations (Bitar et al., 2014; Roberts, 2005). In spite of paramount cautions within the Freudian disciplines, research reviewed by Henretty and Levitt (2010) suggested that surveyed psychodynamic/analytic practitioners tended to disclose only marginally less than therapists from other theoretical persuasions more overtly supportive of disclosure.

Cognitive behavioral therapists are discussed in the literature as at times using TSD as an intervention in service of model-specific treatment goals (Satterly, 2006). Cognitive behaviorists may disclose in an attempt to challenge a client's negative interpretations of their major life events and bolster their motivation to participate in treatment (Dryden, 1990; Freeman, Fleming, & Pretzer, 1990; Goldfried, Burckell, & Eubanks-Carter, 2003). Under this model, therapists may also specifically disclose concrete examples of how they cope in daily life (Bottrill et al., 2010).

To better understand the cognitive behavioral theory of disclosure, Miller and McNaught (2016) conducted in-depth interviews of six cognitive behavioral therapists discussing their histories of intentionally disclosing. Consistent with other models, cognitive behaviorists emphasized they were open to TSD with a clear clinical purpose and relationship to identified treatment goals. Specifically, they mentioned using their therapeutic conceptualization to guide their TSDs. They also reported deciding to or not to disclose based on what was occurring in the relationship in the moment, reflecting upon their decisions to disclose after sessions in order to ensure appropriate boundaries remained in place, and often using TSD as an intervention intended to interrupt client's usual cycles of feeling, thinking, and behaving.

For example, and from the author's vantage point, if a client shared his/her experience of what seemed like a never-ending depression, it might be help-ful for the cognitive behavioral therapist to reflect upon on his/her personal history of depression, momentarily reflect upon major feelings in a prior depressed state, and consider what helped the therapist modulate similarly negative affects. With this conceptualization in mind, the therapist might then help the client to name what are likely to be at least somewhat similar emotional states, and then choose a cognitive behavioral intervention flowing from what may be a parallel experience. Interventions that might be helpful in such interchanges may include the downward arrow (i.e., "what does that say about you?"), Socratic questioning (i.e., "how is this affecting you?"), and encouraging behavioral activation (i.e., "what is one small thing you might be able to do that might help you feel a little better today?").

As reviewed by D'Aniello and Nguyen (2017), Carl Whittaker's experiential therapy advances TSD as a clinical technique. Within this model, overall efficacy and helpfulness of the therapist is seen as directly related if not contingent upon the therapist's capacity for fuller forms of engagement and vulnerability. Whittaker was of the opinion that it was somewhat unfair to expect client vulnerability without some level of therapist reciprocity. This theory was developed based on Whittaker's reflection that his personal investment in therapeutic interactions seemed to associate with maximal therapeutic change.

Feministic therapists advance the usage of tactful (Tabol & Walker, 2008) and yet proactive disclosure about the therapist's professional training and orientation, as well as personal, political, and social values (Audet, 2011; Bitar et al., 2014; Bottrill et al., 2010). In so doing, contemporary feminists self-disclose with the intention to reduce client–therapist power imbalance, promote a collaborative relationship, affirm shared experiences, and allow clients to make better informed decisions concerning therapist selection (Audet, 2011; Bitar et al., 2014; Bottrill et al., 2010). For these reasons, the feminist model of therapy permits a greater level of openness to answering clients' questions directly, essentially, with TSD by request in at least some circumstances (Dean, 2010). An additional underpinning of this approach is that being open and frank with clients encourages them to see their therapist as distinct, which encourages individuation and indeed liberation from power and dependency (Thomas, 2008). Similarly, Michael White's narrative therapy advances general transparency, egalitarianism, and possibly telling clients when and how particular interventions may be inspired by the therapist's personal experiences (D'Aniello & Nguyen, 2017).

Contemporary Clinical Perspectives

In addition to the major theoretical positions noted previously, therapist writers discuss some of the more practical ways in which TSDs may benefit clients. Therapist disclosures driven by empathy and caring (Sturges, 2012) may have positive impacts on the client's perception of the therapist (Henretty & Levitt, 2010) and the therapeutic relationship (Audet & Everall, 2003). Put another way, TSD can decrease client feelings of isolation and disconnection, and increase feelings of hope (Satterly, 2006). As discussed in previous summaries of progressive models of therapy, TSD may encourage clients to be more open, vulnerable, and disclose more intimately (Knox & Hill, 2003).

The prior positions have some support from both client and therapist perspectives as follows. Clients in a qualitative interview study reported that TSDs reduced their feelings of being objectified in therapy and described their disclosing therapists as human and appropriately fallible, genuinely caring and trustworthy, empowering, and collaborative (Audet, 2011). Ziv-Beiman and Shahar (2016), practicing therapists and researchers, reported personally finding that TSD often helped to reduce power imbalances, normalize client experiences, and reduce client shame and self-judgment. Thus, appropriate self-disclosures may lead to client responses commensurate with strengthening therapeutic relationships, as among the most consistent and stable predictors of positive outcome (Hanson, 2005; Horvath, 2000).

TSD may also be an effective therapeutic strategy for addressing clients' chief complaints (Henretty & Levitt, 2010) and attempting to reduce the severity of internalized symptoms (Audet & Everall, 2003). Presumably, therapist disclosures may get clients' attention in-session, distract them from internalized distress, and help them conceptualize their problems from alternate perspectives. Refocusing, distraction, and perspective taking can reasonably be expected to provide clients with some extent of emotional relief. Ziv-Beiman and Shahar (2017) reported that their search of the literature yielded only two articles that experimentally examined a potential relationship between TSD and symptom reduction. These two studies consistently supported an association between self-disclosure and forms of positive benefit to clients, as discussed earlier.

Supporting the potential of TSD to lower symptom severity, Barrett and Berman (2001) conducted a study of 36 clients (mean age of 27 years, with ethnicity not reported) paired with 18 doctoral student therapists. Barrett and Berman (2001) sought to determine whether TSD frequency, duration, intimacy, and similarity to client concerns, as rated by undergraduate coders/reviewers, did or did not associate significantly with client-rated outcome variables. Among other findings, clients who received higher numbers of TSDs reported lower symptom distress and more positive feelings about their therapist. Neither the two studies in Ziv-Beiman and Shahar (2017) nor Barrett and Berman (2001) controlled for *type* or *timing* of disclosure, which will be discussed in upcoming chapters of this text as important to consider with respect to TSD ethics and efficacy. Additionally, each of the aforementioned studies (in this paragraph) included only relatively younger therapist and client dyads.

Contemporary writings offer an expansion of ideas about client disclosures, therapist disclosures, and how reciprocity between the two may lead to positive outcomes. In and of themselves, client disclosures often lead to insights, a growing capacity for intimacy and reciprocity, and may reduce the negative impacts of withdrawal and avoidance of intimacy outside of therapy (Simonds

& Spokes, 2017). Therapist disclosures may lead clients to reveal more about their interpersonal patterns in therapy, so that their patterns outside of therapy begin to change (Henretty & Levitt, 2010). Therapist disclosures *in response to client disclosures* may help clients rethink negative anticipations about how their disclosures might negatively impact the therapist, and in turn how similar showings of vulnerability might be received by others (Simonds & Spokes, 2017). Contrastingly, if clients do not grow out of states of withdrawal and avoidance of intimacy, negative views of themselves may remain unchallenged (Simonds & Spokes, 2017). However, an approaching equal level of client and self-disclosure would risk inappropriately blurring therapeutic boundaries (D'Aniello & Nguyen, 2017).

Contemporary perspectives also maintain some of the early psychoanalytic and ethical cautions. TSD may distract from the focus of treatment (Sturges, 2012), diminish the therapist's credibility (Audet, 2011), and elevate risk management concerns (Audet, 2011). TSD may at times be an inappropriate shortcut to joining, seem seductive, interfere with client fantasies, lead vulnerable or impressionable clients to reflect upon themselves in ways that are more congruent with their therapist's experiences than their own, and increase the likelihood that clients pursue therapist-inspired, inauthentic goals (D'Aniello & Nguyen, 2017; Dean, 2010; Farber, 2006). Consistent with D'Aniello & Nguyen's (2071) position, Ziv-Beiman and Shahar (2017) noted that TSD may be a clinical error when clients experience the subjectivity of the therapist as intrusive due in part to their own earlier deficits in object relations.

Whereas disclosure is often intended to facilitate client–therapist rapport (Bitar et al., 2014), therapist discipline and restraint (LaPorte, Sweifach, & Linzer, 2010) is theorized to maintain the disproportionate give-and-take of the relationship (Audet & Everall, 2003) that is considered central to its uniqueness (LaPorte et al., 2010). Indeed, it may be the uniqueness of the relationship that builds deeper trust and safety (Gutheil & Gabbard, 1993) and results in deeper and lasting changes (Audet & Everall, 2003).

Positions discouraging TSD (or at least a more cautionary approach to it) have some support from research as follows. Interviewed clients have reported that their therapist's disclosures made them feel burdened (Vandenberghe & Silva Silvestre, 2014) or overwhelmed (Audet & Everall, 2003). Additionally, many of the clients in Audet's (2011) interview study reported that disclosures were generally helpful *and* led them to worry that the relationship might become more personal than professional.

Similarly to the last point made by Audet (2011), Bottrill et al. (2010) indicated that clients tend to experience a range of positive and negative reactions to therapist disclosures, thereby suggesting that the impact of disclosure is rarely completely positive *or* negative. Audet and Everall (2003) report that client expectations of disclosure and the extent and quality of therapist disclosure should be understood as interacting variables. Findings suggesting the possibility of positive and negative effects will be elaborated upon in more detail later by author Jennifer Henretty in Chapter 28 of this text.

Conclusions

It will be interesting to see in the future how pervading clinical opinions on TSD may change based on growing factions of evidence-based and 'atheoretical' practitioners. The larger movement of evidence-based practice seeks to encourage reliance on therapeutic models, techniques, and fidelity determined in research to be beneficial to clients in at least some if not many if not most circumstances. Practitioners operating from this basis often make mention of how it is important to use methods with established efficacy and standardization, in which case recipient clients may have reason to expect better results from treatment.

Clinicians from a less theoretical, less research-driven persuasion are often of the opinion that various clinical circumstances, including self-disclosure scenarios, are at least somewhat more unique than similar. It is not uncommon for therapists of this line of thought to view (theory/research-influenced) managed care restrictions on practice methods (which modular approaches often accommodate) as de-individualizing treatment and inhibiting the flow and delivery of professional helping. Thus, theory and research on the whole may be argued to have less applicability to practice than what is often alleged in the evidence-based movement. Primarily, because what tends to more often make a TSD helpful/appropriate or unhelpful/inappropriate are factors related to the therapist, the therapist's understanding of the client's individual needs, and an understanding of the strength and dynamics of the relationship. These points were touched upon within the prior review of contemporary perspectives and conceptual literature, and will also be more thoroughly discussed within upcoming chapters related to timing and types of TSD.

It is reasonable to assume that most practitioners are probably not rigidly ascribed to either side of the previous debate, likely incorporate some extent of research implications and individualization of treatment, and may (nevertheless) lean at least somewhat more strongly in one direction or the other. Whereas some therapists may question the practice-based implications of controlled research, other therapists may question whether reliance on a somewhat uncontrolled myriad and integration of prior experiences, training, and intuition about a client's emotional state is more likely than research to guide effective interventions. In all likelihood, somewhere in between lies the truth in most cases.

From this chapter, major take-aways for the research-informed practitioner include that TSD has not only gained at least a minimally or marginally greater level of acceptance across theoretical orientations, but can also be more actively worked into theoretical conceptualizations and interventional planning. Whereas the theoretical component may appear somewhat of an afterthought to in-the-moment clinical thinking, the research on TSD marks an important step towards reconciling the prior debate. The research suggests that self-disclosing with timing and intentionality relevant to the particular aims of a particular approach may not only be a potent intervention, but may also offer a method of practicing fidelity to a model in an emotionally nearer way.

Whereas certain interventions and techniques may neatly fit into a particular model, a TSD intended to meet similar goals may be received by clients as more authentic, giving to the relationship, and therefore more likely to associate with positive and model-specific outcomes. This idea is put forth as a hypothesis that flowed from the research and warrants follow-up study.

TSD may have a different aim under different theoretical lenses, though the commonality across theories is that there should be a clear purpose of theory-driven disclosures, with respect to the particular aims and goals of the model. For example, psychodynamic practitioners may be more theoretically inclined to self-disclose their immediate emotional reactions, primarily, in an effort to positively impact the client's object relations. Cognitive behavioral practitioners may self-disclose about their methods of coping and problem solving in an attempt to help the client shift their perspective on presenting problems and encourage behavioral activation.

Further study in this area is clearly needed, and with particular attention to whether research-/theory-informed TSDs or non-theory-informed TSDs may be more efficacious in different clinical circumstances. In particular, this research is necessary because research summarized in upcoming chapters will show that positive and negative outcomes associated with self-disclosure are fairly patterned across contexts and highly congruent with theoretical positions noted previously. Thus, it can be argued that results from research being at least somewhat affirming of theoretical positions suggests the potential benefit of *theory-driven decision-making*, as applied to scenarios wherein self-disclosure may be a possibility.

References

Ackerman, S., & Hilsenroth, M. (2003). A review of therapist characteristics and techniques positively impacting the therapeutic alliance. *Clinical Psychology Review*, *23*(1), 1–33.

Audet, C. (2011). Client perspectives of therapist self-disclosure: Violating boundaries or removing boundaries? *Counselling Psychology Quarterly*, *24*(2), 85–100.

Audet, C., & Everall, R. (2003). Counsellor self-disclosure: Client-informed implications for practice. *Counselling and Psychotherapy Research*, *3*(3), 223–31.

Barrett, M., & Berman, J. (2001). Is psychotherapy more effective when therapists disclose information about themselves? *Journal of Consulting and Clinical Psychology*, *69*(4), 597–603.

Bitar, G., Kimball, T., Bermúdez, J., & Drew, C. (2014). Therapist self-disclosure and culturally competent care with Mexican-American court mandated clients: A phenomenological study. *Contemporary Family Therapy*, *36*(3), 417–25.

Bottrill, S., Pistrang, N., Barker, C., & Worrell, M. (2010). The use of therapist self-disclosure: Clinical psychology trainees' experiences. *Psychotherapy Research*, *20*(2), 165–80.

D'Aniello, C., & Nguyen, H. (2017). Considerations for intentional use of self-disclosure for family therapists. *Journal of Family Psychotherapy*, *28*(1), 23–37.

Dean, B. (2010). Therapist self-disclosure: Heterosexual perceptions of sexual minority therapists (Doctoral dissertation). Retrieved from ProQuest Dissertations and Theses database. (No UMI No.).

Dryden, W. (1990). Self-disclosure in rational-emotive therapy. In G. Stricker & M. Fisher (Eds.), *Self-disclosure in the therapeutic relationship* (pp. 61–74). New York: Plenum Press.

Farber, B. (2006). *Self-disclosure in psychotherapy*. New York: Guilford Press.

Freeman, A., Fleming, B., & Pretzer, J. (1990). *Clinical applications of cognitive therapy*. New York: Plenum Press.

Goldfried, M., Burckell, L., & Eubanks-Carter, C. (2003). Therapist self-disclosure in cognitive behavior therapy. *Journal of Clinical Psychology/In Session, 59*(5), 555–68.

Gutheil, T., & Gabbard, G. (1998). Misuses and misunderstandings of boundary theory in clinical and regulatory settings. *American Journal of Psychiatry, 155*(3), 409–14.

Hanson, J. (2005). Should your lips be zipped? How therapist self-disclosure and non-disclosure affects clients. *Counselling & Psychotherapy Research, 5*(2), 96–104.

Henretty, J., & Levitt, H. (2010). The role of therapist self-disclosure in psychotherapy: A qualitative review. *Clinical Psychology Review, 30*(1), 63–77.

Horvath, A. (2000). The therapeutic relationship: From transference to alliance. *Journal of Clinical Psychology, 56*(2), 163–73.

Knox, S., & Hill, C. (2003. Therapist self-disclosure: Research-based suggestions for practitioners. *Journal of Clinical Psychology, 59*(5), 529–39.

LaPorte, H., Sweifach, J., & Linzer, N. (2010). Sharing the trauma: Guidelines for therapist self-disclosure following a catastrophic event. *Best Practices in Mental Health, 6*(2), 39–56.

Miller, E., & McNaught, A. (2016). Exploring decision making around therapist self-disclosure in cognitive behavioural therapy. *Australian Psychologist, 53*(1), 1–7.

Roberts, J. (2005). Transparency and self-disclosure in family therapy: Dangers and possibilities. *Family Process, 44*(1), 45–63.

Satterly, B. (2006). Therapist self-disclosure from a gay male perspective. *Families in Society: The Journal of Contemporary Social Services, 87*(2), 240–7.

Simonds, L., & Spokes, N. (2017). Therapist self-disclosure and the therapeutic alliance in the treatment of eating problems. *Eating Disorders, 25*(2), 151–64.

Sturges, J. (2012). Use of therapist self-disclosure and self-involving statements. *The Behavior Therapist, 35*(5), 90–3.

Tabol, C., & Walker, G. (2008). The practice of psychotherapy: Application. In M. Ballou, M. Hill, & C. West (Eds.), *Feminist therapy theory and practice: A contemporary perspective* (pp. 87–108). New York: Springer.

Tantillo, M. (2004). The therapist's use of self-disclosure in a relational therapy approach for eating disorders. *Eating Disorders, 12*(51), 51–73.

Tsai, M., Plummer, M., Kanter, J., Newring, R., & Kohlenberg, R. (2010). Therapist grief and functional analytic psychotherapy: Strategic self-disclosure of personal loss. *Journal of Contemporary Psychotherapy, 40*(1), 1–10.

Thomas, M. (2008). Shades of gray: Lesbian therapists explore the complexities of self-disclosure to heterosexual clients (Doctoral dissertation). Retrieved from Smith College Theses, Dissertations, and Projects.

Vandenberghe, L., & Silva Silvestre, R. (2014). Therapist's positive emotions in- session: Why they happen and what they are good for. *Counselling and Psychotherapy Research, 14*(2), 119–27.

Ziv-Beiman, S., & Shahar, G. (2016). Therapeutic self-disclosure in integrative psychotherapy: When is this a clinical error? *Psychotherapy, 53*(3), 273–7.

CHAPTER 4

Research on Efficacy and Outcomes

Graham S. Danzer, PsyD

Inherently, therapeutic self-disclosure (TSD) is difficult to research empirically because what leads therapists to disclose under what circumstances and what makes a disclosure impact a client in a particular way depends largely on a multitude of client and therapist personal factors, the therapist's professional training and perspectives, and clinical and vulnerability/cultural considerations that are very difficult to measure and reliably account for (D'Aniello & Nguyen, 2017). In fact, it is this difficulty that makes the current text a necessary addition to the scholarly literature. This text not only addresses each major research confound in its own distinct chapter, but also applies the literature on each factor to more nebulous clinical practice issues. Applied to the current chapter, the learning objective for the research-informed practitioner will be to connect the extent and quality of recurring TSD effects and outcomes to each clinical and contextual factor discussed in each of the chapters within the next two sections.

With concerns about replicability and reliability in mind, TSD research from the 1970s to 2010 was largely of a controlled analogue nature with simulated clients (Audet & Everall, 2003; Henretty & Levitt, 2010). Analogue participants are typically college students presented with a hypothetical therapy session via a written vignette, transcript, or video tape and are asked to rate a particular therapist, intervention, or occurrence in terms of how positive or negative it appears to be (Knox & Hill, 2003).

The sum total of analogue-TSD research yielded mixed findings erring towards supporting the potential efficacy of disclosure in at least some circumstances (Audet, 2011; Henretty & Levitt, 2010; Simonds & Spokes, 2017). A quantitative meta-analysis conducted by Henretty, Currier, Berman, and Levitt (2014), with most studies being analogue, yielded generally supportive findings, as well as a conclusion that TSD significantly predicted greater client perception of therapist positive regard and attractiveness. As reviewed by Simonds and Spokes (2017), analogue studies conducted from 1977 to 2001 supported the benefits of therapists sharing impersonal demographic details and responding to client disclosures with reciprocal disclosures of similar content. Early analogue studies were limited by the usage of simulated clients, selection biases, and small sample sizes (Bottrill, Pistrang, Barker,

& Worrell, 2010; Simonds & Spokes, 2017), as well as controlled laboratory conditions (Henretty & Levitt, 2010; Kelly & Rodriguez, 2007), and a limited number of time points when data was collected (Ackerman & Hilsenroth, 2003).

Henretty and Levitt (2010) qualitatively reviewed 61 studies that were analogue, retrospective, and/or empirical in nature. Among these studies, most supported TSD in general, while relatively few yielded mixed findings, and few studies more overtly suggested that disclosure may generally do more harm than good. Conflicting with progressive theoretical orientation perspectives, client survey research summarized in other parts of this text, and the prior qualitative/meta-analytic review of mostly analogue studies (Henretty & Levitt, 2010), the sum total of research reviewed and quantitatively analyzed in Henretty et al. (2014) concluded no significant/reliable correlation between therapist disclosure and client perceptions of therapist trustworthiness, positive regard, empathy, and higher frequency of client affective expressions. An analogue study by Myers and Hayes (2006) concluded that therapists were perceived as more of an expert when TSD was put forth within a more positively rated therapeutic relationship.

It is reasonable to interpret analogue findings as a caution against assuming that TSD is a quick and unilateral way to build relationships with clients, regardless of other clinical and contextual factors discussed more thoroughly in upcoming chapters. Additionally, simulated clients in analogue studies were often college students who were aware of the intentions and boundaries of the research. Under these circumstances, simulated clients/college students may have responded differently to TSD than non-simulated clients with real suffering, anxiety, and anticipation about becoming open and vulnerable with a historically neutral, emotionally removed, and withholding professional.

As if in answer to the limitations of early analogue research, over the past 20 years, TSD research has generally progressed from a focus on therapist perspectives and qualities to therapeutic process variables and outcomes (Audet, 2011; Audet & Everall, 2003; Bottrill et al., 2010; Henretty & Levitt, 2010; Kelly & Rodriguez, 2007). The focal progression is important in light of the increasing understanding that the client's perspective (rather than the therapist's perspective) tends to be more predictive of outcomes (Audet & Everall, 2003). Outcomes of contemporary research are mostly discussed in terms of immediate impact, which makes clinical sense because TSD is usually put forth as an intervention in service of the therapeutic process, rather than with long-term goals or lasting symptom change in mind (Hill & Knox, 2002).

Consistent with interpretations in the second to last paragraph, the following real client studies tended to report findings that were different from findings as reported in simulated client studies and in a manner consistent with progressive theoretical positions (discussed in Chapter 3). In contrast to the findings from simulated client studies, real clients in qualitative studies reported that they tended to experience disclosing therapists as emotionally warmer (Henretty & Levitt, 2010). As touched upon earlier, warmth is important as it has been identified as a significant correlate of stronger therapeutic relationships (Ackerman & Hilsenroth, 2003). In an additional study of real clients, Hanson (2005) found that clients consistently reported a positive response to TSDs they felt were well attuned and responsive to their needs. These findings are consistent with other research supporting that TSDs perceived by clients as helpful tended to correlate with generally positive outcomes (Simonds & Spokes, 2017).

Levitt et al. (2016) recently studied 52 therapeutic dyads at a university counseling center in order to determine the extent to which types, purpose, and frequency of TSD correlated with the results of treatment. The average length of therapy was 7.44 sessions. A total of 16 therapists were involved in all 52 of the dyads. Of the therapists, 10 were Caucasian, 1 was African American, 3 were Asian or Pacific Islander, and 2 did not specify. Mean length of therapist experience was just over three years. In terms of theoretical orientations, 5 therapists were cognitive behavioral, 3 were humanistic/client-centered, 2 were feminist/multicultural, 2 were integrative/eclectic, 1 was constructivist, 1 was family systems, and 2 did not report. Of the clients in the sample, 36 were Caucasian, 10 were African American, 2 were Latino/a, 1 was of mixed ethnicity, and 2 did not specify. There were 32 women and 20 men.

Consistent with the mention in the introduction of this text (i.e., that most therapists disclose at least some of the time), Levitt et al. (2016) noted that 46 of the 52 dyads included some level of TSD, with approximately 75% of total sessions including between one and four TSDs. Levitt et al. (2016) found that 67.4% of disclosures were of an *intra-therapy* therapy, while 28.4% were *extra-therapy*, and 4.3% were 'asides' (see Chapter 6 on different types of TSD for definition of these terms). According to standardized measures, TSDs presenting the therapist in a neutral rather than a positive light, conveying client–therapist similarity, or intending to have a humanizing effect tended to result in greater symptom reduction, mainly, in areas related to interpersonal problems.

Positive findings from studies of real client experiences versus null findings from analogue studies warrant further discussion. It is first cautioned that null findings may not necessarily suggest wider spread support for conservative ethical and analytic positions. Null findings may have been due to (a) insufficiently warm therapists, (b) TSDs based on insufficient attention to clinical and contextual factors, and/or (c) poorly simulated clients. Thus, it might have been the therapists and not the intervention that failed.

Client survey studies identified some additional ways in which therapist, researcher, and client perspectives may differ significantly. Clients in Audet and Everall's (2003) study rated disclosure as among the most helpful interventions, while therapists rated their disclosures as among the least helpful. Consistent with this discrepancy, therapists and conservative ethicists often worry that TSDs may compromise the therapist's credibility, though client survey data, as reported within literature reviews, suggests that clients tend not to experience disclosing or non-disclosing therapists as more or less professional or credible, though may perceive a disclosing therapist as less of an expert (Audet, 2011; Henretty & Levitt, 2010).

Conclusions

Offering further explanation of the previous discrepancy, client perception of the therapist as expert may have both positive and negative impacts on the therapeutic relationship and outcomes. Some extent of expertness may be necessary to formulate therapeutic goals and maintain client commitment and receptivity, while some extent of egalitarianism may be necessary to encourage client vulnerability and empowerment. An optimal balance between the two may be achieved through the therapist's dynamic understanding of the client and relationship factors over the course of treatment. In turn, this understanding should be what guides clinical thinking in scenarios wherein TSD feels like a possibility.

The sum total of efficacy research yields mixed findings, with what can be considered a moderate level of support for TSD on the whole. It may be of interest or even encouraging for practitioners to have read that most therapists acknowledge intentionally self-disclosing at least some of the time, and that at least some level of TSD is generally supported as beneficial for therapeutic relationships and helpful to clients. Thus, it can be concluded that TSD is a relatively normal and helpful intervention, particularly when brief, conveying similarity, constructive, intended to meet the client's needs from the relationship, and with aims specific to the particular method or theory of treatment (as discussed in Chapters 2 and 3), *and* well-timed, of a type and content relevant to the client's needs, and with appropriate use of supervision or consultation (as discussed in the upcoming 'clinical factor' chapters of this text). As this multitude of clinical and contextual factors can reasonably be assumed to be what makes any intervention effective and helpful to clients, it is reasonable to conclude that appropriate and moderated use of TSD deserves greater and outward acceptance in practice circles, with some acknowledgment that the extent of outcry and controversy may be overblown.

At the same time, previously reviewed efficacy research studies also identified a significant number of therapist and client personal factors, clinical decision-making and technique-related variables, and vulnerability/cultural factors that could not be researched as distinct concepts due to small samples, but are surely influential to outcomes. For example, a heterosexual male Caucasian therapist, with a client of similar cultural and gendered background who chronically arrives and pays late, and shares that the therapist too has had a similar history of irresponsibility in relationships, is likely to be received very differently from that same therapist responding to an African American male client's early disclosure of being discriminated against by acknowledging that the therapist, too, had once held racist beliefs. In real-world practice scenarios, these factors may be experienced and interpreted differently by clients and therapists, at different points in the development of the relationship, and may have immediate, longer standing, and multilayered impacts on the client and therapist as individuals, as well as the therapeutic dyad as an entity.

In essence, the major take-away from this chapter is that TSD is generally beneficial, albeit with a multitude of additional clinical, contextual, and cultural considerations that are the subject of upcoming chapters in this text.

Within the next two sections of chapters will be a review of the scholarly literature on each of the prior factors, with chapter titles flowing from the research, and discussed in their implications for the research-informed practitioner. As noted within the current chapter, findings on positive *and* negative effects, failings of the practitioner and not the technique, and expertness were compelling, and to such an extent that they warrant fuller elaboration in Chapters 26, 28 and 30 of this text, as authored by often cited researchers Jennifer Henretty and Cristelle Audet.

References

Ackerman, S., & Hilsenroth, M. (2003). A review of therapist characteristics and techniques positively impacting the therapeutic alliance. *Clinical Psychology Review*, *23*(1), 1–33.

Audet, C. (2011). Client perspectives of therapist self-disclosure: Violating boundaries or removing boundaries? *Counselling Psychology Quarterly*, *24*(2), 85–100.

Audet, C., & Everall, R. (2003). Counsellor self-disclosure: Client-informed implications for practice. *Counselling and Psychotherapy Research*, *3*(3), 223–31.

Bottrill, S., Pistrang, N., Barker, C., & Worrell, M. (2010). The use of therapist self-disclosure: Clinical psychology trainees' experiences. *Psychotherapy Research*, *20*(2), 165–80.

D'Aniello, C., & Nguyen, H. (2017). Considerations for intentional use of self-disclosure for family therapists. *Journal of Family Psychotherapy*, *28*(1), 23–37.

Hanson, J. (2005). Should your lips be zipped? How therapist self-disclosure and non-disclosure affects clients. *Counselling & Psychotherapy Research*, *5*(2), 96–104.

Henretty, J., Currier, J., Berman, J., & Levitt, H. (2014). The impact of counselor self-disclosure on clients: A meta-analytic review of experimental and quasi-experimental research. *Journal of Counseling Psychology*, *61*(2), 191–207.

Henretty, J., & Levitt, H. (2010). The role of therapist self-disclosure in psychotherapy: A qualitative review. *Clinical Psychology Review*, *30*(1), 63–77.

Hill, C., & Knox, S. (2002). Self-disclosure. In J. Norcross (Ed.), *Psychotherapy relationships that work: Therapist contributions and responsiveness to patients* (pp. 255–65). New York: Oxford University Press.

Kelly, A., & Rodriguez, R. (2007). Do therapists self-disclose more to clients with greater symptomology? *Psychotherapy: Theory, Research, Practice, Training*, *44*(4), 470–5.

Knox, S., & Hill, C. (2003). Counselor self-disclosure: Research-based suggestions for practitioners. *Journal of Clinical Psychology: Special Issue: In Session: Self-Disclosure*, *59*(5), 529–39.

Levitt, H., Minami, T., Greenspan, S., Puckett, J., Henretty, J., Reich, C., & Berman, J. (2016). How therapist self-disclosure related to alliance and outcomes: A naturalistic study. *Counselling Psychology Quarterly*, *29*(1), 7–28.

Myers, D., & Hayes, J. (2006). Effects of counselor general self-disclosure and countertransference disclosure on ratings of the counselor and session. *Psychotherapy: Theory, Research, Practice, Training*, *43*(2), 173–85.

Simonds, L., & Spokes, N. (2017). Therapist self-disclosure and the therapeutic alliance in the treatment of eating problems. *Eating Disorders*, *25*(2), 151–64.

Part II
Clinical Factors

CHAPTER 5

Timing and Decision-Making

Graham S. Danzer, PsyD and Kevin Andresen, MA

It is important to first recall that the nebulous and multi-faceted nature of therapist decisions on whether or not to self-disclose in different circumstances makes it essential to review and discuss scholarly perspectives on the subject, as an additional source of information on one of the most controversial clinical subject matters. Short of suggesting a more rigid approach to decision-making, the scholarly literature will be shown to provide a helpful overview of factors related to the decision-making process and timing considerations of therapeutic self-disclosure (TSD). In turn, these considerations will be shown to correlate with the guiding principles of disclosure ethics and efficacy mentioned in the prior section of chapters in this text.

Probably due to the inherent difficulty of measuring in the moment decision-making variables, literature on decision-making and timing is largely conceptual, though converges with prior empirical research findings in ways that will be shown to be clinically informative. Germaine to the larger subject matter of this text, the primary author of this chapter was encouraged to find that recurrent therapist writer perspectives on timing and decision-making variables were largely in line with prior research findings. Convergence suggests the possibility that generally accepted clinical thinking and research findings on TSD may not be as divergent as some might think. In effect, it may be that maximally ethical and helpful self-disclosures are intuitively consistent with the research, even when not by design or intention. Whereas managed care restrictions and the evidence-based movement advance the more purposeful and predetermined application of *research to practice*, alignment between therapist writer intuitions/perspectives and outcomes suggests that it may be as clinically valuable to apply *practice considerations to research*. This may be of particular consideration when it comes to nebulous clinical practice variables, such as TSD timing and decision-making, which may be very difficult (if not impossible) to research empirically.

Deciding Whether or Not to Self-Disclose?

The decision to disclose or not to disclose is first and foremost clinical and cannot be made entirely based on pre-determined procedures and parameters (Bottrill, Pistrang, Barker, & Worrell, 2010). In therapy, opportunities to disclose arise suddenly and do not usually allow time for careful reflection and implementation planning (Bottrill et al., 2010). When these opportunities arise, the therapist will have a lot of information to consider and a very short amount of time to decide what to do (Henretty & Levitt, 2010). Accordingly, therapist uncertainty in such scenarios is not uncommon (LaPorte, Sweifach, & Linzer, 2010) and is probably an appropriate showing of therapeutic reservation, restraint, and critical thinking as discussed in Chapter 2 of this text. How therapists make such decisions may vary considerably depending on their unique personal qualities (Kelly & Rodriguez, 2007).

What makes TSD beneficial or potentially harmful to the client depends largely on the specific therapeutic dyad and framework (Aron, 1996; Greenberg, 1995; Mitchell, 1997), as understood by a therapist, based on his or her combination of personality skills and features (Henretty & Levitt, 2010). The ideal personality of the disclosing therapist is described similarly by different researchers. Preferred qualities include a high level of self-awareness (LaPorte et al., 2010), discernment and forethought (Hanson, 2005), intuition, vulnerability, authenticity, and judiciousness (Bitar, Kimball, Bermúdez, & Drew, 2014), and tact, timing, patience, humility, perseverance, and sensitivity (Henretty & Levitt, 2010). Such a repertoire of 'clinical-personality skills' are something of a base from that therapists make maximally appropriate and helpful decisions about whether or not to self-disclose in different clinical circumstances.

The inherent subjectivity and controversy of the ideal personality of the self-disclosing therapist warrants additional scrutiny and exploration. While it is reasonable to assume face validity of researchers' prior positions, it is also reasonable to assume that therapists, researchers, and clients probably differ considerably in terms of who they would opine to be highly self-aware, discerning, authentic, appropriately vulnerable, humble, persevering, and sensitive. It is likely that some therapists, if viewed in practice by other *competent* therapists, might be seen as clearly having *or lacking* the preferred qualities described in the previous paragraph. It is also likely that many therapists might not be so obvious in their presentation and goodness or badness of fit (i.e., to self-disclose). Moreover, it is reasonable to suspect that therapists who might be generally regarded as self-serving, impulsive, disregarding, and poorly attuned would be the least likely to be aware of these limitations and exercise additional restraint. Paradoxically, if therapists were to acknowledge such shortcomings and exercise restraint, they might be demonstrating the ideal qualities they doubt themselves to have, and may in turn be more capable of self-disclosing ethically and helpfully than what they might have initially assumed. Such multi-layered possibilities and implications related to clinical competency speak to the importance of teaching clinical thinking, decision-making, and encouraging a deeper process of reflection and maturation in training and education, which will be discussed in more detail in the next chapter of this text.

One of the major challenges in deciding whether or not to disclose is that it is difficult to know (a) what clients do or do not want to know about their therapists, and (b) what the effects of a TSD may or may not be (Roberts, 2005). Client responses may depend significantly and perhaps unexpectedly on manifest aspects of their personalities, as well as aspects of their personal histories and early lives (which may or may not be known to the therapist), and situational therapeutic relational dynamics. Similarly, therapists may differ in their ability to identify and anticipate client curiosities, underlying motivations, and possible/likely reactions to disclosure. For such reasons, the anticipated risks and rewards of TSD need to be weighed carefully, with an acknowledgment that therapist predictions are likely to be at least somewhat inaccurate or imprecise (Gibson, 2012). Ultimately, the full impact of a TSD may never be fully known by a therapist (Thomas, 2008).

Within their review of TSD studies, Henretty and Levitt (2010) noted that disclosure/non-disclosure decisions should be considerate of the client's expectations and preferences for the nature of therapy and whether disclosure content is positive or negative/confrontational, similar/dissimilar to the client's experience, reactive, or well-thought-out, and volunteered by the therapist or requested by the client. Consistent with progressive theoretical orientations, as well as Henretty and Levitt's (2010) larger findings, surveyed clients in other studies consistently reported a desire for their therapist's decisions to (or not to) disclose to be based primarily on the therapist's assessment of what was happening in the relationship at the time, rather than basing their decisions on pre-determined rules (Audet & Everall, 2003; Bitar et al., 2014).

There is also the perspective in some research studies that therapists should consider formulating a personal policy on TSD before opportunities suddenly arise (Bottrill et al., 2010; Henretty & Levitt, 2010). Consistent with prior cautions about TSD and self-care, Bottrill et al. (2010) noted that the therapist's personal policy should be based on the range of potentially positive and negative effects of TSD on both themselves and the client. Research cited within Henretty and Levitt's (2010) review indicated that therapists might first consider orienting clients to the therapist's TSD policy and then consider asking the client's permission to disclose when opportunities arise in session, rather than making an executive decision in the moment.

Therapeutic Timing Considerations

The timing of TSD is important to discuss through the lens of scholarly literature, indeed, because it is elusive and difficult to conceptualize. It is likely that what makes a particular TSD helpful to a client is more about timing, as well as authenticity, rather than frequency or the intimacy of content (Tantillo, 2004).

Timing is particularly difficult to account for in cases where clients come to therapy with multiple problems that require multiple interventions that are in turn vulnerable to multiple interaction effects (Ziv-Beiman & Shahar, 2016). Within the conceptual literature and research is a modest level of discussion about how TSD may be put forth and received by clients at the beginning of therapy, during termination, and as a strategy for addressing and working through therapeutic ruptures.

Within the conceptual literature are positions for and against TSD in the initial rapport-building stage of therapy. Early TSDs, usually of a non-threatening and even superficial nature, have been discussed as helping to lower initial client anxieties, contributing to the formation of therapeutic relationships, and inspiring discussion and development of treatment goals (Audet & Everall, 2003; Bitar et al., 2014; Ziv-Beiman, 2013). In furtherance of the prior objectives, content of early TSDs may include the therapist's education, licenses, professional experience and training, and areas of specialty or expertise (Dean, 2010).

Historically, disclosure in the initial stage of therapy has been discouraged for reasons consistent with ethical and early analytic cautions discussed in prior chapters (Strasburger, Jorgenson, & Sutherland, 1992; Watkins & Schneider, 1989). To review, while early disclosures may be intended to build rapport, they also risk sending the client a mixed message about therapeutic boundaries and roles, and can distract from the focus of treatment. For such reasons, it has been recommended within some research articles that TSDs be withheld or at least put forth infrequently until the relationship is more firmly established (Gelso & Palma, 2011; Henretty & Levitt, 2010). In so doing, the possibility of client burden associated with disclosure may be lowered (Audet & Everall, 2003).

The conceptual literature also contains more middle-ground perspectives on early self-disclosures. Roberts (2005) recommended that early disclosures for the purpose of joining should be limited and probably withheld to a greater degree as the therapy progresses. As an additional form of compromise, it has been recommended that therapists at least refrain from high-intimacy disclosures early in the relationship (Audet & Everall, 2003). This strategy may help the therapist to learn more objectively about the client's expectations for therapy and begin to anticipate their reactions to a disclosing therapist (Audet & Everall, 2003).

Levitt et al. (2016) recently explored similar hypotheses about early disclosure through naturalistic research on 52 client–therapist dyads in a university counseling setting. Somewhat conflicting with prior cautions, Levitt et al.'s (2016) findings indicated no significant correlation between frequency of early disclosure and scores on standardized measures of therapeutic alliance. Early disclosures that tended to associate with lower symptom severity at the end of sessions were intended to portray the humanity and humility of the therapist, convey therapist-client similarity, and were fairly neutral in terms of the disclosure not presenting the therapist in either a clearly positive or negative light. Therefore, these results were somewhat affirming of the humanistic and client-centered conceptualizations of how TSD may work into treatment.

Disclosure during termination has been discussed as helping clients to consolidate grief and growth experiences (Henretty & Levitt, 2010; Knox & Hill, 2003). Progressive therapeutic models at times encourage a more authentic and open-hearted termination as a way to solidify and deepen therapeutic gains (Tsai, Plummer, Kanter, Kanter, Newring, & Kohlenberg, 2010). Controversially, therapists may write goodbye letters and/or become openly tearful or humorous when doing so may help clients grow in their capacities for healthy intimacy and reciprocity (Tsai et al., 2010). It may even be that TSDs during termination can help to ward off client regression and model a healthier and more authentic way of saying goodbye. In such cases, clients may have a truer form of attachment experience and be more receptive to resuming or continuing therapy as needed in the future.

Within the conceptual literature are perspectives on how TSD may be an intervention in service of working through therapeutic ruptures and mistakes (Fox, Strum, & Walters, 1984; Henretty & Levitt, 2010). Although the impact and helpfulness of TSD necessarily depends on the therapeutic dyad and circumstances at hand, it is also reasonable to expect that most clients experiencing a misattunement or interpreting a therapist statement as unduly critical or irrelevant would probably appreciate and respond at least somewhat favorably to a therapist transparently acknowledging his or her mistake and being open to a discussion of a revised or perhaps more mindful approach in the future. These positions on how TSD can help address or repair therapeutic ruptures are consistent with prior research findings supporting the benefits of real-time feeling (i.e., *self-involving* disclosures, as discussed in the next chapter), as well as prior mentions of therapists appropriately modeling vulnerability, and potentially opening the door to intense and clinically productive en-vivo work.

Conclusions

From a review of the conceptual literature emerges important implications for the research-informed practitioner. It must first be acknowledged that decisions to or not to self-disclose are necessarily clinical, based primarily on in-the-moment considerations, and cannot be navigated entirely based on predetermined rules or lines of thinking. At the same time, prior preparation and consideration may be helpful, as moments in which TSD may be a possibility are fleeting and give the therapist a lot of information to consider in a relatively short period of time. A high level of self-awareness, tact, timing, patience, attentiveness to moment-to-moment client *needs* (i.e., as opposed to client desires for gratification), and forethought are among the therapist qualities if not independent variables most likely predictive of relatively successful navigation of these circumstances, which are in turn likely to be among the most clinically fruitful *and* hazardous.

Also from the conceptual literature emerge forms of advice for therapists considering TSD during different stages of therapy. Positions for and against using TSD to build rapport in the early stage of relationship building are reconciled by *permitting* judicious, brief, lower intimacy, and modulated forms of TSD, at least in some therapeutic relationships, and in a manner consistent with ethical and theoretical positions noted in previous chapters of this text. When put forth by a well-attuned and well-boundaried therapist, such forms of TSD are likely to appropriately convey the humanity, sincerity of desire to help, and emotional accessibility of the therapist. Early TSDs of a more excessive, lengthy, or irrelevant nature are expected to complicate therapeutic relationships.

More broadly, this last point suggests that what ultimately makes TSD ethically appropriate/inappropriate *and* helpful/unhelpful clients may not be fundamentally different from what determines the relative appropriateness and helpfulness of other interventions. Thus, a therapist's ability *to disclose* ethically and helpfully, in light of the prior multitude of considerations and complications, may be something of a barometer of clinical competency on the whole. This possibility will be explored further in upcoming discussant chapters of this text.

Additionally, TSD is discussed in the conceptual literature in its potential to help work through therapeutic ruptures or mistakes, and to solidify client gains during the termination stage of treatment. It is reasonable to assume that most clients, on some level, would appreciate a therapist's transparent acknowledgment of misunderstanding them, not attending sufficiently to their needs, or otherwise engaging in a relatively normal, non-egregious, and at least somewhat expectable form of clinical blunder. As discussed in more detail in Chapter 2 of this text, therapist writers advise that such an acknowledgment be followed by the therapist attempting to quickly return to topics of therapeutic discussion or dynamics that have in the past seemed to help build and maintain the relationship.

In a similar vein, therapists are advised to consider TSD in the form of a more authentic and transparent goodbye. While some therapist writers advise letter writing and more heartfelt emotional expressions, the primary author of this chapter infers that a more moderated form of boundary expansion, to permit sharing and receiving of personal feelings, *may* in some cases be warranted. It is also reasonable to conclude that any real and lasting clinical gains have been at least partially the result of therapist transparency and accessibility, as well as forms of restraint, discipline, and not impulsively or instantly gratifying client requests. Therefore, it may be advantageous to consider TSD during times of therapeutic rupture or termination, though not to an extent well beyond the therapist's practice-of-usual. In the latter case, a well-boundaried and forethinking therapist who suddenly presents very differently to a client at the time of goodbye may be perceived by the client as communicating a desire for a personal relationship. In such a case, a suddenly and perhaps impulsively disclosing therapist may be disregarding his or her clinical mindset, which can be considered the engine to psychotherapy, as the vehicle for real, lasting, and meaningful client change.

References

Aron, L. (1996). *A meeting of minds: Mutuality in psychoanalysis*. London: Analytic Press.

Audet, C., & Everall, R. (2003). Counsellor self-disclosure: Client-informed implications for practice. *Counselling and Psychotherapy Research*, 3(3), 223–31.

Bitar, G., Kimball, T., Bermúdez, J., & Drew, C. (2014). Therapist self-disclosure and culturally competent care with Mexican-American court mandated clients: A phenomenological study. *Contemporary Family Therapy*, 36(3), 417–25.

Bottrill, S., Pistrang, N., Barker, C., & Worrell, M. (2010). The use of therapist self-disclosure: Clinical psychology trainees' experiences. *Psychotherapy Research*, 20(2), 165–80.

Dean, B. (2010). Therapist self-disclosure: Heterosexuals' perceptions of sexual minority therapists (Doctoral dissertation). Retrieved from the University Digital Conservancy database.

Fox, S., Strum, C., & Walters, H. (1984). Perceptions of therapist disclosure of previous experience as a client. *Journal of Clinical Psychology*, 40(2), 496–8.

Gelso, C., & Palma, B. (2011). Directions for research on self-disclosure and immediacy: Moderation, mediation, and the inverted-U. *Psychotherapy*, 48(4), 342–8.

Gibson, M. (2012). Opening up: Therapist self-disclosure in theory, research, and practice. *Clinical Social Work Journal*, 40(3), 287–96.

Greenberg, J. (1995). Self-disclosure: Is it psychoanalytic? *Contemporary Psychoanalysis*, 31(2), 193–205.

Hanson, J. (2005). Should your lips be zipped? How therapist self-disclosure and non-disclosure affects clients. *Counselling & Psychotherapy Research*, 5(2), 96–104.

Henretty, J., & Levitt, H. (2010). The role of therapist self-disclosure in psychotherapy: A qualitative review. *Clinical Psychology Review*, 30(1), 63–77.

Kelly, A., & Rodriguez, R. (2007). Do therapists self-disclose more to clients with greater symptomology? *Psychotherapy: Theory, Research, Practice, Training*, 44(4), 470–5.

Knox, S., & Hill, C. (2003). Therapist self-disclosure: Research-based suggestions for practitioners. *Journal of Clinical Psychology*, 59(5), 529–39.

LaPorte, H., Sweifach, J., & Linzer, N. (2010). Sharing the trauma: Guidelines for therapist self-disclosure following a catastrophic event. *Best Practices in Mental Health*, 6(2), 39–56.

Levitt, H., Minami, T., Greenspan, S., Puckett, J., Henretty, J., Reich, C., & Berman, J. (2016). How therapist self-disclosure relates to alliance and outcomes: A Naturalistic study. *Counselling Psychology Quarterly*, 29(1), 7–28.

Mitchell, S. (1997). Two quibbles: Commentary on Kenneth A. Frank's paper. *Psychoanalytic Dialogues*, 7(3), 319–22.

Roberts, J. (2005). Transparency and self-disclosure in family therapy: Dangers and possibilities. *Family Process*, 44(1), 45–63.

Strasburger, L., Jorgenson, L., & Sutherland, P. (1992). The prevention of psychotherapist sexual misconduct: Avoiding the slippery slope. *American Journal of Psychotherapy*, 46(4), 544–55.

Tantillo, M. (2004). The therapist's use of self-disclosure in a relational therapy approach for eating disorders. *Eating Disorders*, 12(1), 51–73.

Thomas, M. (2008). Shades of gray: Lesbian therapists explore the complexities of self-disclosure to heterosexual clients (Doctoral dissertation). Retrieved from Smith College Theses, Dissertations, and Projects.

Tsai, M., Plummer, M., Kanter, J., Newring, R., & Kohlenberg, R. (2010). Therapist grief and functional analytic psychotherapy: Strategic self-disclosure of personal loss. *Journal of Contemporary Psychotherapy*, *40*(1), 1–10.

Watkins, C., & Schneider, L. (1989). Self-involving vs. self-disclosing counselor statements during an initial interview. *Journal of Counseling and Development*, *67*(6), 345–9.

Ziv-Beiman, S. (2013). Therapist self-disclosure as an integrative intervention. *Journal of Psychotherapy Integration*, *23*(1), 59–74.

Ziv-Beiman, S., & Shahar, G. (2016). Therapeutic self-disclosure in integrative psychotherapy: When is this a clinical error? *Psychotherapy*, *53*(3), 273–7.

CHAPTER 6

The Different Types of Self-Disclosure

Graham S. Danzer, PsyD and Kevin Andresen, MA

It is important to discuss the various *types* of therapeutic self-disclosure (TSD) as not all are the same and in fact differ significantly in terms of intentionality, intimacy, and implications for treatment (Bottrill, Pistrang, Barker, & Worrell, 2010; Henretty & Levitt, 2010). Different types of TSD discussed in this chapter may have significantly different effects on clients and overall results of treatment (Thomas, 2008). In a broader sense, nonverbal and unintentional forms of TSD are qualitatively different from verbal TSDs (Dean, 2010). The ways in which types of TSD are different and may have different impacts are discussed as follows.

Intentionally or unintentionally, therapists may reveal a lot about themselves through office pictures and décor, a wedding ring, pregnancy, religious head coverings, how they behave during random/chance encounters with clients in the community, or how they respond to clients suddenly asking personal questions in-session (Henretty & Levitt, 2010; LaPorte, Sweifach, & Linzer, 2010). Revealing qualities or characteristics also include the therapist's gender and race (Cabaj, 1991), demeanor, body language, tone of voice, and facial expressions (Russell, 2006; Thomas, 2008; Zur, 2007), and/or the presence of LGBTQ-affirmative insignia (Daley, 2012). Ultimately, and whether intentionally or unintentionally, therapists are disclosing aspects of themselves every time they speak to clients (Gutheil & Gabbard, 1993).

Thus, unintentional TSDs are mentioned somewhat frequently in the conceptual literature and with good reason. From a diversity perspective, it is important to consider not only individual differences between the therapist and client, such as mannerisms, ways of thinking, or interpersonal and communication style, but also *between group differences*. Applied to the subject of TSD, and with additional consideration of factors discussed in prior chapters, clients may not only react differently to a particular TSD depending on timing, intimacy of content, brevity, relevance, and therapist personality skills. Additionally, clients are likely to react at least somewhat differently when a similar TSD is put forth by a therapist who is male, female, or gender nonconforming, of African American, Caucasian, Latino, or Asian American ethnicity, presenting with religious head covering or insignia, who is or is not pregnant, and is or is not wearing a wedding ring.

The subject of unintentional TSD has been insufficiently researched in terms of the extent to which various forms associate with outcomes and under what clinical circumstances. As a result, the research-informed practitioner reader is cautioned to consider and prepare for potential ramifications of unintentional disclosures and continue reviewing the literature in case further study occurs in the future. Intentional TSDs are discussed in the conceptual literature, researched to a greater extent, and are therefore the primary subject of this chapter.

Self-Involving TSDs

Self-involving disclosures are defined as therapist's direct and transparent sharing of real-time thoughts or feelings with the client (Bottrill et al., 2010). For example, a therapist may share feelings of frustration with a client who is frequently tardy to session (Audet, 2011). These types of disclosures not only reveal to the client how he/she is experienced by the therapist (Audet, 2004; Casement, 1988), but also inform the client about how he or she may affect others in like circumstances (Audet, 2011). Such a form of therapeutic confrontation may help to decrease the frequency of aversive client behaviors (Goldfried, Burckell, & Eubanks-Carter, 2003). Although this explanation is most consistent with psychodynamic theory, self-involving TSDs are considered a crucial ingredient in all therapies (Bottrill et al., 2010).

Self-involving disclosures are not only mentioned in the conceptual literature, but also have support from empirical research. Therapist writers have purported different benefits of self-involving TSDs, including increasing client retention (Watkins & Schneider, 1989), building and repairing therapeutic relationships (Sturges, 2012), and enhancing client perception of therapist genuineness, likeability, and trustworthiness, and decreasing client anxiety (McCarthy Veach, 2011). Potential benefits may also include modeling healthy communication and feedback-receiving skills (Sturges, 2012), helping to illustrate therapeutic points (Eifert & Forsyth, 2005), and addressing lack of client motivation (Goldfried et al., 2003) in the somewhat confrontive manner noted previously. As TSDs of reactions or feelings can be intense, it is important for a therapist to first assess that his or her relationship with the client is strong enough to withstand and support the range of possible impacts (Sturges, 2012). Supporting the efficacy of these positions, in client survey studies reviewed by Henretty and Levitt (2010), self-involving TSDs elicited more positive responses from clients than TSDs of factual or historical content. These findings suggest the possibility that occasional null findings, in general disclosure research, may have failed to account for different impacts of self-involving and potentially less helpful historical disclosures.

Aron's (2016) psychoanalytic paper provided a clinically informative example of the benefits of sharing real-time feelings in a group therapy context, with attention to some of the client interpersonal/attachment variables mentioned in prior chapters. Aron's (2016) group had been meeting for over two years and included a relatively smaller number of higher functioning clients in a private practice setting. Among the members was a 40-year-old man described as having a conflicted early attachment history that he manifested in an alternately charismatic and aggressive personality, as well as a tendency to be absent from group therapy approximately once per month. At one point, the group had progressed into a somewhat emotionally detached discussion of prior grief and loss issues. Aron (2016) reflected that her initial interpretations, exploratory questions, and reflections did not appear to move group members into deeper exploration and affective expression. When the 40-year-old man shared his desire to depart from the group permanently, Aron (2016) transparently shared her feelings of anger at his frequent absences, tendency to orbit the group, and avoid intimacy in a manner consistent with his losses in earlier life. Group member responses and reactions varied, though were generally introspective, constructive, and contributed to a larger group dynamic that was clearly more productive and vibrant. This demonstrates how self-involving TSDs may inspire deeper therapeutic engagement and change-inspiring (i.e., corrective) experiences.

Within the conceptual literature are recurring mentions that therapists sharing positive feelings towards clients may help to reassure them, improve their self-image, and reinforce their progress (Goldfried et al., 2003; Hill & Knox, 2002; Sturges, 2012). Research on both client and therapist perspectives offers some support for this position. Supporting the therapist perspective, Vandenberghe and Silva Silvestre (2014) conducted a grounded theoretical research study of 26 therapists identified by colleagues as appropriately mindful and professionally critical of their own practice. The researchers concluded in favor that therapists should consider sharing positive emotions when appropriate. Somewhat in divergence from traditional ethical precautions, the researchers recommended competent therapists should not be dissuaded from sharing positive feelings on the basis of undue personal discomfort or concern about losing therapeutic focus.

Further supporting the sharing of positive emotions, from the client perspective, Simonds and Spokes (2017) conducted a study of 120 eating disorder clients, 84% of whom reported that therapists disclosed their positive feelings (directly to them). Clients reported that TSDs of positive feelings were the most helpful type of disclosure. Types of TSD rated lower by clients in Simonds and Spokes' (2017) study included a therapist's theoretical orientation or training background, life experiences, personal background, therapeutic mistakes, cultural factors, personal values, and sexuality (presented in order of client rating from most to least positive). Additionally, it is noteworthy that clients in Simond and Spokes' (2017) study tended to rate disclosures of most and least helpful content in a manner consistent with prior research on what clients generally do and do not want to hear about from their therapists.

Historical TSDs

Whereas self-involving TSD are generally present and object relations focused, historical TSDs are necessarily past and either empathy or insight focused (Bottrill et al., 2010). Typical content pertains to the therapist's biographical details, education, professional training, theoretical orientation, or beliefs about the relative effectiveness of psychotherapy, as well as acknowledging therapeutic mistakes, and sharing personal insights, coping strategies, attitudes, and personal experiences (Audet & Everall, 2003; Hill & Knox, 2002; Thomas, 2008). Unlike therapist disclosures of feelings/reactions, disclosures of historical content more directly shift the therapeutic focus from the client to the therapist (Audet, 2011). Commensurate with the aims of humanistic and client-centered schools, this type of TSD is usually intended to build rapport, convey the humanness of the therapist, make the therapeutic relationship more egalitarian, model or encourage new perspectives and behavior, or acknowledge and validate client experiences (Audet, 2011; Hill & Knox, 2002). These disclosures may be well received by clients preferring a relational rather than a traditional intrapsychic focus (Audet, 2011).

When therapists disclose factual or historical information, content should convey similarity on a personal level though maintain differentiation on a professional level (Audet, 2011). The balance of similarity and differentiation is important because disclosing overly similar content risks collusion with dysfunctional client attitudes and minimization of uniqueness (Bitar, Kimball, Bermúdez, & Drew, 2014; Goldstein, 1994; Stolorow & Atwood, 1992).

To the latter end, potentially appropriate content of *lower intimacy* historical disclosures may include the therapist's education, training, and theoretical orientation (Audet, 2011). Potentially appropriate content for higher intimacy disclosures may include therapist acknowledgment of interventional mistakes and therapists having been in therapy themselves (Fox, Strum, & Walters, 1984; Henretty & Levitt, 2010).

As follows, research comparing the efficacy of historical and self-involving TSDs had small samples and yielded mixed findings. Interviewed clients reported that therapist revelation of personal and historical information increased therapist likeability and improved their perception of treatment efficacy (Kelly & Rodriguez, 2007). Schimmel's (1994) dissertation research on 54 adolescent males in an early stage of therapy yielded no significant differences depending on whether adolescents were assigned to a therapist utilizing self-involving or historical TSD, or was more fully non-disclosing. Pinto-Coelho, Hill, and Kivlighan (2015) explored the impacts of 185 TSDs over the course of 16 cases of psychodynamic therapy. As predicted earlier, TSDs of feelings and insights (to a greater extent than historical TSDs) correlated with more positive client ratings of the therapeutic relationship.

Findings from client survey data were consistent in terms of what historical content clients do and do not want to hear about. Consistent with prior ethical precautions, clients consistently reported a preference for TSDs to be more general/lower intimacy and convey therapist-client similarity in terms of experiences and personal values (Audet, 2011; Audet & Everall, 2003; Bitar et al., 2014). Consistent with the cognitive behavioral view, clients have indicated high interest in the therapist's personal feelings, methods of coping with problems, interpersonal-relational strategies, and general successes and failures (Audet & Everall, 2003). Aligning with the humanistic/client-centered position, clients in Bitar et al.'s (2014) qualitative study reported positive responses to TSDs of therapist's weekend activities and that therapists, like the client they served, had also experienced periods of depression. In Audet's (2011) qualitative study, a client who thought the therapist might be too young and inexperienced responded positively to hearing about the therapist's life successes. Clients in multiple studies reported not wanting to hear about therapist sexual experiences or relationship failings (Audet, 2011; Audet & Everall, 2003).

What Makes TSD an Intervention Versus a Reaction?

D'Aniello and Nguyen (2017) propose a method of differentiating TSD as an intervention from TSD that is spontaneous if not impulsive. Disclosure as an intervention is described as having a clear purpose related to the therapeutic process, being used infrequently, offering the client a somewhat unique opportunity to look into him or herself, and shifting the therapeutic process without causing role reversal. In contrast, spontaneous/impulsive TSDs often occur when therapists are asked a question by a client and answer the question almost automatically. These disclosures are suspected to occur more frequently. Although these disclosures may build rapport, they also move the basis of connection into a more personal realm and away from theoretical orientation and professional experience.

D'Aniello and Nguyen (2017) offer additional perspectives and insights into the nature of various client inquiries about the therapist. Client questions about the therapist's age, training, and experience are often intended to inform the client's prediction about whether the therapist can be helpful. Client questions about the therapist's personal experiences are generally in inquiry as to whether or not therapists can be empathic. Beneath the surface, personal inquiries may be intended to reduce client anxiety about the therapeutic process, level the inherent power imbalance in the relationship, or signify feelings of vulnerability or powerlessness. In such instances, it may be advantageous for the therapist to explore these client feelings. This opportunity may be missed if therapists answer client inquiries directly and without consideration of how doing so may impact the therapeutic process.

D'Aniello and Nguyen (2017) also offer something of a form of sympathy to therapists struggling to maintain a focus on the process. It is acknowledged that simply responding to client inquiries is socially desirable, so that it becomes difficult for therapists not to gratify client curiosities. Therapists who do not answer client inquiries directly may expect and even fear the possibility of clients becoming angry, experiencing the non-disclosure as a rejection, and expressing dissatisfaction with the therapist and the treatment. As discussed in Chapter 2 of this text, it would also be reasonable to suspect that therapists who surrender to client inquiries may be susceptible to progressing into more serious forms of boundary violation.

Conclusions

Research-informed practitioners should reflect upon prior and potential future TSDs, in part, by considering the potential meanings and impacts of *the type*, as well as the timing, intimacy of content, treatment purpose, and relevance to the client's needs, as discussed in prior chapters of this text. Therapists reflecting on what may be disclosed to clients (of different ages, races, genders, personality types, and needs from therapy) with consideration of the impact of the therapist's race, gender, religious insignia, pregnancy, wedding ring, style of dress, and either self-involving or historical disclosures, are embarking on an important exercise in TSD training.

Therapists considering and more deeply reflecting upon the multitude of interaction effects between the aforementioned self-disclosure variables are likely to later approach TSD scenarios with at least a marginally greater level of forethought, attention to factors known to associate with outcomes, and at least partially due to greater preparatory learning and training. Such a deeper and more reflective clinical mindset is particularly necessary to put forth self-involving TSDs of the therapist's real-time feelings in a manner that may in turn helps clients reflect upon ways in which they may impact the therapist as a symbol of other, acknowledge counter-productive behavior in relationships, and even progress towards taking greater responsibility for immediate and future behavior change. To this end, some degree of knowledge about what *types* of TSD tend to be most and least beneficial to clients, with additional attention to and consideration of factors noted in prior chapters of this text, is likely to be helpful to incorporate within a conceptualization of a scenario where-in TSD feels like a possibility. Contrastingly, therapists impulsively disclosing positive or negative feelings to clients, and without initial forethought, reflection on relevant factors, and a conceptualization of in-the-moment relationship dynamics at least partially informed by relevant research may be less well-informed and probably less well attuned to the client's needs from the relationship.

Inferred from the prior review of research is the general advisement that self-involving TSDs and historical TSDs are likely to be helpful when put forth with appropriate timing, consideration of therapeutic relational dynamics, and with content relevant to the client's needs from the relationship. While historical TSDs may help to communicate empathy, similarity, and understanding, TSDs of feelings and reactions may help clients to have insights into their impacts on others. As research on both therapist and client perspectives most consistently offers a greater level of support for self-involving/feeling TSDs, therapist preference for the latter type may be most advisable in many clinical circumstances.

This discussion does not necessarily make a definitive case for a TSD in any particular circumstance. However, consideration of the type of disclosure and potential impacts on clients is likely to be a helpful component of the therapist's conceptualization of what is happening in the relationship and whether a particular TSD may be appropriate. As a result, decisions to *or not to disclose* may be more likely to be beneficial to clients.

References

Aron, L. (2016). The conductor's self-disclosure of negative countertransference in group analytic psychotherapy. *Group Analysis*, *40*(4), 385–97.

Audet, C. (2004). Client experiences of therapist self-disclosure (Doctoral dissertation). Retrieved from ProQuest Dissertations and Theses database (UMI No. NQ96235).

Audet, C. (2011). Client perspectives of therapist self-disclosure: Violating boundaries or removing boundaries? *Counselling Psychology Quarterly*, *24*(2), 85–100.

Audet, C., & Everall, R. (2003). Counsellor self-disclosure: Client-informed implications for practice. *Counselling and Psychotherapy Research*, *3*(3), 223–31.

Bitar, G., Kimball, T., Bermúdez, J., & Drew, C. (2014). Therapist self-disclosure and culturally competent care with Mexican-American court mandated clients: A phenomenological study. *Contemporary Family Therapy*, *36*(3), 417–25.

Bottrill, S., Pistrang, N., Barker, C., & Worrell, M. (2010). The use of therapist self-disclosure: Clinical psychology trainees' experiences. *Psychotherapy Research*, *20*(2), 165–80.

Cabaj, R. (1991). Sexual orientation of the therapist. In R. Cabaj & E. Stein (Eds.), *Textbook of homosexuality and mental health* (pp. 513–24). Washington, DC: American Psychiatric Publishing.

Casement, P. (1988). *Learning from the patient*. New York: Guilford Press.

Daley, A. (2012) Becoming seen, becoming known: Lesbian women's self-disclosures of sexual orientation to mental health service providers. *Journal of Gay & Lesbian Mental Health*, *16*(3), 215–34.

D'Aniello, C., & Nguyen, H. (2017). Considerations for intentional use of self-disclosure for family therapists. *Journal of Family Psychotherapy*, *28*(1), 23–37.

Dean, B. (2010). Therapist self-disclosure: Heterosexuals' perceptions of sexual minority therapists (Doctoral dissertation). Retrieved from the University Digital Conservancy database.

Eifert, G., & Forsyth, J. (2005). *Acceptance and commitment therapy for anxiety disorders: A practitioner's treatment guide to using mindfulness, acceptance, and values-based behavior change strategies*. Oakland, CA: New Harbinger.

Fox, S., Strum, C., & Walters, H. (1984). Perceptions of therapist disclosure of previous experience as a client. *Journal of Clinical Psychology*, *40*(2), 496–8.

Goldfried, M., Burckell, L., & Eubanks-Carter, C. (2003). Therapist self-disclosure in cognitive behavior therapy. *Journal of Clinical Psychology/In Session*, *59*(5), 555–68.

Goldstein, E. (1994). Self-disclosure in treatment: What therapists do and don't talk about. *Clinical Social Work Journal*, *22*(4), 417–33.

Gutheil, T., & Gabbard, G. (1993). The concept of boundaries in clinical practice: Theoretical and risk-management dimensions. *American Journal of Psychiatry*, *150*(2), 188–96.

Henretty, J., & Levitt, H. (2010). The role of therapist self-disclosure in psychotherapy: A qualitative review. *Clinical Psychology Review*, *30*(1), 63–77.

Hill, C., & Knox, S. (2002). Self-disclosure. In J. Norcross (Ed.), *Psychotherapy relationships that work: Therapist contributions and responsiveness to patients* (pp. 255–65). New York: Oxford University Press.

Kelly, A., & Rodriguez, R. (2007). Do therapists self-disclose more to clients with greater symptomology? *Psychotherapy: Theory, Research, Practice, Training, 44*(4), 470–5.

LaPorte, H., Sweifach, J., & Linzer, N. (2010). Sharing the trauma: Guidelines for therapist self-disclosure following a catastrophic event. *Best Practices in Mental Health, 6*(2), 39–56.

McCarthy Veach, P. (2011). Reflections on the meaning of clinician self-reference: Are we speaking the same language? *Psychotherapy, 48*(4), 349–58.

Pinto-Coelho, K., Hill, C., & Kivlighan, D. (2015). Therapist self-disclosure in psychodynamic psychotherapy: A mixed methods investigation. *Counselling Psychology Quarterly, 29*(1), 29–52.

Russell, G. (2006). Different ways of knowing: the complexities of therapist disclosure. *Journal of Gay and Lesbian Psychotherapy, 10*(1), 79–94.

Schimmel, L. (1994). The effects of therapist verbal self-disclosure on adolescent male offenders' engagement in an initial clinical interview (Doctoral dissertation). Retrieved from ProQuest Dissertations and Theses database (No UMI No.).

Simonds, L., & Spokes, N. (2017). Therapist self-disclosure and the therapeutic alliance in the treatment of eating problems. *Eating Disorders, 25*(2), 151–64.

Stolorow, R., & Atwood, G. (1992). *Contexts of being: The intersubjective foundations of psychological life.* Hillsdale, NJ: Analytic Press.

Sturges, J. (2012). Use of therapist self-disclosure and self-involving statements. *The Behavior Therapist, 35*(5), 90–3.

Thomas, M. (2008). Shades of gray: Lesbian therapists explore the complexities of self-disclosure to heterosexual clients (Doctoral dissertation). Retrieved from Smith College Theses, Dissertations, and Projects.

Vandenberghe, L., & Silva Silvestre, R. (2014). Therapists' positive emotions in- session: Why they happen and what they are good for. *Counselling and Psychotherapy Research, 14*(2), 119–27.

Watkins, C., & Schneider, L. (1989). Self-involving vs. self-disclosing counselor statements during an initial interview. *Journal of Counseling and Development, 67*(6), 345–9.

Zur, O. (2007). *Boundaries in psychotherapy: Ethical and clinical explorations.* Washington, DC: American Psychological Association.

CHAPTER 7

Supervision and Training Considerations

Graham S. Danzer, PsyD

As summarized by Bottrill, Pistrang, Barker, and Worrell (2010), clinical training is a time of exploration and growth. Through educational and experiential learning, trainees are introduced to a multiplicity of clinical theories, approaches, and techniques that they must think through, reflect upon, and reconcile in areas that seem to diverge. Indeed, thinking and consulting through discrepancies and dissonance is one of the primary ways in which trainees mature in their competence and develop stronger professional identities. However, the early stages of this process are often wrought by confusion and anguish until the relative uncertainty and nebulousness of psychotherapy becomes at least somewhat familiar and even invigorating.

For the prior reasons, Bottrill et al. (2010) noted that trainees often feel uncertain and vulnerable when attempting to choose between standard interventions and when to implement them, let alone the particularly complicated process of deciding whether or not to self-disclose to different clients, in different clinical circumstances, and with historical precautions and some level of graduate-educational or supervisory discouragement in mind. Early dilemmas regarding therapeutic self-disclosure (TSD) may be among trainees' foundational experiences of bridging their personal and professional selves, a process of reconciliation/refinement that continues throughout a therapist's career (Bottrill et al., 2010).

Within conceptual writings are concerns about how TSD may not be sufficiently addressed and attended to as part of the supervisory process. It has been suspected that supervisors often avoid a more critical discussion of TSD, or at least do not make it a priority in training (Bottrill et al., 2010). Within, it is common for disclosure to be discouraged, as a *don't ask, don't tell* subject (Bottrill et al., 2010; Henretty & Levitt, 2010). Trainees may require encouragement from their supervisor to candidly discuss issues pertaining to TSD, while supervisors may require similar encouragement from their parent agencies (Bottrill et al., 2010). Consistent with this point, and as summarized within Burkard, Knox, Edwards, Smith, and Schlosser (2008), different research studies have found that therapists and clients often conceal potentially important and relevant information from each other, which is often detrimental to the relationship, and with greater disclosure in supervision usually being beneficial in this respect.

Without at least some level of encouraged openness to TSD, trainees may feel inclined to err on the side of demonstrating fidelity to particular models and may then miss opportunities to appropriately self-disclose for the purpose of joining with clients (D'Aniello & Nguyen, 2017). In such cases, it is possible that trainees may conceptualize clients and intervene in an overly cognitive manner that is relatively disconnected from clients' emotional needs. In turn, clients' emotional needs may, at times, be met through moderated, brief, relevant, well-timed, and well-attuned use of TSD, as discussed in prior chapters of this text, and in service of building relationships and engendering trust in a necessarily two-person therapeutic relationship.

Supervisory avoidance of the topic of TSD is ill-advised because disclosure competence tends not to come naturally, even for therapists who are actively engaged in personal counseling and ongoing supervision (Bitar, Kimball, Bermúdez, & Drew, 2014). Thus, it may be unreasonable and even detrimental to assume that TSD competency will naturally generate over time and thereby negates the need for supervisory attention. As a result, educational and training programs virtually ignoring the issue may indirectly and inadvertently be doing a disservice to clients (Henretty & Levitt, 2010). Insufficient education and training may lead trainees to omit, misuse, or ineffectively use TSD (Carew, 2009). Per a practitioner interviewed by Felloney (2010, p. 76): "In hindsight, I wish I would have learned it [TSD] a littler earlier, to try to use it. I think it may be one of the gifts that worked well for me."

With similar precautions in mind, Bitar et al. (2014) recommended that TSD should be among the agenda topics to cover as part of clinical supervision. D'Aniello and Nguyen (2017) interpreted discrepancies between widespread ethical precautions and generally positive research findings (as discussed in prior chapters of this text) as an indication that doctoral students of advanced candidacy might be appropriately trained *to self-disclose* in ways that are appropriate, therapeutic, and healing. Bottrill et al. (2010) offered something of a reconciliation of pro and con positions by noting that it may be appropriate to advise trainees to be cautious about disclosure early in their training, though unwise to avoid the issue altogether based on the assumption that trainees necessarily lack the necessary experience and clinical wherewithal to disclose ethically and effectively.

Research Findings

Further supporting the positive potential of more fully incorporating TSD in clinical training, Anchor, Strassberg, and Elkins (1976) conducted a study of supervisors' perceptions of trainee disclosure and clinical competence, maturity as a therapist, and clinical sophistication. Supervisor ratings of trainee willingness to self-disclose correlated with significantly higher supervisor ratings of trainee competence and sophistication. TSD ratings did not correlate significantly with supervisory ratings of trainee maturity. Findings were interpreted as suggesting the possibility that (a) TSD may be more independent of the training process than competence and sophistication, and (b) that trainee willingness to self-disclose, as manifested in clinical contexts, may be more of a trait than a state-like personality characteristic.

Recent qualitative research of trainees' experiences suggest a possibility if not likelihood that graduate programs and supervisors, in general, may need to make TSD a greater priority in education and training. In Burkard, Knox, Goren, Perez, and Hess' (2006) qualitative study of 11 trainees, it was common for trainees to report having received minimal or no training in TSD during graduate studies. In Bottrill et al.'s (2010) study of 14 doctoral psychology trainees, it was similarly common for trainees to express reluctance to inquire of their supervisors about disclosure, particularly with a supervisor who they anticipated would be unreceptive or might evaluate them negatively.

Findings on trainee usage of self-involving or historical disclosures are mixed. In Bottrill et al.'s (2010) study, it was found that most trainee TSDs were factual/historical and not of real-time feelings. This finding is of concern in light of prior mentions that self-involving disclosures tend to be more positively impactful on clients. Outside of therapy, honest and transparent disclosures of feelings and reactions tend to occur less frequently and are often difficult for trainees to utilize effectively (Bottrill et al., 2010). Contrastingly, in Kircanski's (2015) dissertation research on five videotaped sessions with trauma survivors, trainees tended to utilize *more* self-involving TSDs. Samples in both studies were too small to reliably analyze within group differences, such as whether a particular type of disclosure was used more or less frequently depending on the level of trainee education and experience.

Within research as follows, some of the potentially *negative* ramifications of de-prioritizing self-disclosure in clinical training are highlighted. Audet and Everall (2003) noted it is not uncommon for the issue of TSD to first come up via clients unexpectedly asking trainees personal questions. In Bottrill et al.'s (2010) study, trainees frequently reported feeling caught off guard, flustered, and uncomfortable when clients asked them questions of a conversational nature that they felt unprepared to answer. Trainees also expressed uncertainty about whether TSD was appropriate (in general) and how to avoid disclosing without offending the client (Bottrill et al., 2010). Such findings are consistent with prior positions on disclosure scenarios evoking complex and client-paralleling emotional states in the therapist, as well as TSD being a multi-layered, multi-faceted bridge of the therapist's personal and professional factors not reasonably addressed in an entirely prescriptive manner.

There are opinions within the literature about whether lesser or more experienced practitioners disclose more or less, though research findings are ultimately mixed and inconclusive. As noted in Henretty and Levitt (2010), experts on the subject have speculated that beginning therapists may self-disclose too frequently. However, five studies conducted from 1989–2001 collectively suggested that less experienced therapists tended to disclose *less frequently* than more experienced therapists (Henretty & Levitt, 2010). Consistently, Bottrill et al.'s (2010) qualitative interview study suggested trainees were quite concerned about over/inappropriate TSDs and reported discomfort with disclosing much of anything. Generally, early career therapists may disclose less and for different reasons, such as a fear that clients may question the therapist's mental health (Henretty & Levitt, 2010).

It is also not uncommon for licensed practitioners to become somewhat less consultative and disclose more frequently and inappropriately as they become independent and feel relatively freer to do so (D'Aniello & Nguyen, 2017). Somewhat consistently with this occurrence, Ladany and Lehrman-Waterman (1999) noted that trainees often reported that supervisors disclosed more about their personal lives (i.e., marital status or religious affiliation) rather than disclosing about their clinical experiences and perspectives. Doremus' (2012) dissertation study of 59 psychologists (42 of whom were male, 52 of whom were Caucasian, and 49 had a PhD) concluded that more years in practice did not significantly predict higher levels of TSD.

Supervision Approaches to Self-Disclosure

As summarized by Farber (2006), supervisors must maintain an at times tenuous balance between giving supportive and critical feedback in order to facilitate trainee growth. This balance is necessary for trainees to become increasingly clinically skilled, though without becoming resistant to a degree that is counter-productive. Among the key tools/methods of maintaining or at times correcting this balance is supervisor disclosure to trainees. Farber (2006) elaborated that supervisor disclosures are often intended to strengthen the relationship, share what the supervisor learned from prior experiences and with some indication of building trainee insight, and providing trainees with feedback about their clinical work.

In turn, trainees need specific advisement on how to disclose appropriately (Bitar et al., 2014). Training programs may begin by openly acknowledging that therapists do self-disclose and that the technique has both merits and risks (Henretty & Levitt, 2010). Student-therapists may benefit from being educated about how to think through the *who, what, why, when*, and *how* of appropriate disclosure (Henretty & Levitt, 2010). It may be difficult to teach the skills that contribute to effective disclosures, such as tact, timing, patience, humility, perseverance, and sensitivity (Henretty & Levitt, 2010). What can be more easily and perhaps even taught in a prescriptive manner are the precepts, rules, criteria, and cognitive processes that guide effective clinical decision-making and alliance building (Ackerman & Hilsenroth, 2003; Henretty & Levitt, 2010). As discussed previously, this process of teaching clinical thinking may be informative to trainees learning about how and when to disclose self-involving feelings and reactions to clients (Bottrill et al., 2010). Beginning therapists should also be helped to understand the clinical utility of their positive emotions and how the presence and sharing of those emotions can positively affect the quality of their clinical work on the whole (Vandenberghe & Silva Silvestre, 2014). Further, trainees may benefit from learning that what makes a TSD helpful to a client is more likely related to authenticity and timing and less related to frequency or intimacy/intensity of content (Tantillo, 2004).

Within the conceptual literature are discussions of the advantages of both highly structured and less structured/more supportive approaches to TSD training and supervision. A more structured and didactic approach flowing from a particular theoretical base may be experienced by trainees as helpful and valuable (Bottrill et al., 2010). It is possible that structured training helps to assuage early and at times counter-productive anxieties in the face of unfamiliarity and uncertainty that eventually becomes better understood, accepted, and even invited as trainees become more experienced. In addition, less structured and more supportive supervision can help guide trainees during a parallel process of client-trainee growth, as the trainee more critically wrestles with the decision of whether or not to disclose and under what circumstances (Broadbent, 2013). It is likely that a supportive approach may be preferred for trainees wrestling with TSD for reasons of a more personal or countertransference nature.

Conclusions

Supervisors should be actively introducing the topic of TSD into clinical supervision and didactic training. With support from the results of qualitative interviews studies, it would be reasonable to assume that graduate students are likely to have been cautioned against disclosing, with advice limited to the general and clinically uncritical 'only when in the best interest of the client,' and without further elaboration or discussion of clinical and contextual factors discussed in prior chapters of this text as essential considerations in scenarios wherein TSD feels like it may be helpful to clients. A more general and cautionary advisement at least somewhat in discouragement to TSD negates the possibility that TSD may benefit clients in at least some circumstances. Limiting TSD instruction and training may in turn associate with trainees approaching TSD scenarios in a more prescriptive manner discussed previously as clinically inappropriate. In contrast, it is the multiplicity of aforementioned clinical factors that provides necessary context for the research-informed practitioner and trainee's understanding of individual client's needs from therapy, and how those needs may be addressed via forms of TSD or perhaps clinical restraint.

Absent more critical discussion in clinical supervision, trainees are likely to approach complicated scenarios in which TSD might be a possibility with undue anxiety and reservation. Trainees may then attempt to manage these difficulties through a more formulaic or modular approach that may in turn be effective when predetermined and with client–therapist agreement from the onset of treatment, though likely to be experienced by clients as a misattunement when defaulted to, essentially, as a way for trainees *to help themselves* cope with clinical uncertainty and complexity. In and of itself, supervisors directly mentioning these possibilities to trainees is likely to be beneficial during the process of learning about how to make decisions to or not to self-disclose in ways that are maximally helpful and beneficial to clients.

From the literature flowed recommendations for supervisors seeking guidance on how best to teach trainees about TSD. A starting point for supervisors is to reflect upon their own relative comfort with the subject, prior times when they have disclosed to clients and how clients reacted, and in turn how the supervisors' prior experiences with TSD are likely to affect the flow of supervisory instruction and discussion of the subject. This thinking process carried forth into supervision is expected to maintain supervisor awareness of potentially helpful and problematic experiences to draw from and consider as a guide for future supervisory advice and direction.

A review of the relevant literature suggests that supervisors should directly introduce the topic of TSD, possibly as a topic for didactic instruction. Supervisors should err towards exploring the trainees' relative level of knowledge on the subject, identifying their personal feelings about disclosure, and encouraging them to go beyond cautionary advisements typical of graduate educational institutions. Supervisors should also encourage trainees to reflect upon different interchanges with specific clients and anticipate how they might have reacted to a particular type of TSD, at a particular time in therapy, and as discussed in prior chapters of this text. This exploration should be connected to what is known about the client's earlier life and object relations history, personality structure, relative level of engagement in the therapy, and needs from the therapeutic relationship.

Trainee participation in the dialogue may be encouraged by supervisors informing trainees that most therapists do disclose intentionally and directly at least some of the time. Trainees may also find it helpful to learn that ethically appropriate and maximally helpful TSDs are usually brief, infrequent, relevant to the client's need from the therapy, conveying of therapist-similarity, flowing from consideration of the relative strength of the relationship and how the relationship might be affected by TSD, and reflection upon the impacts of visible differences such as age, gender, and race. This point of instruction is also likely to be informative to practice, beyond what trainees usually learn in graduate programs, and may provide a framework for discussion and application to individual clients on the trainee's caseload.

Thereafter, and due to the likelihood that trainees may still fear criticism and negative evaluation, supervisors may need to revisit the general topic and inquire about whether TSD has occurred with clients on an ongoing basis and as discussed in prior supervisory sessions. Supervisors are advised to remind trainees about the major TSD guidelines discussed previously as flowing from the prior review of literature, and with support from empirical studies, qualitative interviews, studies of client experiences, and therapist perspective papers in example of wisdom from practice. The sum total of this instructional method may not only help trainees prepare *to disclose* in appropriate circumstances in the future, but may also teach them by example about how to approach the subject with their own trainees when in supervisory roles themselves, and thereby contribute to expanding general TSD awareness and competency on the whole.

Yielding conclusions of a similar nature, to those mentioned previously, Knox et al. (2008) conducted a qualitative interview study of 16 supervisors in exploration of their experiences and regard for self-disclosing to trainees. Consistent with prior mentions of TSD to clients, therapists in Knox et al.'s (2008) study most frequently reported judiciously disclosing to trainees in effort to contribute to their professional development and normalize their experiences. Supervisors often disclosed when supervisees appeared to be struggling and when sharing the supervisors' reactions to his or her clients, or the trainees' clients, seemed helpful. Interviews yielded that supervisor disclosure consistently had positive effects on supervisors themselves, as well as their supervisory relationships, and interestingly, supervisors' supervision of other trainees.

References

Ackerman, S., & Hilsenroth, M. (2003). A review of therapist characteristics and techniques positively impacting the therapeutic alliance. *Clinical Psychology Review*, *23*(1), 1–33.

Anchor, K., Strassberg, D., & Elkins, D. (1976). Supervisors' perceptions of the relationship between therapist self-disclosure and clinical effectiveness. *Journal of Clinical Psychology*, *32*(1), n.p.

Audet, C., & Everall, R. (2003). Counsellor self-disclosure: Client-informed implications for practice. *Counselling and Psychotherapy Research*, *3*(3), 223–31.

Bitar, G., Kimball, T., Bermúdez, J., & Drew, C. (2014). Therapist self-disclosure and culturally competent care with Mexican-American court mandated clients: A phenomenological study. *Contemporary Family Therapy*, *36*(3), 417–25.

Bottrill, S., Pistrang, N., Barker, C., & Worrell, M. (2010). The use of therapist self-disclosure: Clinical psychology trainees' experiences. *Psychotherapy Research*, *20*(2), 165–80.

Broadbent, J. (2013). 'The bereaved therapist speaks.' An interpretive phenomenological analysis of humanistic therapists' experiences of a significant personal bereavement and its impact upon their therapeutic practice: An exploratory study. *Counselling and Psychotherapy Research*, *13*(4), 263–71.

Burkard, A., Knox, S., Goren, M., Perez, M., & Hess, S. (2006). European American TSD in cross-cultural counseling. *Journal of Counseling Psychology*, *53*(1), 15–25.

Burkard, A., Knox, S., Edwards, L., Smith, J., & Schlosser, L. (2008). Supervisors' reports of the effects of supervisor self-disclosure on supervisees. *Psychotherapy Research*, *18*(5), 543–59.

Carew, L. (2009). Does theoretical background influence therapists' attitudes to therapist self-disclosure? A qualitative study. *Counselling & Psychotherapy Research*, *9*(4), 266–72.

D'Aniello, C., & Nguyen, H. (2017). Considerations for intentional use of self-disclosure for family therapists. *Journal of Family Psychotherapy*, *28*(1), 23–37.

Doremus, B. (2012). Psychologist self-disclosure with court-mandated and self-referred clients (Doctoral dissertation). Retrieved from Engaged Scholarship Archive.

Farber, B. (2006). *Self-disclosure in psychotherapy*. New York: Guilford Press.

Felloney, R. (2010). A qualitative analysis of school-based mental health professionals' views on the use of self-disclosure and humor (Doctoral dissertation). Retrieved from PCOM Psychology Dissertations and Theses Database.

Henretty, J., & Levitt, H. (2010). The role of therapist self-disclosure in psychotherapy: A qualitative review. *Clinical Psychology Review*, *30*(1), 63–77.

Kircanski, K. (2015). Student therapists' use of self-disclosure with clients who have experienced trauma (Doctoral dissertation). Retrieved from ProQuest Dissertations and Theses database. (No UMI No.).

Ladany, N., & Lehrman-Waterman, D. (1999). The content and frequency of supervisor self-disclosures and their relationship to supervisor style and the supervisory working alliance. *Counselor Education and Supervision, 38*(3), 143–60.

Tantillo, M. (2004). The therapist's use of self-disclosure in a relational therapy approach for eating disorders. *Eating Disorders, 12*(1), 51–73.

Vandenberghe, L., & Silva Silvestre, R. (2014). Therapists' positive emotions in- session: Why they happen and what they are good for. *Counselling and Psychotherapy Research, 14*(2), 119–27.

Part III
Vulnerability Factors

CHAPTER 8

Trauma, Physical Illness, and Mortality

Graham S. Danzer, PsyD

Within this chapter is a review of literature suggesting how therapists should conceptualize scenarios in which the client and therapist are afflicted with similar/shared traumas or when the therapist or client is facing critical illness and mortality. In such scenarios, the literature will be shown to suggest that unintentional therapeutic self-disclosure (TSD) is somewhat inevitable, while more direct TSD may be helpful, and at times, necessary. It is overwhelmingly likely that a client will sense the affliction or suffering of a therapist practicing (a) alongside the client in a war-torn community, (b) progressively declining in physical health, or (c) working with a client who is progressively declining. Further, it is unlikely that a therapist could remain fully neutral in such circumstances even if it were so desired, and unlikely that a client would benefit from what would essentially amount to a therapist's refusal to acknowledge the obvious (Alexander, Kolodziejski, Sanville, & Shaw, 1989; Pizer, 2016; Rabinor & Nye, 2003). For these reasons, and in the general spirit of this text, it is therefore necessary to go beyond the more conservative subject of whether or not to disclose *in contexts of trauma and illness*, acknowledge that at least some forms of TSD in these contexts may be ethically appropriate and helpful to clients, review the extant research on the subject, and then apply the research to a more critical discussion regarding implications for practitioners.

When the Therapist Too Has Been Traumatized

Therapist writers and researchers have broached the topics of whether or not therapists practicing in war or disaster-torn communities alongside client-victims should or should not acknowledge and directly disclose aspects of their similar experiences. Common themes within therapist perspective papers and research studies on Hurricane Katrina (LaPorte, Sweifach, & Linzer, 2010), the 9–11 attacks (Frawley-O'Dea, 2003), and Hurricane Sandy (Rao & Mehra, 2015) will be presented. Frawley-O'Dea (2003) and Rao and Mehra (2015) wrote about their experiences in the first person as therapist survivors continuing to practice in spite of disasters. LaPorte et al. (2010) interviewed 103 social workers about their experiences. Therapists and clients living in disaster afflicted communities experienced parallel and overwhelming feelings of grief, despair, and destruction to personal life and property (Frawley-O'Dea, 2003; LaPorte et al., 2010; Rao & Mehra, 2015). Nevertheless and courageously, therapists and social workers consistently reported feeling a sense of duty not to abandon their clients, continue practicing, and essentially channeling (i.e., sublimating) their own acute traumatization into helping similarly afflicted others (Frawley-O'Dea, 2003; LaPorte et al., 2010; Rao & Mehra, 2015).

Points in more specific illustration of the previous paragraph are as follows. Following Hurricane Sandy, Rao and Mehra (2015) reported that their personal loss of home and devastation to family and friends paralleled the losses clients endured and grieved. Frawley-O'Dea (2003) described herself and other therapists living and practicing in the aftermath of 9–11 affected communities as coping side by side with clients, struggling to provide good enough therapeutic environments in the face of overwhelming terror, horror, and sorrow, and struggling with self-acceptance when they felt unable to contain or resolve similar/parallel emotional turbulence in their clients. Consistent with the perspectives of Rao and Mehra (2015) and Frawley-O'Dea (2003), LaPorte et al. (2010) found that social workers practicing in the aftermath of Hurricane Katrina displayed greater emotional accessibility, availability, and modulated vulnerability, which in turn helped model for clients how to be in touch with and actively cope with traumatic stress. This interpretation is further validated by its consistency with primary and research-supported theories of trauma and recovery (Herman, 1996).

Whereas such occurrences could be scrutinized if not pathologized, the totality of the circumstances warrants consideration to the contrary. If therapists and social workers halted their practices for the sake of self-care, large numbers of acutely traumatized clients would not be served. As discussed previously, and will be demonstrated in more detail in upcoming subsections of this chapter, it is not realistic to expect that therapists or social workers afflicted by such critical events could remain neutral nor that doing so would be well-received or otherwise helpful to clients. Therefore, continuing to practice fell in line with ethical mandates related to duty and commitment, though required adaptive/defensive strategy to undergo safely, with stability, and competently. To this end, sublimation is indeed among the healthiest defensive/adaptive strategies (Mitchell & Black, 1995).

After deciding if not resolving themselves to continue practicing, therapists and social workers tended to reflect upon boundary considerations and then decide to alter traditional boundaries in an informed and purposeful manner. Within LaPorte et al. (2010), it was cautioned that TSD during disasters is not necessarily warranted, may be problematic in light of heightened possibilities of therapist indulgence, and may nevertheless warrant greater than usual consideration because traditional therapeutic boundaries were not created with shared traumatic experiences in mind. Consistently, there were ethical reservations about TSD, alongside concern that traditional neutrality in the face of overwhelming and omnipresent disaster would possibly and even likely be experienced by clients as outrageous, alienating, and deepening their post-traumatic isolation (Frawley-O'Dea, 2003; LaPorte et al., 2010; Rao & Mehra, 2015). As an example of how boundaries were modified, Frawley-O'Dea (2003) indicated that therapists in her community practicing after 9–11 sometimes allowed clients to use their phones in-session and permitted sessions to be canceled free of charge.

Frawley-O'Dea (2003), Rao and Mehra (2015), and most social workers in LaPorte et al.'s (2010) study seemed to increase the frequency of TSD described in a manner suggesting TSDs were modulated, conversational, and well attuned, as recommended in prior chapters of this text. All three sets of authors concurred that TSDs of this nature tended to be experienced by clients as appropriately human, fallible, relieving, non-abandoning, and supportive. Rao and Mehra (2015) indicated that tempered therapist participation in discussion of community suffering and disaster relief efforts helped clients progress into deeper discussions of other areas of life in which there was similar and symbolic wreckage, including marriage and family. It was elaborated in the discussion and concluding sections of all three papers that therapists continuing to practice in the aftermath of disaster and appropriately altering traditional therapeutic boundaries enabled a necessary sense of client and therapist co-recovery, resilience-building, and reconnection to a recovering other as a symbol of a rebuilding society.

Therapists Facing Grief, Physical Illness, and Mortality

Within the scholarly literature there has been some discussion about TSD when therapists are facing significant personal issues in this area. Articles reviewed and synthesized will include a qualitative interview study (Broadbent, 2013) and a collection of essays (Adelman & Malawista, 2013) on therapists who were either dying or working with dying clients, Pizer's (2016) psychoanalytic exploration of disclosing his blindness to clients, Nye's case study (authored by Rabinor & Nye, 2003) on self-disclosing her auto-immune disease and resulting hair loss, and Alexander et al.'s (1989) paper on their experience as a consultation group for a colleague who was terminally ill with cancer and seeking guidance on how to impart the news to her clients and simultaneously prepare for her own impending death. Consistent with findings in the prior subsection, all five studies reviewed in this subsection concluded in favor of transparent and yet well-thought-out TSDs of grief, illness, and mortality (in select circumstances) being ethically appropriate, helping to address client issues of anger and abandonment, and helping clients transition into addressing other important personal issues of grief, loss, and reconnection.

Articles on TSD in contexts of grief, illness, and mortality each began with similar discussions of professional ethics and cautions related to self-disclosure of inherently high-intensity content. Therapists in Broadbent's (2013) study consistently reported that, prior to disclosing, they first explored their underlying motivations in supervision, consultation, and/or as needed personal therapy. Therapists considered potential boundary problems, as well as the client's capacity to receive and make use of invariably high-intensity disclosures (Broadbent, 2013). Consistent with prior positions on TSD as a self-care issue, both Adelman and Malawista (2013) and the consultation group in Alexander et al. (1989) noted that therapist disclosure of illness, as well as mortality in general (and as discussed more thoroughly in Chapter 25 by Asha Wilkus-Stone on TSD in contexts of suicide), can be severely discomforting and even disorienting *for the therapist*. Similarly, Pizer (2016) acknowledged that initiating uncomfortable and yet necessary discussions with clients about his blindness was exceedingly difficult, gradually became more familiar over time, and yet still led him to question his motivations for disclosing in light of strong and multi-layered client responses. Within Rabinor and Nye (2003), Nye not only acknowledged seeking consultation, but more openly discussed her consultations as focused on the client's inevitable knowing, potential ramifications of disclosing an issue she had not yet fully accepted or reconciled, and with consultation necessarily preceding TSD.

Articles in this subsection frequently identified the manner in which sincere and transparent disclosures appeared to inspire mutual growth among therapists and clients, with appropriate self-care considerations. Rabinor and Nye (2003) presented a case study in which Nye consulted and processed her struggles with auto-immune disease and hair loss and decided to inform clients in light of otherwise obvious physical changes. Within Rabinor and Nye (2003), Nye thereafter shared with an eating disorder client how she came to a greater level of acceptance of her hair loss, albeit with periods of regression and progress, and as an example of how her client could eventually learn to live without compulsive exercise. Therapists in Broadbent's (2013) study, Adelman and Malawista's (2013) essays on working with dying clients, and Pizer's (2016) reflections on his blindness similarly described their well-timed TSDs of illness and mortality factors as deepening here-and-now experiences and inspiring vibrant client reflections on their current and prior experiences of growth and deterioration. Pizer (2016) noted that TSDs of disability, in general, may significantly *and necessarily* alter the course of therapy, in service of helping the client grow in his or her capacity for intimacy. Adelman and Malawista (2013) noted that TSD in contexts of trauma, illness, and mortality brings therapists into immediate awareness of the fragility, unpredictability, and false senses of security in daily life, which may in turn bring them closer to client suffering.

As a particular showing of courage and commitment, the dying therapist discussed in Alexander et al. (1989) made great efforts to remain adherent to the traditional rules of the profession, though progressed in her openness to care for herself and face her own mortality. With the help of consultation, the dying therapist in Alexander et al.'s (1989) study both embraced and transcended professional obligations by sharing mutual testimonials with clients and achieving a progressively greater sense of relief and acceptance, first, as her sessions with clients came to an end, and finally, as her own life came to an end.

Conclusions

Research in this section offers helpful implications and suggestions for practitioners considering TSD in contexts of shared trauma, debilitating physical illness, and mortality. The major implication is that therapists should, in many of these cases, consider cautiously expanding therapeutic boundaries of usual, which may be a form of intervention in these contexts, in and of itself. So doing is expected to be helpful and at times necessary to build, maintain, and deepen therapeutic relationships in situations where the trauma or illness may otherwise disconnect if not alienate the suffering individual from humanity in its entirety.

Supporting this position, reviewed research offered minimal if any support for maintaining what can be considered a standard or traditional level of clinical restraint. It may be somewhat relieving and affirming to hear from researchers that traditional neutrality and a high level of emotional reservation cannot reasonably be expected, nor is it likely to be helpful to the client when both members of the dyad share disaster-trauma experiences or one or the other within the dyad is physically declining or dying. Alternatively, more than usual (though still clinically motivated and modulated) emotional expression may model for clients appropriate vulnerability, self-care, and active coping with trauma and illness. To this end, the literature suggests that therapists may consider TSD of a more conversational and lower intimacy nature, a strategy also referenced in Chapter 5 of this text.

Second, well-thought-out and almost modular/theoretically informed boundary modification may also be necessary for therapist self-preservation. Therapist writers and practitioners showed immense courage and commitment by continuing to practice after surviving catastrophic disasters, physically declining, and preparing to die. Short of suggesting therapist self-indulgence or self-prioritization, expanding boundaries to permit greater TSD may grant both therapists and clients greater access to the more real part of the relationship that is increasingly acknowledged in progressive models of therapy. In contexts of trauma, illness, and mortality, so doing may encourage client and therapist co-recovery, reciprocity, and growth, albeit with the client as the primary benefactor. Due to the complexity of considering whether or not to disclose in contexts of trauma, illness, and mortality, implications will be further specified and applied to practice scenarios in Chapter 20 by Tyson Bailey.

Interpersonal Traumas

An unaddressed area in the research deserving of further discussion is the subtopic of *interpersonal traumas*. Whereas the scholarly research frequently mentioned the impacts of environmental traumas and physical health complications, the current author was unable to locate any research on the pros, cons, or ramifications of a therapist disclosing a similar history of, for example, being physically or sexually abused as a child or adult, or being the victim of hate crimes. Such disclosures would necessarily be of a higher intensity nature, with potential to both build and complicate therapeutic relationships. As discussed in prior chapters of this text, impacts on clients likely depend in part on the strength of the therapeutic relationship, the therapist's underlying intentionality, the timing, technique, and delivery of the (trauma or illness-focused) TSD, and the client's prior history of interpersonal relationships and object relations.

From the current author's vantage point, a direct disclosure of the therapist's similar interpersonal trauma history, in most (if not all) circumstances, would be deserving of scrutiny. Unlike environmental traumas or physical health decline, interpersonal traumas are not ordinarily visible or obvious, so that the therapist has a greater degree of discretion. Also discussed in prior chapters of this text, a store of clinical restraint and forethought are prerequisites to making sound decisions *to or not to* self-disclose. Such forms of professional discipline if not self-control are particularly necessary with clients with histories of abuse and interpersonal trauma who are coming into therapy with a significant history of having their boundaries violated.

In such cases, it is not uncommon for clients to be sensitive to what might otherwise be considered smaller forms of boundary approaching or crossing, become distracted from their therapeutic processing, and/or experience the TSD of similar trauma as imposing, role reversing, and/or making the relationship more personal than professional. It is difficult for the current author to conjure up a clinical scenario in which a TSD of similar interpersonal trauma history would *not* strongly and inappropriately shift the focus of therapy to the therapist (i.e., as a negative occurrence), or clearly deepen the client's reflections or understanding of their own experience (i.e., as a positive occurrence). Instead, it would seem more beneficial for a therapist to reflect upon his or her similar trauma, consider the ways in which his or her experience and the client's is similar *and* different, consult and seek supervision, and use the similar experience as a less direct and more conceptual frame of reference for exploring and understanding the client's emotions, ways of thinking, and efforts to adjust and adapt during different stages of the trauma and recovery process.

Whereas TSD of similar interpersonal traumas might build the therapeutic relationship and engender feelings of trust, a competent and professional psychotherapist should always be able to find other ways to achieve such objectives and with less risk to the client. Should clients ask therapists directly about whether or not they have been abused, assaulted, etc., prior discussions of restraint and fore thinking would first apply. In cases where these principles were disregarded or only minimally considered, it could be argued that the intervention was no longer in the realm of professional psychotherapy and had moved into the direction of peer counseling.

As noted by D'Aniello and Nguyen (2017), though admittedly in contexts of lower intimacy, clients with such direct questions about a therapist's personal history would most often be seeking to determine whether the therapist could be empathic, reduce client anxiety about the therapeutic process, level the inherent power imbalance in the relationship, or signify feelings of vulnerability or powerlessness. Again, from the current author's perspective, it is reasonable to go a step further in considering that a direct question about another person (i.e., the therapist's) trauma history would ordinarily be considered intrusive, suggest interpersonal boundary problems, and would likely be initiated by clients in an effort to manage discomfort and potentially avoid deeper topics of discussion (in turn likely related to the client's own trauma and conflicted early family and relationship history).

In cases where the therapist might be asked directly about whether they have a similar interpersonal trauma history, it will most likely be most helpful to explore the client's feelings underneath his or her request, reflect upon how gratifying the client's request may affect the therapeutic process, and acknowledge that therapeutic pull to disclose is likely stemming from expectation and even fear that clients may become angry, experience the non-disclosure as a rejection, or express dissatisfaction with the therapist or treatment (D'Aniello and Nguyen, 2017). In such cases, a client's ability to accept and move beyond a therapist's *empathic and well-informed* restraint may be diagnostic of his or her appropriateness for psychotherapy. At the same time, further research is clearly needed to better address the question of TSD in contexts of interpersonal trauma and with a maximally empirical basis, as advanced throughout this text.

References

Adelman, A., & Malawista, K. (2013). *The therapist in mourning: From the faraway nearby*. New York: Columbia University Press.

Alexander, J., Kolodziejski, K., Sanville, J., & Shaw, R. (1989). On final terminations: Consultation with a dying therapist. *Clinical Social Work Journal*, *17*(4), 307–24.

Broadbent, J. (2013). 'The bereaved therapist speaks.' An interpretive phenomenological analysis of humanistic therapists' experiences of a significant personal bereavement and its impact upon their therapeutic practice: An exploratory study. *Counselling and Psychotherapy Research*, *13*(4), 263–71.

D'Aniello, C., & Nguyen, H. (2017). Considerations for intentional use of self-disclosure for family therapists. *Journal of Family Psychotherapy*, *28*(1), 23–37.

Frawley-O'Dea, M. (2003). When the trauma is terrorism and the therapist is traumatized too. *Psychoanalytic Perspectives*, *1*(1), 67–89.

Herman, J. (1996). *Trauma and recovery: The aftermath of violence—from domestic abuse to political terror*. New York: Basic Books.

LaPorte, H., Sweifach, J., & Linzer, N. (2010). Sharing the trauma: Guidelines for therapist self-disclosure following a catastrophic event. *Best Practices in Mental Health*, *6*(2), 39–56.

Mitchell, S., & Black, M. (1995). *Freud and beyond*. New York: Basic Books.

Rabinor, J., & Nye, S. (2003). Healing through connection: Self-disclosure in psychotherapy. *Eating Disorders*, *11*(3), 235–40.

Pizer, A. (2016). Do I have to tell my patients I'm blind? *Psychoanalytic Perspectives*, *13*(2), 214–29.

Rao, N., & Mehra, A. (2015). Hurricane Sandy: Shared trauma and therapist self-disclosure. *Psychiatry*, *78*(1), 65–74.

CHAPTER 9

Caucasian Therapists and Multicultural Clients

Graham S. Danzer, PsyD

Multicultural therapeutic approaches have long recognized TSD as a skill or competency (Bitar, Kimball, Bermúdez, & Drew, 2014; Henretty & Levitt, 2010). It has been discussed as an intervention that may build trust and credibility in cross-cultural contexts (Constantine & Kwong-Liem, 2003; Henretty & Levitt, 2010; Sue & Sue, 1999). Disclosure may impress upon the client the therapist's willingness to take risks, be experienced as a gesture of openness, convey cultural sensitivity, and encourage reciprocal client disclosure (Constantine & Kwong-Liem, 2003; Terrell & Terrell, 1984). These potentially positive impacts are of interest in light of the high early dropout rates among clients of color paired with Caucasian therapists (Chang & Berk, 2009). From these findings it is reasonable to hypothesize that traditional therapeutic neutrality may, in many circumstances, exacerbate longstanding and historical trust barriers, so that a more humanizing and two-person relationship may be necessary to prevent withdrawal.

In addition to the aforementioned upsides, Caucasian therapists are cautioned against insincere or even patronizing self-disclosures such as random mentions of having friends of color or over-emphasizing perceived similarities (Constantine & Kwong-Liem, 2003; LaPorte, Sweifach, & Linzer, 2010). In such cases, insincere and even condescending disclosures are likely to be as harmful to relationships as authentic and humanizing disclosures are likely to build them. For example, and as detailed in Felloney (2010), a Caucasian male school-based mental health counselor reported in an interview study that, when paired with a student of an unspecified cultural minority background, and after an initial period of attempting to joke around with him, the counselor made up a story about having an African American male roommate in college who was from 'the hood.' The story backfired when the student client reportedly responded that the counselor 'knew nothing about the hood.'

Similarly, Tantillo (2004) advises female therapists to refrain from TSDs that err toward universality of women's experiences, and regardless of differences in race, class, sexual orientation, and age, as well as socioeconomic factors such as education employment, and resources. Although not further specified, and likely to avoid controversy, Tantillo's (2004) point clearly suggests that Caucasian female therapists seek other ways to connect with cultural minority clients rather than by drawing parallels between cultural and gender-based marginalization, irrespective of racial privilege and socioeconomic considerations noted previously, and in the presumptive and subtly micro-aggressive manner noted in Felloney (2011). In a broader sense, the relationship between racial/ethnic identity and gender/gender identification is not always so clear (Masuda et al., 2009).

Additional clinical considerations are noted in the conceptual literature. Cultural factors specific to the client and racial composition of the particular therapist-client dyad strongly influence client perceptions of whether or not TSD may be appropriate and under what circumstances (Simonds & Spokes, 2017). Per Chang and Berk (2009), it may be particularly challenging for Caucasian therapists to self-disclose ethically and effectively to clients of color in light of research suggesting that problematic cross-racial countertransference is common and, as discussed in prior clinical chapters, somewhat greater than usual self-awareness and clinical skill is necessary *to self-disclose* ethically. These points will be shown to have implications for interpreting the research on this subject, and will be referenced in upcoming discussions of how the research applies when considering TSD in cross-cultural contexts.

Research Findings

Earlier research on cross-cultural client experiences with TSD was based on interviews with college students. Borrego, Chavez, and Titley (1982) conducted an analogue study of 124 Mexican American and Caucasian college students who filled out questionnaires and were asked if certain scenarios, if experienced by them, would lead them to return for a second therapy session. There was a significant difference depending on therapist technique, with 63% of participants (or 78) reporting they would return to see the therapist who used probing statements, 46% (or 57) returning to the therapist who self-disclosed, and 37% (or 46) returning to a therapist who used reflecting statements, with no significant differences in these findings depending on analogue-client ethnicity.

Cherbosque (1987) surveyed 100 Mexican/Mexican American and 100 Caucasian students in an effort to explore the relationship between self-reported adherence to cultural norms and expectations regarding TSD. Mexican/Mexican American students in this study expressed stronger preferences for counselor formality and lower levels of disclosure. Cherbosque (1987) noted this finding was consistent with aspects of cultural norms, though partially explainable as a function of TSD having less relevance for younger clients (as will also be discussed in more detail in Chapter 14 on TSD with children and adolescents). Among the limitations, Cherbosque (1987) acknowledged that simulated clients/college students may not be representative of real-world clients in therapy.

With an aim similar to Cherbosque (1987), Cashwell, Scherbakova, and Cashwell (2003) conducted a prospective interview study of 444 undergraduates. Of the 444, 294 (or 66.2% of the sample) were African American. The aim of Cashwell et al. (2003) was to determine whether racial matching/mismatching would predict a significantly higher level of client preference for higher or lower frequency of TSD. African American students under study reported a significantly stronger preference for more TSD when paired with a Caucasian therapist. Consistent with previously discussed conceptual positions, it was hypothesized by Cashwell et al. (2003) that African American students' desire for greater amounts of cross-cultural TSD was reminiscent of historical trust barriers associated with ethnic differences. Thus, a comparison of research findings indicated that African American though not Mexican American college students tended to prefer higher levels of Caucasian therapist TSD.

Studies of real therapy clients of color consistently indicated that Caucasian therapist TSD had positive impacts on the therapeutic relationship and outcomes *when* TSDs were commensurate with the client's cultural values. With a design similar to Cherbosque (1987), Kim et al. (2003) studied the relationship between clients' adherence to traditional values and extent of TSD in a single therapy session, for a sample of 62 Asian American clients paired with Caucasian therapists. Kim et al. (2003) sought to determine the extent to which client adherence to traditional Asian cultural values would predict whether or not TSDs tended to be received in a positive manner. One hypothesis was that self-disclosure might model and encourage reciprocal client disclosure and might help to address client beliefs and experiences of the therapist as an agent of an oppressive system. Commensurate with Asian cultural norms, clients reported more positive responses to TSDs of problem-solving strategies rather than more emotionally-focused reassurance, therapist credentials, or feelings.

Kim et al. (2003) hypothesized that this finding on culturally congruent TSDs might generalize to clients from other cultures as well. Meaning, clients from all cultures may or may not find TSDs helpful depending, in part, on whether or not the TSD is congruent with their cultural values and individual expression of them. Thus, intervening in a manner commensurate with the client's cultural values is not only culturally appropriate, but also clinically and ethically appropriate, and likely to drive TSDs that are helpful to clients of all backgrounds.

As if to follow up on the generalizing implication in Kim et al. (2003), Lokken and Twohey (2004) conducted a retrospective interview study of 17 Native American clients paired with Caucasian therapists. The researchers sought to identify common factors in cross-cultural relationships experienced by Native clients as strong and helpful. In addition to a respectful and caring attitude, casual demeanor, and empathic listening, six of the 13 clients reported that TSD helped to build trust and enhance the therapist's credibility in a manner consistent with positions noted earlier in the summary of conceptual literature. Participants endorsing the benefits of TSD frequently noted that TSD helped to establish a sense of mutuality and common ground akin to tribal values for communalism and interconnection.

Qualitative studies of smaller samples of both Caucasian therapist (Burkard, Knox, Goren, Perez, & Hess, 2006) and cultural minority clients (Bitar et al., 2014; Chang & Berk, 2009) consistently identified positive therapeutic outcomes associated with Caucasian therapist TSDs in general and of therapist personal experiences with racism in particular. Chang and Berk (2009) conducted a qualitative interview study of 16 ethnic minority clients paired with Caucasian therapists. Chang and Berk (2009) identified a significant positive association between TSD and minority client satisfaction with treatment. Bitar et al. (2014) conducted a study of 10 court-mandated Mexican American male clients, who consistently reported that TSD encouraged their participation in treatment, lessened the negative effects of hierarchy, modeled appropriate male vulnerability, and normalized their feelings and experiences. Bitar et al. (2014) hypothesized that Caucasian therapist TSDs were well received *because* the timing, content, and context was consistent with Mexican American cultural values for respect, dignity, and equality. Consistently, Carlton's (1993) dissertation study of 60 mixed gender adolescents indicated that Latino youth tended to disclose more to therapists who disclosed general and limited information to them. Thus, research on Mexican American college students (noted earlier in this chapter) as well as real adolescent and adult clients suggests that some extent of therapist revelation is likely to be helpful. The research also suggests that TSD should probably occur infrequently and in more moderated forms with younger Mexican American clients, and with potentially greater frequency and/or intimacy with adult clients and when an additional layer of coercion/oppression (i.e., the criminal justice system) further impedes the development of trust.

Caucasian therapists in Burkard et al.'s (2006) study frequently indicated that sharing sincere outrage at client victimization and tactfully acknowledging that they too had held racist beliefs appeared to deepen therapeutic relationships with African American, Latino, and Asian American clients. Therapists also reported that, subsequently, racism TSDs seemed to help clients progress and address other important personal issues in therapy. A similar therapist observation was also noted in prior studies of TSD from therapists in contexts of shared environmental trauma and critical physical illness. Implications from Chang and Berk's (2009) study included that TSD, particularly Caucasian therapist revelations about racism, might begin to bridge social and power imbalances between Caucasian therapists and cultural minority clients as a foundation for change-inspiring relationships.

Offering a finding to the contrary, Wetzel and Wright-Buckley (1988) conducted a study of 33 African American women paired with either an African American or Caucasian therapist. It was determined that greater frequency of disclosure predicted more reciprocal disclosure *only* when clients were paired with an African American therapist, though not with a Caucasian therapist. Wetzel and Wright-Buckley (1988) interpreted the findings as indicative of a trust barrier in the manner described earlier in this chapter. These findings may also be interpreted as supporting the prior position against assuming that TSD will always have a positive effect, regardless of paramount client and therapeutic relationship variables compartmentalized within the two prior sections of chapters in this text. Wetzel and Wright-Buckley's (1988) finding, in combination with other findings, suggests multicultural clients may respond differently to Caucasian therapist TSD depending in part on gender. This hypothesis warrants further study.

Conclusions

Research suggests that Caucasian therapists paired with multicultural clients should conceptualize TSD as an intervention that has the potential to help work through trust barriers, facilitate engagement, and lower early termination rates. The research also suggests that, in order for cross-cultural TSD to be ethically and culturally appropriate, and otherwise helpful to clients, TSD must be an authentic and genuine expression of interest in building a relationship. From the research emerges the likelihood/advisement that decisions to or not to use TSD in a particular cross-cultural context should be made based on the individual client circumstances at hand, with the conceptualization of those circumstances based in part on the prior review of research and with particular attention to the client's cultural values and related expectations regarding hierarchy versus egalitarianism in the relationship. Although the literature on this subject was primarily conceptual, and the few available studies had very small samples, it was informative that findings and key positions were consistent, and that samples of different cultural minority clients tended to express a generally positive reaction to Caucasian therapist TSDs, albeit for different reasons in turn consistent with cultural values. Thus, cross-cultural self-disclosure decisions should be based on both individual *and* between-group differences.

Whereas the literature reviewed on TSD in general suggests that maximally ethical and helpful self-disclosures are usually brief and of lower intimacy/intensity, it was mentioned if not recommended in research in this chapter that Caucasian therapists should refrain from somewhat superficial, disingenuous, and perhaps unintentionally offensive TSDs. Rather, should multicultural clients disclose personal experiences of being oppressed, practitioners may in some cases respond by acknowledging their position as oppressor, and some of the ways in which they too have been racist. It was noted in the conceptual literature that such TSDs might be particularly difficult for Caucasian therapists to implement in light of significant likelihood of cross-cultural countertransference, but strike the current author as a compelling way to try to move the therapy into a more vibrant here-and-now dynamic. Prior recommendations on monitoring for countertransference, quickly returning the focus to the client, and asking the client how he or she felt about the racism disclosure would apply. In fact, and in light of the great potential for misunderstandings and therapeutic rupture, it may be advantageous if not necessary to first discuss the possibility of reciprocal-racism disclosure in supervision and possible cross-cultural consultation, as an additional check on therapist personal motives. In addition, further empirical research on this intervention would be a great contribution to this field of study.

Beyond Racial Considerations

Further study is also needed to better understand the impacts of TSD within cultural minority dyads in general, with attention to the specific cultural makeup of a particular dyad, with additional considerations of age, gender, sexuality, intersectionality, and treatment variables discussed in prior and upcoming chapters of this text. It would be uncritical and indeed inappropriate to presume that the impact of TSD is locused in a cultural vacuum, without consideration of the client's *and the therapist's* age, gender, sexuality, and other important personal identities. Rather, how a client receives and responds to a TSD will not only relate, in part, to the client's and the therapist's culture, as well as the strength of the therapeutic relationship, timing, type, relative brevity and frequency, relevance, and delivery of the TSD. In addition, impact will also differ depending on whether the client and therapist are male, female, or transgender, of similar or different age groups, and of similar or different sexual identity. So doing may offer balanced attention to all aspects of a client's identity, which in turn influence how he or she relates to the therapist, expresses cultural values as an individual, and perhaps determine goodness-of-fit for cross-cultural pairing.

References

Bitar, G., Kimball, T., Bermúdez, J., & Drew, C. (2014). Therapist self-disclosure and culturally competent care with Mexican-American court mandated clients: A phenomenological study. *Contemporary Family Therapy*, 36(3), 417–25.

Borrego, R., Chavez, E., & Titley, R. (1982). Effect of counselor technique on Mexican American and Anglo-American self-disclosure and counselor perception. *Journal of Counseling Psychology*, 29(5), 538–41.

Burkard, A., Knox, S., Goren, M., Perez, M., & Hess, S. (2006). European American therapist self-disclosure in cross-cultural counseling. *Journal of Counseling Psychology*, 53(1), 15–25.

Carlton, C. (1993). The effect of therapist self-disclosure and explanation of confidentiality on adolescent clients' willingness to self-disclose and therapist preference (Doctoral dissertation). Retrieved from ProQuest Dissertations and Theses database (No UMI No.).

Cashwell, C., Scherbakova, J., & Cashwell, T. (2003). Effect of client and counselor ethnicity on preference for counselor disclosure. *Journal of Counseling and Development*, 81(2), 196–201.

Chang, D., & Berk, A. (2009). Making cross-racial therapy work: A Phenomenological study of clients' experiences of cross-racial therapy. *Journal of Counseling Psychology*, 56(4), 521–36.

Cherbosque, J. (1987). Differences between Mexican and American clients in expectations about psychological counseling. *Journal of Multicultural Counseling and Development*, 15(3), 110–14.

Constantine, M., & Kwong-Liem, K. (2003). Cross-cultural considerations of therapist self-disclosure. *Journal of Clinical Psychology, 59*(5), 581–8.

Felloney, R. (2010). A qualitative analysis of school-based mental health professionals' views on the use of self-disclosure and humor (Doctoral dissertation). Retrieved from PCOM Psychology Dissertations and Theses Database.

Henretty, J., & Levitt, H. (2010). The role of therapist self-disclosure in psychotherapy: A qualitative review. *Clinical Psychology Review, 30*(1), 63–77.

Kim, B., Hill, C., Gelso, C., Goates, M., Asay, P., & Harbin, J. (2003). Counselor self-disclosure: East Asian American client adherence to Asian cultural values, and counseling process. *Journal of Counseling Psychology, 50*(3), 324–32.

LaPorte, H., Sweifach, J., & Linzer, N. (2010). Sharing the trauma: Guidelines for therapist self-disclosure following a catastrophic event. *Best Practices in Mental Health, 6*(2), 39–56.

Lokken, J., & Twohey, D. (2004). American Indian perspectives of Euro-American counseling behavior. *Journal of Multicultural Counseling and Development, 32*, 320–31.

Masuda, A., Anderson, P., Twohig, M., Feinstein, A., Chou, Y., Wendell, J., & Stormo, A. (2009). Help-seeking experiences and attitudes among African American, Asian American, and European American college students. *International Journal for the Advancement of Counselling, 31*(3), 168–80.

Simonds, L., & Spokes, N. (2017). Therapist self-disclosure and the therapeutic alliance in the treatment of eating problems. *Eating Disorders, 25*(2), 151–64.

Sue, D. W., & Sue, D. (1999). *Counseling the culturally different: Theory and practice* (3rd ed.). New York: John Wiley & Sons.

Tantillo, M. (2004). The therapist's use of self-disclosure in a relational therapy approach for eating disorders. *Eating Disorders, 12*(1), 51–73.

Terrell, F., & Terrell, S. (1984). Race of counselor, client sex, cultural mistrust level, and premature termination from counseling among Black clients. *Journal of Counseling Psychology, 31*(3), 371–5.

Wetzel, C., & Wright-Buckley, C. (1988). Reciprocity of self-disclosure: Breakdowns of trust in cross-racial dyads. *Basic and Applied Social Psychology, 9*(4), 277–88.

CHAPTER 10

Sexuality

Graham S. Danzer, PsyD

The already complicated issue of therapeutic self-disclosure (TSD) is even more complicated when the disclosure is of the therapist's sexual orientation (TSDO) (Satterly, 2006). There is considerable debate in the scholarly literature because TSDO cannot easily be categorized alongside the disclosure of other demographic details (i.e., marriage status or age) nor compared to other historical disclosure content (Dean, 2010; Lea, Jones, & Huws, 2010; Moore & Jenkins, 2012; Thomas, 2008) *because* the therapist's sexuality is concealable (Moore & Jenkins, 2012), yet cannot reasonably be expected to be unimportant (Hearn & West-Olatunji, 2015), *and* may be an issue of informed consent and client right-to-know (Dean, 2010; Thomas, 2008) and therapist credibility (Hearn & West-Olatunji, 2015). Moreover, non-disclosure *or* TSDO is likely to impact the therapeutic relationship, the ways in which therapists and clients relate and communicate, and particularly when clients are of an LGBTQ background (Hearn & West-Olatunji, 2015). As is true for all forms of TSD, decisions to or not to disclose sexuality must be made on a case-by-case basis (Guthrie, 2006). In many cases, the question is not whether or not the therapist should disclose his or her sexuality at all, but rather, when, how, and under what circumstances TSDO should occur (Bjork, 2004; Harris, 2015; Thomas, 2008).

While the subject of TSDO is discussed in the literature as essential consideration among LGBTQ therapists, it is also important for heterosexual therapists to explore as one of many LGBTQ issues they are unlikely to be familiar with (Carroll, Gauler, Relph, & Hutchinson, 2011; Hearn & West-Olatunji, 2015). LGBTQ issues, including but not limited to TSDO, are often under-emphasized and deserving of greater priority in graduate training, multicultural education, and clinical supervision (Carroll et al., 2011; Hearn & West-Olatunji, 2015; Lea et al., 2010; Russell & Greenhouse, 1997). Under-emphasis is detrimental to the professional development of LGBTQ therapists in training, who are often paired with supervisors less knowledgeable about LGBTQ issues, struggling with anxiety and fear related to clients not knowing their sexuality, and may miss TSDO opportunities due to anxiety and over-reliance on predetermined rules (Farber, 2006; Harris, 2015; Russell & Greenhouse, 1997; Satterly, 2006).

For such reasons, supervisors with LGBTQ trainees should explicitly address LGBTQ identification and possibly TSDO as part of supervision (Hearn & West-Olatunji, 2015; Russell & Greenhouse, 1997). Suggesting a possibility that TSDO competency may not necessarily grow over time, a study of 53 LGBTQ therapists yielded no significant relationship between number of years in practice and likelihood of disclosing sexuality (Harris, 2015).

Moreover, general guidelines for TSD (as discussed in previous chapters of this text) tend not to overtly consider the multi-faceted and unique nature of disclosing sexual identity, or have implications that presume heterosexism (Thomas, 2008). Among the effects of living in a heterosexist society is that most people, including but not limited to therapists, are presumed to be heterosexual (Thomas, 2008). In turn, it is not uncommon for clients of either LGBTQ or heterosexual identity to come into therapy and talk to the therapist in a dialogue clearly presuming the therapist is of a similar sexuality (Satterly, 2006).

Further suggesting TSDO should not solely be of interest to LGBTQ therapists, research studies consistently found that LGBTQ clients often seek out a similarly identified therapist, considered matching and TSDO to be helpful though non-essential, and frequently indicated that the therapist being knowledgeable about LGBTQ community issues or LGBTQ-affirming was more important than the therapist also being LGBTQ identified (Bashan, 2004; Dean, 2010; Liddle, 1997). Thus, further learning in the area of TSDO is important from a cultural competency and diversity perspective, and for therapists of all sexual orientations and gender identifications. Further learning may be specifically necessary for heterosexual male therapists, who were rated as least helpful to LGBTQ clients, as compared to gay men and lesbian, bisexual, or heterosexual women (Liddle, 1996, 1997).

A Must Consider for LGBTQ-Identified Therapists?

Avoidance of coming out to clients does not necessarily mean they will not sense the therapist's identity or discover it in some other way (Goldstein & Horowitz, 2003). As discussed by Satterly (2006), given limited options for dating and socializing in many communities, LGBTQ therapists often encounter current or potential clients at community events, or in social situations such as gay/lesbian bars where client or potential client observations (i.e., drinking or flirtatious singles behavior) may complicate therapy. Attending such events often presumes LGBTQ identity. In effect, a therapist seen in attendance by a client, who had not previously disclosed LGBTQ identity, would almost certainly be seen as inauthentic. As a result, LGBTQ therapists, particularly in smaller gay communities, often feel pressured to disclose their orientation or answer direct questions about their sexuality based in part on informed consent and right to know considerations, as well as anticipation of by-chance meetings with clients/potential clients in social situations. In turn, early and pre-emptive discussion between LGBTQ therapists and LGBTQ clients about the possibility of by-chance encounters may be warranted. This may not only prevent later and unintentional client discovery, but may also build trust within the therapeutic relationship (Dean, 2010). Thus, the subject of whether therapists should be 'out' to clients is a particularly provocative subject, has implications for how LGBTQ therapists should manage sexual and personal identity in a professional context, and requires considerable psychological energy for LGBTQ therapists to explore and work through (Carroll et al., 2011).

Potentially negative impacts *of non-disclosure*, as well as common occurrences and positive impacts of TSDO of gay, lesbian, and bisexual identity, are discussed frequently by therapist writers and researchers. Non-disclosure may implicitly send homophobic messages to clients (Carroll et al., 2011), be rooted in or lead to client perception of therapist shame (Dean, 2010; Farber, 2006; Harris, 2015), and (therefore) interfere with therapeutic focus on clients (Harris, 2015). In a similar vein, non-disclosure of sexuality may exacerbate LGBTQ therapist fears/anticipation of client judgment, homophobic comments, and the extent of internalized homophobia projected onto the client (Hearn & West-Olatunji, 2015), as well as feelings of stress (Harris, 2015), misleading clients (Thomas, 2008), and loneliness, isolation, and inauthenticity (Carroll et al., 2011). Interestingly, non-disclosure of sexuality may then have similar ramifications to non-disclosure in contexts of trauma, illness, and eating disorder, as discussed in other 'vulnerability' chapters within this section of chapters.

TSDO: Occurrences, Benefits, and Cautions

Survey studies of LGBTQ professionals consistently revealed that most therapists (a) have disclosed their sexuality to a client at some point in their career, (b) were generally 'out' to some clients and not others, (c) had mixed perceptions on the impact of TSDO, and (d) had both favorable and precautionary perceptions supported in other research findings discussed later in this chapter (Harris, 2015; Houston, 1997). TSDO often occurs through suggestive conversation, office art or books, pro-gay symbols, clothing, or insignia, and/or information on the Internet, provided to insurance companies, or in advertisements (Carroll et al., 2011; Thomas, 2008). The following review of therapist writer perspectives suggests implicit agreement with Satterly (2006): That it may be less helpful for the client, particularly of LGBTQ background, *not to know* the therapist's sexual orientation and more helpful *to* know it.

Benefits of TSDO are frequently discussed as having a role-modeling and social justice component. As identity maturation and security integrates without making exclusive one's LGBTQ identity, TSDO may serve a role-modeling function, with the importance locused in the general lack of gay and lesbian role models in society (Carroll et al., 2011; Hearn and West-Olatunji, 2015). TSDO may be very helpful to LGBTQ clients who are 'coming out,' demonstrate the therapist's commitment to social justice and fighting oppression, and challenge stereotypes (Thomas, 2008). Further, TSDO may open dialogues with cultural minority clients about their experiences of oppression, though may not be well received when put forth with intention to suggest similarity, irrespective of racial privilege, and in a manner cautioned against in Chapter 9 of this text (Thomas, 2008).

Therapist writer and researcher positions on outcomes and technique are as follows. Satterly (2006) noted that TSDO often increases client disclosure, therapist
empathy and positive regard, and mutual and reciprocal spontaneity, intimacy,
confidence, openness, flexibility, as well as commitment to treatment, and often
increases the appropriateness and helpfulness of other forms of disclosure. Satterly
(2006) elaborated that TSDOs which actualize upon the aforementioned goals are
likely to come from an LGBTQ therapist whose sexual identity is relatively secure
and mature. In terms of technique, TSDO should be mindful, timely, and for the
benefit of the client, like all TSDs in general (Hearn & West-Olatunji, 2015). Timing
is crucial, as clients with higher levels of shame, denial, boundary problems, and/
or internalized or externalized homophobia are more likely to respond negatively
(Thomas, 2008).

Within the literature are recurring cautions with respect to TSDO decision-
making, technique, delivery, and impacts on both clients and therapists. LGBTQ
therapists thinking through the possibility of TSDO must consider the impacts
of their own and the client's internalized homophobia and projections, whether
they may be over-identifying with the client, the relevance of TSDO to treatment,
and the foreseeable impacts of TSDO on the therapeutic relationship, the balance
between therapeutic neutrality and authenticity, and the intersection between social
and professional identity (Harris, 2015; Satterly, 2006; Thomas, 2008). Thus, TSDO
risks meeting the therapist's own needs, giving the impression of flaunting one's
sexuality, sending simplistic "its ok to be gay" messages, and near-abruptly discon-
firming client presumptions in a way that can damage the relationship (Carroll
et al., 2011; Harris, 2015, p. 38; Hearn & West-Olatunji, 2015; Lea et al., 2010).

Gay male therapists in focus group studies have reported feeling it is beyond the
scope of therapy to challenge clients' homophobic attitudes, essentially, without
a clear connection to treatment or client goals (Satterly, 2006). LGBTQ therapists
may also conceal their identities due to legitimate concerns about how TSDO
may affect their personal safety and career stability (Thomas, 2008). Clients in
Simonds and Spokes' (2017) study of eating disorder clients tended to rate TSD
of sexuality as the least helpful form of disclosure, though without specification
of therapist and client sexualities, and the possibility of a less clear relationship
between the therapist's sexuality and the client's primary treatment issue (in cases
of eating disorder).

In addition, it is important to consider how TSDO occurrences and impacts
may differ depending on the gender and sexual orientation of the client and therapist. Sexual identity development cannot be assumed to be the same for men
or women, nor in cases of heterosexual or LGBTQ identity (Mohr & Fassinger,
2003). For these reasons, research on specific populations is summarized and
integrated as follows.

TSDO in Gay Male Dyads

Disclosure of sexuality in gay male dyads has come up somewhat frequently
in the TSD literature over the last decade. Gay male clients frequently have a
desire to know the therapist's sexual orientation, often based on a desire for

assurance of physical and emotional safety, and to anticipate the likely extent of understanding, affirmation, and reassurance that the therapist will not express a more overt and re-traumatizing form of homophobia (Cole & Drescher, 2006; Guthrie, 2006; Henretty & Levitt, 2010; Russell, 2006; Satterly, 2006). In gay male dyads, TSDO may help to reduce both the client's and the therapist's internalized homophobia, shame, and self-hatred (Cornett, 1993; Henretty and Levitt, 2010; Kronner & Northcut, 2015). In effect, self-disclosure of gay male sexuality may transcend the heterosexual-normative policy of 'don't ask don't tell' (Cole & Drescher, 2006).

Attachment-focused research was conducted by Mohr and Fassinger (2003) on 288 lesbian and bisexual women and 201 gay and bisexual men, 84.9% (or 415) were Caucasian, with multiple indicators that the sample was generally composed of individuals who were of middle-higher socioeconomic background. There were significant associations between attachment insecurity, avoidance, and anxiety in relationships, and a lower extent of 'outness.' Associations between variables were far stronger for gay men than lesbian women. There were indications of more significant impact of paternal (than maternal) support for coming out and LGBTQ identity in general. Thus, *lack of* TSDO may be damaging in gay male therapist-client dyads, and at least partially due to generally more negative response to gay male than lesbian female sexuality, or hetero-sexuality (Mohr & Fassinger, 2003; Thomas, 2008). In such cases, TSDO in gay male dyads may be empowering, whereas non-disclosure may be shaming.

The research also supports that gay male therapists tend to approach such scenarios with appropriate restraint and forethought as indicators of good clinical practice in general. Qualitative interview studies in furtherance of these points have been conducted on both gay male therapist (Jeffrey & Tweed, 2015; Lea et al., 2010; Satterly, 2006) and gay male client (Kronner, 2013; Kronner & Northcut, 2015) experiences with TSDO. Interview transcripts in Kronner (2013), Jeffrey and Tweed (2015), and Kronner and Northcut (2015) consistently indicated that gay male therapists, from both the therapist and client perspective, tended to use TSDO (1) with appropriate professional caution and reflection, (2) no more often than they disclosed in terms of other historical content, and (3) without implication of exceeding the frequency of TSDs noted by most therapists in TSD studies reviewed in the background chapters of this text.

Across all five studies of self-disclosure in gay sexuality contexts, TSDO as well as TSD of a more implicit nature, was described as central to therapeutic bonding, reducing client anxiety that otherwise inhibited their disclosures, and affirming gay sexuality and self-esteem. In Kronner and Northcut's (2015) study, clients indicated 73% of historical disclosures (including but limited to therapist's sexuality) were rated/perceived as positive, 24% were neutral, and only 3% were negative. Clients with sexuality-disclosing therapists often responded in kind (Jeffrey & Tweed, 2015), and demonstrated more tolerance for therapeutic mistakes (Kronner, 2013).

Qualitative interview studies of gay male therapists also yielded themes consistent with the aforementioned key points in the non-gender specific TSDO conceptual literature. Lea et al.'s (2010) interview study of six gay male therapists yielded consistent therapist perception of TSDO as beneficial to the client and contributing to the development of the therapeutic relationship. Consistent with prior mentions reminiscent of inevitable discovery, therapists often reported that clients used language suggesting they knew the therapist was gay before he disclosed, while direct revelations of gay sexuality were often conversational and essentially not of the high-intimacy, focus-shifting nature that might otherwise be presumed, particularly by heterosexual readers (in the current author's opinion). Satterly's (2006) focus group study of 26 gay male therapists revealed perspectives that appropriate use of TSDO required understanding, awareness, and consideration of where personal and professional identities converged and should converge, the culture and openness of their employers and colleagues, and theoretical orientations. Gay male therapists in focus groups also discussed themes of realness and authenticity (particularly with respect to heterosexual clients), as well as their own projections and foreseeable boundary issues, and the likely extent of client benefit or negative response.

TSDO to and from Lesbians

There is a growing, albeit still limited body of literature focusing on TSDO from lesbian identified therapists (Thomas, 2008). At least some level of self-disclosure of lesbian women's sexuality, both from clients to therapists and from therapists to clients, is discussed as important for the development of the therapeutic relationship, as well as women's health and well being in general (Daley, 2012). As discussed by Thomas (2008), lesbian identity may impact the therapeutic relationship whether or not revealed directly, though TSDO may be complicated, multifaceted, and even more so when the client is heterosexual. In and out of therapy, disclosure of lesbian sexuality is often an expression of pride and empowerment (Thomas, 2008).

Loughran's (1993) dissertation was an analogue study of 120 participants with comparable representation of LGBTQ and heterosexual male and female college students. Results were that TSDO of any orientation was more highly regarded than non-disclosure and across sexual orientations. TSDO of LGBTQ sexuality to LGBTQ clients consistently and positively affected the analogue client's willingness to see the therapist in the future, with lesbian therapist to lesbian client TSDO being more positively impactful (in this regard) than TSDO in gay male dyads. Thus, Loughran's (1992) findings are somewhat affirming of the prior positions advanced in Thomas (2008) and Daley (2012).

Disclosure may also depend on the extent of the woman's directness-passivity, timing considerations, gender identity, race/cultural factors, intersectionality, and general comfort and security with lesbian identity (Daley, 2012). Thus, some lesbian therapists may openly share their identity, many do not, and to an extent that generalizing TSDO impacts is difficult (Thomas, 2008). As discussed by Goldstein and Horowitz (2003), lesbian therapists in various states of discomfort may at times be non-disclosive on the whole, which may in turn impede the development of relationships with clients.

Consistent with this last point, Thomas (2008) interviewed 12 lesbian social worker-therapists of a range of theoretical orientations. Therapists consistently indicated some level of anxiety, worry, or fear about self-disclosing their sexuality, with these feelings often related to fear of loss of clients, and anticipation that the client might react differently to her subsequent to TSDO. Respondents consistently reported a general view of TSD and TSDO as potentially beneficial if used sparingly, with clear relation to treatment goals, and thereby in a manner consistent with research summarized previously in this text. Respondents in Thomas' (2008) study also indicated they would usually reveal their sexuality to a client that posed a direct question, though would also base their decisions on relative comfort and an underlying sense of the client's intention in asking. Fear of loss of clients was also identified in another qualitative interview study conducted by Harris (2015). Loss of clients may not only be a financial loss, but of particular concern for lesbian therapists preferring to maintain a caseload of both LGBTQ and heterosexual clients (Thomas, 2008).

TSD to Heterosexual Clients

While TSDO has been researched to a greater extent in recent history, comparatively less research has been conducted on LGBTQ-TSDO to presumed heterosexual clients (Moore & Jenkins, 2012). While LGBTQ clients frequently find it affirming when LGBTQ therapists reveal similar identity, heterosexuals may not necessarily react the same way (Dean, 2010). In some cases, heterosexual clients may make discriminatory remarks, put forth moralistic judgments, not want to hear about the therapist's sexual orientation, or perceive TSDO as not highly impactful/relevant to the therapeutic process (Bashan, 2004; Dean, 2010; Satterly, 2006). In some cases, and in a manner consistent with prior research findings, LGBTQ therapists may anticipate such reactions as a form of projecting their internalized homophobia onto the heterosexual client, which may be more likely after working with openly discriminatory clients (Satterly, 2006). TSDO to heterosexual clients may be beneficial when it permits them to explore previously unasked questions they may have about their sexuality (Dean, 2010; Thomas, 2008).

Research on therapist perspectives, and further addressing the possibilities noted in the last paragraph, is now summarized. Harris' (2015) review of four qualitative studies, as well as Moore and Jenkins' (2012) qualitative review of eight practicing therapists (six women and two men), revealed similar findings. Across studies, therapists were generally apprehensive about using TSDO with heterosexual clients, questioned the relevance of TSDO to their treatment, and acknowledged that their reticence was largely related to their own internalized homophobia projected onto clients, and particularly in light of their heterosexual client's prior responses to TSDO often being positive. In Moore and Jenkins' (2012) study, therapists reported that heterosexual clients often made statements or interacted with them in ways suggesting their presumption of therapist heterosexuality, which at times led therapists to feel compelled to answer in an affirmative/corrective manner. Therapists in Moore and Jenkins' (2012) study at times expressed reservations around disclosing same-sex orientation to a client of the same gender, for fear of being perceived as suggesting sexual attraction or intentionality, or disclosing to clients who expressed strong religious beliefs. Moore and Jenkins (2012) discerned no major difference in these outcomes depending on whether therapist-respondents were gay men or lesbian women.

Both Carroll et al. (2011) and Dean (2010) conducted analogue studies of heterosexual clients, who participated by reviewing transcripts of TSDO in client–therapist dyads of different genders and sexual orientations. Carroll et al. (2011) and Dean (2010) reported findings that were consistent with previously summarized therapist perspective studies. Students in Carroll et al.'s (2011) study rated disclosing gay and lesbian therapists as more trustworthy than non-disclosing gay and lesbian therapists, likely due to a relationship between TSDO and perceived authenticity, as identified as of pivotal importance in other contexts of culture and diversity, as discussed in Chapter 9 of this text. Interestingly, non-disclosing heterosexual therapists and disclosing gay and lesbian therapists were rated as similarly trustworthy, with heterosexual non-disclosers rated higher than heterosexual disclosures, and without gay and lesbian or heterosexual therapists being rated differently in terms of attractiveness or expertness. Dean (2010) concluded that heterosexual client ratings of LGBTQ therapists were less impacted by TSDO and anti-gay attitudes, and were more impacted by general help-seeking attitudes. The sum total of these findings should be at least somewhat encouraging for heterosexual practitioners who may otherwise presume a need for LGBTQ clients to be paired with LGBTQ therapists, and for LGBTQ therapists who may presume or anticipate homophobic responses from heterosexual clients.

Conclusions

TSDO is generally well received by many clients of all sexual orientations. Generally positive outcomes can be expected by research-informed practitioners who put forth TSDO with appropriate consideration of the client's needs from the relationship, relevance to treatment, and appropriate therapeutic timing and delivery, as discussed in prior chapters of this text. This perspective is supported by general benefits of TSDO being similarly and consistently described in studies both of client and therapist perspectives. Decisions to or not to disclose sexuality should also be considerate of both the client's and therapist's internalized and externalized homophobia, projections, comfort, and safety considerations.

Population-specific implications flow from the scholarly literature. In dyads of gay men or lesbian women, TSDO frequently has clinical benefits related to role modeling, encouraging client self-esteem, and building client self-respect. TSDO may also meet social justice aims of empowerment and fighting oppression, as may the LGBTQ therapist's aim when correcting heterosexual clients' presumptions of similar sexuality. Research indicated that TSDO in gay male dyads was most often experienced by clients as particularly affirming, validating, and possibly even necessary to address internalized homophobia and stigma. Research indicated that lesbian women showed a stronger preference for being matched with a lesbian female therapist. Therefore, TSDO in lesbian female dyads may be necessary to ensure informed consent and in a manner consistent with the feminist perspective discussed earlier. In other studies, heterosexual clients often reported that TSDO from an LGBTQ-identified therapist was well received as a showing of authenticity, and was discussed by therapists as at times giving heterosexual clients permission to explore questions about their sexuality. From these findings, practitioners are advised that TSDO may in many cases be beneficial, depending in part on the clinical and contextual factors discussed previously, and regardless of client or therapist sexual orientation, though with greater likelihood of positive impact in gay male and lesbian female dyads.

Implications for Heterosexual Practitioners

Heterosexual male practitioners are encouraged not to discount their potential to be helpful to LGBTQ clients on grounds of different sexual orientations, and instead, seek training and consultation in effort to improve therapeutic engagement and outcomes. LGBTQ identification was not determined via client survey studies to suggest qualification to treat, though knowledge of LGBTQ community issues and an affirming attitude was generally seen as more important. This encouragement is also a challenge in light of findings suggesting heterosexual male therapists are typically regarded by LGBTQ clients as least helpful, as compared to heterosexual women or LGBTQ-identified practitioners.

Should heterosexual male competency in LGBTQ issues be increased, it might be of particular, ancillary, and associated benefit to gay male clients in light of previously discussed research indicating a greater multitude of paternal (rather than maternal) and male role-modeling implications for mental health. Male role-modeling benefits cannot reasonably by achieved through pairing with heterosexual women, which has thus far yielded better outcomes, though may operate at a loss due to gender mismatching, and unless male heterosexual therapists improve in LGBTQ-related knowledge and competencies.

It was of interest that non-disclosure of heterosexuality was regarded more favorably (than TSDO), though also consistent with prior findings: That TSDs tend to be more beneficial to clients when conveying client–therapist similarity. This may suggest heterosexual therapists should be more cautious in revealing their sexuality directly, and possibly err towards answering client inquiries with a process-oriented response. Further study is needed on the benefits and drawbacks of disclosing or not disclosing heterosexual identification in completely heterosexual dyads. The absence of this research, on the whole, is consistent with prior researcher concerns about widespread presumptions of heteronormity (Thomas, 2008).

Intersectionality Considerations

A major limitation of the TSDO research, which in its turn limits the extent to which results can be generalized into implications for practice, is recurring and insufficient inclusion of participants from diverse racial groups, socioeconomic and employment statuses, religious beliefs, and gender identities (Daley, 2012; Dean, 2010; Mohr & Fassinger, 2003; Satterly, 2006). TSDO research predominantly included Caucasian participants of college education, and/or middle to higher socioeconomic status. Transgender and bisexual individuals were at times included in larger samples, rather than analyzed as distinct groups. Further, most of the TSDO research had relatively smaller convenience samples with recruitment occurring at LGBTQ events, community centers, or in online networks. In effect, it may be more accurate to say that the implications of prior research pertain specifically to therapists and clients who are Caucasian and cisgendered men or women with a college education, middle to higher socioeconomic status, and at least a marginal level of contact with LGBTQ networks. Intersectionality considerations will be discussed and applied to psychotherapeutic contexts in more detail in Chapter 18 by Apryl Alexander, while gender considerations will be discussed in more detail by Ryan Barbeau in Chapter 24.

References

Bashan, F. (2004). Therapist self-disclosure of their sexual orientation from a client's perspective (Doctoral dissertation). Retrieved from ProQuest Dissertations and Theses database (UMI No. 3156916).

Bjork, D. (2004). Disclosure and the development of trust in the therapeutic setting. *Journal of Lesbian Studies*, *8*(1–2), 95–105.

Carroll, L., Gauler, A., Relph, J., & Hutchinson, K. (2011). Counselor self-disclosure: Does sexual orientation matter to straight clients? *International Journal for the Advancement of Counseling*, *33*(2), 129–48.

Cole, G., & Drescher, J. (2006). Do tell: Queer perspectives on therapist self-disclosure introduction. *Journal of Gay and Lesbian Psychotherapy*, *10*(1), 1–6.

Cornett, C. (1993). *Affirmative dynamic psychotherapy with gay men*. Northvale, NJ: Jason Aronson.

Daley, A. (2012). Becoming seen, becoming known: Lesbian women's self-disclosures of sexual orientation to mental health service providers. *Journal of Gay and Lesbian Mental Health*, *16*(3), 215–34.

Dean, B. (2010). Therapist self-disclosure: Heterosexual perceptions of sexual minority therapists (Doctoral dissertation). Retrieved from ProQuest Dissertations and Theses database (No UMI No.).

Farber, B. (2006). *Self-disclosure in psychotherapy*. New York: Guilford Press.

Goldstein, E., & Horowitz, L. (2003). *Lesbian identity and contemporary psychotherapy: A Framework for clinical practice*. Hillsdale, NJ: The Analytic Press.

Guthrie, C. (2006). Disclosing the therapist's sexual orientation: The meaning of disclosure in working with gay, lesbian, and bisexual patients. *Journal of Gay & Lesbian Psychotherapy*, *10*(1), 63–77.

Harris, A. (2015). To disclose or not to disclose? The LGBT therapist's question (Doctoral dissertation). Retrieved from ProQuest Dissertations and Theses database (No UMI No.).

Hearn, B., & West-Olatunji, C. (2015). Deciding to disclose: The LGBTQ counselor's unique challenge. *VISTAS Online*, *74*, 1–8.

Henretty, J., & Levitt, H. (2010). The role of therapist self-disclosure in psychotherapy: A qualitative review. *Clinical Psychology Review*, *30*(1), 63–77.

Houston, A. (1997). Lesbian and bisexual therapist's desire for authenticity: Self-disclosure vs. nondisclosure of sexual orientation in therapy and supervision (Doctoral dissertation). Retrieved from ProQuest Dissertations and Theses database (UMI No. 9941948).

Jeffrey, M., & Tweed, A. (2015). Clinician self-disclosure or clinician self-concealment? Lesbian, gay, and bisexual mental health practitioners' experiences of disclosure in therapeutic relationships. *Counselling and Psychotherapy Research, 15*(1), 41–9.

Kronner, H. (2013). Use of self-disclosure for the gay male therapist: The impact on gay males in therapy. *Journal of Social Service Research, 39*(1), 78–94.

Kronner, H., & Northcut, T. (2015). Listening to both sides of the therapeutic dyad: Self-disclosure of gay male therapists and reflections from their gay male clients. *Psychoanalytic Social Work, 22*(2), 162–81.

Lea, J., Jones, R., & Huws, J. (2010). Gay psychologist and gay clients: Exploring therapist disclosure of sexuality in the therapeutic closet. *Psychology of Sexualities Review, 1*(1), 59–73.

Liddle, B. (1996). Therapist sexual orientation, gender, and counseling practices as they relate to ratings of helpfulness by gay and lesbian clients. *Journal of Counseling Psychology, 43*(4), 394–401.

Liddle, B. (1997). Gay and lesbian clients' selection of therapists and utilization of therapy. *Psychotherapy: Theory, Research, Practice, Training, 34*(1), 11–18.

Loughran, M. (1993). Counselor self-disclosure of sexual orientation: Effects of gender and similarity (Doctoral dissertation). Retrieved from ProQuest Dissertations and Theses database (UMI No. 9304272).

Mohr, J., & Fassinger, R. (2003). Self-acceptance and self-disclosure of sexual orientation in lesbian, gay, and bisexual adults: An attachment perspective. *Journal of Counseling Psychology, 50*(4), 482–95.

Moore, J., & Jenkins, P. (2012). 'Coming out' in therapy? Perceived risks and benefits of self-disclosure of sexual orientation by gay and lesbian therapists to straight clients. *Counselling & Psychotherapy Research, 12*(4), 308–15.

Russell, G. (2006). Different ways of knowing: The complexities of therapist disclosure. *Journal of Gay & Lesbian Psychotherapy, 10*(1), 79–94.

Russell, G., & Greenhouse, E. (1997). Homophobia in the supervisory relationship: An invisible intruder. *Psychoanalytic Review, 84*(1), 27–42.

Satterly, B. (2006). Therapist self-disclosure from a gay male perspective. *Families in Society: The Journal of Contemporary Social Services, 87*(2), 240–7.

Simonds, L., & Spokes, N. (2017). Therapist self-disclosure and the therapeutic alliance in the treatment of eating problems. *Eating Disorders, 25*(2), 151–64.

Thomas, M. (2008). Shades of gray: Lesbian therapists explore the complexities of self disclosure to heterosexual clients (Doctoral dissertation). Retrieved from Smith College Theses, Dissertations, and Projects.

CHAPTER 11

Mental Illness and Personality Disorders

Graham S. Danzer, PsyD and Andrea Che, PhD

Attention is now turned to the subject of therapeutic self-disclosure (TSD) in cases where clients *and/or therapists* may have mental illnesses or personality considerations/disorders. As discussed by de Vos, Netten, and Noordenbos (2016), there has in the last two decades been a large scale shift from a medical model understanding of clients as sick people in need of treatment to a bio-psychosocial-spiritual model of recovery with a peer-helping component. Within, a therapist's personal experiences with mental illness can give them unique and powerful insights into clients' recovery processes (de Vos et al., 2016). A major oversight of the recovery movement is that large numbers of professional therapists have experiential knowledge from their own recovery process (de Vos et al., 2016).

According to Dixon et al. (2001), TSD may not be used as often in these contexts due in part to a lack of guidelines, as well as the possibility that a disclosing therapist could be more harmful than beneficial to a treatment already high in vulnerability concerns. Although TSD often associates with reduced mental health symptoms (Ziv-Beiman & Shahar, 2016), further discussion is necessary because clients with mental illnesses and personality disorders often misinterpret interactions of a more personal and connective nature (i.e., TSD). It is also not uncommon for more severely disturbed clients to respond to changes in boundary structure by recreating problematic dynamics. The specific nature of their responses and recreations is likely reminiscent of their earlier interpersonal difficulties and reinforcing of their interpersonal problems outside of therapy.

Within the literature are credible arguments for and against TSD in contexts of mental illness, boundary problems, and personality disorder. Empirical research suggests that therapists are frequently reluctant to disclose to symptomatic clients and for boundary-related reasons as mentioned in the previous paragraph (Kelly & Rodriquez, 2007). Similarly, other research suggests that therapists' personal issues often associated with mental health or boundary problems, including substance abuse, personal crises, or physical health complications, can lead to inappropriate TSD (Lawson & Venart, 2005). Still other research suggests that disclosure of mental illness primarily in peer-helping relationships can be particularly beneficial to client–provider relationships, and may be empowering, de-stigmatizing, and role modeling when the client and provider are both from a cultural background where mental illness is taboo (Marino, Child, & Krasinski, 2016). As discussed in the prior and subsequent chapters on trauma, substance abuse, and eating disorders, the question for professional therapists becomes: How much can (if not should) boundaries be modified to build therapeutic relationships and address clients' presenting complaints? And if boundaries are modified, at one point is professional therapy no longer professional therapy? Due to a lack of empirical research on peer-helping interventions applied in therapy contexts of serious mental illness, further commentary is warranted.

The First Author's Perspective

In the first author's professional experience, appropriate TSDs *to* severely ill and personality-disordered populations may convey a stable and professional therapist's sincerity of interest in building a genuine relationship with a client. Often, a marginally higher frequency of tactful, well-thought-out, and low-intimacy TSDs at least somewhat necessary to build relationships with clients who are so severely disordered they are largely if not completely intolerant of ambiguity and resistant to more cognitive forms of empathy (i.e., surface level reflections).

Again, in the first author's experience, psychotherapy with individuals with multiple, severe, and comorbid conditions, and from highly marginalized and stigmatized backgrounds, tend to enter professional relationships with a much greater level of distrust and even aversion and alienation to contact with professionals (and particularly for such clients who have adverse contacts with prior professionals, as discussed in Chapter 23 by Tyson Bailey). As a result, such individuals are likely to be of the mental health and personality structure deemed unsuitable for traditional individual therapy, particularly among therapists who are more accustomed or prefer to treat higher functioning, neurotic, and 'worried well' clients. Moreover, when severely disturbed clients come to therapy, it is likely that they do so based on some extent of pressure or coercion from other mental or physical health providers, family members, social service or legal authorities, or as a requirement to either become or remain eligible for basic needs resources. Therefore, and in such cases, an understandable level of resistance often requires a greater level of concession and interpersonal outreach to forge a genuine, trusting, and motivating therapeutic relationship.

Elsewise, 'less voluntary' and severely disordered clients may recreate a therapeutic relationship that appears similar to that of a probationer and probation officer, with ongoing assessment perceived as monitoring, and answers to the therapist's questions consistently being to the client's self-interest. For example, clients may report a lack of psychotic symptoms, substance abuse, arrests, or interpersonal conflicts in attempt to prevent the therapist from documenting their self-reports in a manner that may ultimately threaten their livelihood.

The Coauthor's Perspective

Both capacity and motivation for clients with severe mental illnesses, such as schizophrenia spectrum disorders, are frequently affected by the severity of their symptoms and neuropsychological dysfunction (e.g., attention and concentration, executive functions, and verbal and working memory) (Bowie & Harvey, 2006; Hill et al., 2013). Accordingly, these clients' abilities to benefit from and comply with traditional individual psychotherapy may be somewhat limited by the nature of their conditions. As an alternative, clients may benefit from a more active, conversational, task-oriented, and largely non-transferential therapy, including case management services, and at least until a more solid relationship is established.

A more superficial level of rapport generally sufficient to begin treatment with higher functioning clients is often insufficient in cases of severe mental illnesses (SMI). In many of such cases, a conversational or social dialogue with casual forms of TSD, as well as a seemingly prolonged engagement period, may be helpful or necessary *to begin* treatment due to the nature of symptoms (e.g., paranoia, delusions, hallucinations and other psychotic symptoms, possible trauma, and comorbid psychological/medical diagnoses) as well as boundary/ personality considerations mentioned previously. In the coauthor's experiences, active and casual forms of TSD in individual, group, and day treatment activities in the company of peers have been beneficial in enhancing the therapeutic relationship and overall flow and outcome of treatment; a perspective that is also consistent with earlier research studies on the subject (Dies, 1973).

Implications for Practice Scenarios and Considerations

With potential benefits and harmful effects in mind, TSD in cases or contexts of SMI must be approached with caution and for reasons mentioned in the prior introductory, general research, and types of disclosure chapters of this text. In addition to the points made in the previous paragraph of this chapter, it is not uncommon, in the first author's experience, for severely ill and personality disordered clients to respond adversely to TSDs that seem overly empathic, are incongruent with their natural ways of relating and connecting with others (i.e., attachment style), and in ways expectable of one with their particular psychopathology.

For example, clients may at times experience and respond to the disclosing therapist as another intrusive, pressuring family member. TSDs of positive coping skills and maintenance may be experienced as pressuring a client out of affect and into cognition, or as a lack of understanding, appreciation, or respect for his or her emotional solitude. Clients with psychotic symptoms may presume (to a greater extent than clients without psychosis) that the disclosing therapist desires a social relationship or, in the case of paranoid clients, has hidden mal-intentions. In either case, the therapist's efforts to reach out to the client may result in greater withdrawal and defensive maneuvering. A very informative review of how various personality structures can affect various clinical processes underlying TSD considerations is contained in McWilliams (1994).

Following McWilliams' (1994) early work, McWilliams (2011) discusses clients with psychotic disorders as frequently benefitting and perhaps requiring a more active and at times disclosive therapist. McWilliams (2011, p. 76) mentions the necessity of "unwavering honesty," which may include a supportive approach to answering client inquiries, and gently flowing into a more process-style of inquiry. For example, McWilliams (2011) noted that a psychotic client who inquires about whether the therapist is angry with him or her might do well to acknowledge feelings of irritation if present, offer an explanation that is supportive and congruent with treatment aims, and gently ask about the client's intentions behind his or her inquiry. So doing may help to counteract a psychotic client's fantasies or presumptions of malevolence, help to generate emotional relief from symptoms, and provide the client with what may be a rare opportunity to participate in a more genuine and egalitarian interchange.

As depicted in Carl Jung's (2015) conceptualization of the *Wounded Healer*, therapists may conduct therapy in the first place because of their own personal struggles and desire to help similarly afflicted clients. A therapist whose personal tragedies mirror that of a client's symptoms may assume sameness of experience, unintentionally interrupt the client's story, and intuitively finish it with their own. Contrastingly, a self-aware, careful, appropriately restrained, and intervention-minded therapist is more likely to reflect upon similar experiences and carefully consider areas of convergence and divergence. A more mindful, aware, and client-centered therapist may then maintain silence to see what the client does next, carefully word questions intended to facilitate exploration and insight, or put forth reflections intended to encourage emotional/affective expression related to the perceived shared experience of illness and interpersonal conflict.

How is the therapist to know if, when, and how to share their parallel experiences of illness or suffering? This question is challenging to answer when it is considered that a majority of previously reviewed research suggests therapists should err on the side of infrequent, brief, and lower intimacy disclosures. However, this research has yet to be thoroughly applied to seriously mentally ill populations for whom traditional therapeutic boundaries often result in early termination and associated client suffering or other unfavorable outcomes, and in the manner reminiscent of points made by McWilliams (2011). As detailed in other chapters in this section of chapters, research on therapists sharing similar personal experiences in other contexts of vulnerability (e.g., eating disorders, substance abuse, religion, and LGBTQ identity) has been found to be helpful. Therefore, further research should attempt to determine whether somewhat transferable findings may apply in other cases of SMI and identify major implications for practitioners.

Supervision, consultation, and reflection upon the relevant research are likely to help determine whether a particular TSD is ethically appropriate and likely to be helpful/unhelpful for severely mentally ill clients of various psycho-diagnostic categories and psychosocial histories. Reflecting upon the prior clinical conceptualization, it would be reasonable to consider a possible disclosure during therapy, temporarily refrain, consult/seek supervision after the session concludes, review the relevant research, and then re-approach similar scenarios in the future when informed by the full caucus of information available. A conceptualization of the individual client in some ways informed by the therapist's intuitive understanding, supervisory guidance, and relevant research may be chiefly ethical *and* likely to be more beneficial to the client.

With the latter goal in mind, research on TSD in contexts of therapist and client mental illness and personality factors is reviewed in the next section of this chapter. Interestingly, nearly the entirety of available research was on therapist perspectives, both on disclosing to mentally ill populations and disclosing aspects of the therapist's own illness or wounding. This research will be presented in its common themes, limitations, and implications for practitioners. Further study on the perspectives of severely mentally ill and personality disordered clients, who are frequently screened out of research (and therapy), is clearly needed.

Therapist Attitudes about TSD to this Population

Therapists surveyed in multiple studies consistently reported that they tended to self-disclose less to seriously ill or personality disordered clients (Gelso & Palma, 2011; Gibson, 2012; Henretty & Levitt, 2010; Kelly & Rodriguez, 2007). Among the explanations for this position, TSD may reinforce unhealthy preconceived notions of relationships among personality disordered individuals (Priest, 2005), and for eating disordered clients in particular (Stone, 2014). Similarly, TSD may lead substance-abusing clients to worry about triggering the therapist or inspire an unhealthy sense of competition in-session (Henretty & Levitt, 2010; LaPorte, Sweifach, & Linzer, 2010). Thus, clients with severe conditions may benefit from non-disclosure/less disclosure as a therapeutic approach helping them to maintain focus on themselves (Henretty & Levitt, 2010; Kelly & Rodriguez, 2007).

For example, non-disclosure/less disclosure can help individuals with borderline personality disorder to focus on learning skills to decrease target behaviors, rather than trying to regulate via enmeshing and creating other forms of boundary problems. As indicated in Chapter 22 of this text (on forensics), refraining from TSD and maintaining a more matter-of-fact and neutral demeanor with antisocial or psychopathic clients may impress upon them the therapist's inability to be bullied, corrupted, manipulated, or exploited. Non-disclosure or less disclosure may also afford the hysterical and interpersonally/emotionally intrusive client a corrective experience in terms of providing them with the more stable, secure, reliable, and nonreactive caregiver they are likely to have lacked in early life. Non/less disclosure in an effort to maintain client self-focus may be especially beneficial for clients who demonstrate victim mentalities, have a tendency to externalize blame, and whose illnesses or personality factors may predispose them to ineffective and self-defeating thought patterns.

Kelly and Rodriguez (2007) conducted a study of 22 therapists (18 of whom were women, 21 of whom were Caucasian) serving 88 clients in a hospital setting. The purpose was to determine whether therapists' perception that higher frequency of TSD with seriously mentally ill clients was or was not significantly impactful on therapeutic relationships and outcomes. Kelly and Rodriguez (2007) concluded no significant association between TSD in general, the strength of therapeutic relationships, and overall treatment efficacy. Finding similar results, Doremus' (2012) dissertation study of 59 participants (42 of whom were male, 52 of whom were Caucasian, and 49 reported having a PhD) revealed that psychologists tended to disclose less to court-mandated rather than voluntary clients, and disclosed more to court-mandated clients with acute conditions, rather than psychotic or personality disorders.

These last two findings (largely on Caucasian male and female practitioner perspectives) were somewhat in conflict with Bitar, Kimball, Bermúdez, & Drew's (2014) finding from an in-depth qualitative interview study of 10 court mandated Mexican American male clients, who consistently reported favoring Caucasian therapist self-disclosure, as well as McWilliams' (2011) recommendations regarding a higher level of disclosure often being needed to facilitate engagement with psychotic clients. Thus, the relevant research suggests a possibility of cultural differences of perspective on TSD between Caucasian therapists (both male and female) and clients of diverse backgrounds with more stigmatizing mental disorders or legal circumstances. These possibilities are discussed in more detail in Chapters 9 and 29 of this text and make it necessary for this chapter to review research addressing cultural and stigma factors, which is as follows.

Marino et al. (2016) conducted a mixed methods quantitative study of 117 professionals and para-professionals (17 identified as clinician-participants) in order to explore perceptions on the risks and benefits of sharing their personal experiences of mental illness with clients. Participants most frequently reported that their TSDs were intended to benefit the client-provider relationship, inspire hope, and normalize/de-stigmatize the client's experience. Participants also reported basing their decisions to or not to self-disclose on their sense of comfort or safety (which may in turn offer a partial explanation for therapist reluctance to disclose, as discussed in the previous paragraph of this chapter). Additional provider-perceived benefits were related to TSD promoting authenticity in the relationship and reduced stigma. Marino et al.'s (2016) findings were, in effect, consistent with findings and mentions in prior and upcoming chapters on TSD ethics, theoretical conceptualizations, and contexts of vulnerability and risk (i.e., cross-culture, forensic settings, eating disorder, LGBTQ identity, and suicide risk). Interviewed African American and Native American practitioners in Marino et al.'s (2016) study reported that TSD of their mental health history, to clients from their same ethnic background, served a modeling function and frequently helped clients become more open to discussion of mental health issues in spite of culturally related stigma.

Ziv-Beiman and Shahar (2016), practicing therapists and researchers, reported their perspective that TSD is generally helpful, even in cases of SMI and high risk for suicidality (as discussed in more detail in Chapter 25 on suicide). Commensurate with recurring-prior positions, Ziv-Beiman and Shahar (2016) recommended a process-oriented conceptualization of disclosure scenarios with SMI clients, as something of an alternative to a more rule-bound discouragement of TSD.

Conclusions

There is clearly limited research in the area of TSD *to and from* severely disordered, wounded, and personality disordered populations (i.e., clients *and* therapists). Further, most research is focused solely on therapist perspectives and lacks inclusion of client perspectives discussed earlier in this text as generally more predictive of outcomes (Audet & Everall, 2003). Thus, the perspective flowing from research in favor of discouraging TSD in contexts of illness and personality disorders, and for fairly standard clinical/boundary-related reasons, is considered by the first author to have been insufficiently tested. To more fully and empirically address if not answer questions posed in this chapter, more therapists with histories of trauma and mental illness may need to come forward and participate in such research.

Decisions to or not to self-disclose are complicated in cases where clients are severely disordered, suffering, mandated to attend therapy, and have difficulty tolerating traditional approaches. In such cases, it may be equally likely that TSD may benefit *and/or* complicate therapeutic relationships, which must nevertheless grow in spite of deeply ingrained illness and personality-driven resistance. As a result, TSD may paradoxically be as contra-indicated as it is vital to treatment even beginning, let alone progressing towards outcome. For these reasons, the first author of this text concurs with the positions of McWilliams (2011): That a more transparent and open approach to therapy is likely necessary in these cases.

With previously discussed research findings in mind, it is possible that TSDs to seriously mentally disordered populations, both of lower intimacy content and even directly about the therapist's own wounding or illness considerations, may be of greater value and help to clients than therapists realize. Further, it is possible that tactful, appropriate, and well-timed disclosures of similar illnesses or emotional wounding may be hope-inspiring to clients so severely afflicted that recovery seems impossible (as also mentioned in Chapter 12 on eating disorders).

However, TSDs of such high intensity may also be pulled for by mentally and personality disordered clients seeking enmeshment, boundary dissolution, exploitation, or avoidance of the self-focused treatment that may be required for deeper and lasting changes to occur. Although the clinical and

TSD research typically does not include severely/complexly disordered and/ or frequently hospitalized/incarcerated populations, the current authors cautiously assert that a more conversational, task-focused, and casually self-disclosing therapy is likely necessary, as is more common in practice in SMI treatment than what is often acknowledged overtly. A comprehensive search of the literature yields no studies on such an approach. Therefore, further research and discussion in clinical circles is warranted.

References

Audet, C., & Everall, R. (2003). Counsellor self-disclosure: Client-informed implications for practice. *Counselling and Psychotherapy Research, 3*(3), 223–31.

Bitar, G., Kimball, T., Bermúdez, J., & Drew, C. (2014). Therapist self-disclosure and culturally competent care with Mexican-American court mandated clients: A phenomenological study. *Contemporary Family Therapy, 36*(3), 417–25.

Bowie, C., & Harvey, P. (2006). Cognitive deficits and functional outcome in schizophrenia. *Neuropsychiatric Disease and Treatment, 2*(4), 531–6.

De Vos, J., Netten, C., & Noordenbos, G. (2016). Recovered eating disorder therapists using their experiential knowledge in therapy: A qualitative examination of the therapist's and the patient's view. *Eating Disorders, 24*(3), 207–23.

Dies, R. (1973). Group therapist self-disclosure: An evaluation by clients. *Journal of Counseling Psychology, 20*(4), 344–8.

Dixon, L., Adler, D., Braun D., Dulit, R., Goldman, B., Siris, S., . . . Grant, J. (2001). Reexamination of therapist self-disclosure. *Psychiatric Services, 52*(11), 1489–93.

Doremus, B. (2012). Psychologist self-disclosure with court-mandated and self-referred clients (Doctoral dissertation). Retrieved from Engaged Scholarship Archive.

Gelso, C., & Palma, B. (2011). Directions for research on self-disclosure and immediacy: Moderation, mediation, and the inverted-U. *Psychotherapy, 48*(4), 342–8.

Gibson, M. (2012). Opening up: Therapist self-disclosure in theory, research, and practice. *Clinical Social Work Journal, 40*(3), 287–96.

Henretty, J., & Levitt, H. (2010). The role of therapist self-disclosure in psychotherapy: A qualitative review. *Clinical Psychology Review, 30*(1), 63–77.

Hill, S., Reilly, J., Keefe, R., Gold, J., Bishop, J., Gershon, E., . . . Sweeney, J. (2013). Neuropsychological impairments in schizophrenia and psychotic bipolar disorder: Findings from the bipolar-schizophrenia network on intermediate phenotypes (B-SNIP) study. *American Journal of Psychiatry, 170*(11), 1275–84.

Jung, C. (2015). *Carl Jung: Wounded healer of the soul.* London: Watkins Publishing.

Kelly, A., & Rodriguez, R. (2007). Do therapists self-disclose more to clients with greater symptomology? *Psychotherapy: Theory, Research, Practice, Training, 44*(4), 470–5.

LaPorte, H., Sweifach, J., & Linzer, N. (2010). Sharing the trauma: Guidelines for therapist self-disclosure following a catastrophic event. *Best Practices in Mental Health, 6*(2), 39–56.

Lawson, G., & Venart, B. (2005). Preventing counselor impairment: Vulnerability, wellness, and resilience. In G. Walz & R. Yep (Eds.), *Vistas: Compelling perspectives on counseling* (pp. 243–6). Alexandria, VA: American Counseling Association.

Marino, C., Child, B., & Krasinski, V. (2016). Sharing experience learned firsthand (SELF): Self-disclosure of lived experience in mental health services and supports. *Psychiatric Rehabilitation Journal, 39*(2), 154–60.

McWilliams, N. (1994). *Psychoanalytic diagnosis: Understanding personality structure in the clinical process* (1st ed.). New York: Guilford Press.

McWilliams, N. (2011). *Psychoanalytic diagnosis: Understanding personality structure in the clinical process* (2nd ed.). New York: Guilford Press.

Priest, T. (2005). Comments on Hanson [Review of the book *Should your lips be zipped? How therapist self-disclosure and nondisclosure affects clients*, by Hanson, J.]. *Counselling & Psychotherapy Research*, 5(2), 96–104.

Stone, M. (2014). Psychotherapist self-disclosure of personal recovery in treatment of clients with eating disorders: Effects on predicted treatment outcome (Doctoral dissertation). Retrieved from ProQuest Dissertations and Theses database (UMI No. 3643897).

Ziv-Beiman, S., & Shahar, G. (2016). Therapeutic self-disclosure in integrative psychotherapy: When is this a clinical error? *Psychotherapy*, *53*(3), 273–7.

CHAPTER 12

Eating Disorders

Graham S. Danzer, PsyD

Both the pros and cons of therapeutic self-disclosure (TSD) may be magnified when TSD is put forth with eating disorder (ED) clients given (a) their usual avoidance of authentic interpersonal connections, as one of the major precipitants of their suffering, (b) their high rates of early treatment termination, (c) the potential of TSD to deepen connection and increase retention, and (d) the higher likelihood of mortality following ED client disengagement (Stone, 2011; Tantillo, 2004). While many interventions may improve retention, TSD in contexts of ED is of interest because, according to research studies, between 20–47% of ED therapists acknowledge having their own personal history of ED (de Vos, Netten, & Noordenbos, 2016; Stone, 2014; Williams & Haverkamp, 2015). A similar personal history may have the advantages of increasing therapist empathy, challenging ED client narcissism and grandiosity, avoiding stagnation in therapy, maintaining therapist authenticity and a hopeful outlook on treatment, and instilling in clients feelings of hope, safety, motivation, understanding, and reduced shame (Costin & Johnson, 2002; de Vos et al., 2016). In addition, 67% of surveyed ED therapists reported using TSD in different forms in their treatment approach (Bloomgarden, Gerstein, & Moss, 2003). Thus, the large peer-helping component of the ED field, the alienation and isolation characteristics of ED, and the humanizing benefits of TSD (as discussed in prior chapters of this text) converge in a manner suggesting TSD may be among the interventions that helps to improve ED client engagement and outcomes.

However, there is also debate within the ED field about whether therapists with similar personal histories should or should not treat clients with ED, under what circumstances it may be appropriate to disclose a similar personal history, and what actually constitutes recovery from ED on the whole (de Vos et al., 2016). Therapists with similar personal histories may over-identify or become over-involved with ED clients, be easily triggered or at-risk for relapse, lack objectivity, or reinforce negative emotional traits characteristic of EDs, as discussed later in this chapter (de Vos et al., 2016). Disclosures specifically of ED history (i.e., ED-TSD) may be problematic given the possibility that therapists, and particularly those in earlier stages of their careers, may have more active and less under-control EDs (Williams & Haverkamp, 2015).

With these possibilities in mind, a comprehensive review of a small research base (including non-published dissertations) will be presented. First, there will be a review of the common features and presentation of ED clients, followed by the ways in which TSD may be beneficial or harmful, and research in support or dispute of working theories. Reviewed research will focus on TSD *in contexts of ED treatment* as well as ED-TSD, as both are relevant to treatment and the available research on each is limited. This chapter will conclude with a summary of implications for practitioners.

The Congruence of ED Symptoms and TSD

ED behavior occurs in shame and secrecy (Basile, 2004). ED clients frequently feel interpersonally ineffective, have difficulty accessing, naming, trusting, and regulating their emotions, are confused about the behavior of others, exhibit irrational and black and white thinking, and have internalized negative images of themselves, their relationships with others, and how they expect others will respond to them (Tantillo, 2004). ED clients often present as critical, impatient, judgmental, and overly driven (de Vos et al., 2016). These difficulties may be exacerbated by their malnourishment and health complications, and in turn contribute to a paradoxical hunger for *and fear of* emotional connection with others in some ways addressed through their issues with food (Tantillo, 2004). More specifically, ED clients frequently desire to share their deeper thoughts and feelings with their therapists and others, but have difficulty due to societal disapproval and personal embarrassment about their ED behavior, which then manifests in symptoms and interpersonal difficulties such as those noted earlier (Basile, 2004).

Tantillo's (2004) conceptualization of relational therapy for ED clients includes a description of how ED clients are likely to respond to a greater level of therapeutic neutrality and non-disclosure, why TSD is often preferred and even necessary, and how therapists can put forth TSD in a manner that is likely to be beneficial in many cases. Given their aforementioned self-perceptions of interpersonal ineffectiveness, non-disclosure may communicate to ED clients they have no emotional impact on their therapists. In turn, non-disclosure may be reinforcing of their core negative beliefs and be experienced as an abandonment, betrayal, or re-traumatization. In such cases, ED clients are likely to increase the intensity of their distress until the therapist's emotional responsiveness demonstrates understanding and resonance. Should non-disclosure and emotional under-responsiveness continue, dropout is likely to occur.

A more active and at least marginally disclosive therapist communicates to ED clients that the therapist is emotionally present, clarifies how a symbolic other is affected by them, and therefore (yet empathically) challenges the client's negative image of their expected-negative interpersonal impacts. From a developmental perspective, TSD is important since many ED clients are in an adolescent stage of psychosocial maturity, trying to define themselves in relationships, and therefore responsive to a therapist who they see as a role model. Thus, when ED clients become vulnerable, disclose to greater degrees, and therapists respond with validating TSDs, clients may become more trusting of themselves and how they desire to express their emotions. This way of working clinically may be of particular consideration for therapists paired with cognitively rigid ED clients who are in severe stages of decline and risk, as is a common association among ED clients, and is discussed in other contexts in Chapter 25 by Asha Wilkus-Stone.

Per Tantillo (2004), and as in the case of TSD with other vulnerable and at-risk populations discussed in the current section of chapters, TSD should promote mutuality and encourage reciprocal client disclosure. Specific to ED, TSD is likely to be helpful when it helps the client to move out of isolation and rigid/self-critical thinking, and into a sense of communality and connection. For similar reasons, a higher than usual level of therapeutic activity *and TSD* is advised, as it may help often disoriented and malnourished ED clients become more grounded, connected to others, and emotionally present.

In furtherance of the prior aims, TSD may be beneficial when it normalizes client imperfections and areas of growth, includes humorous or irreverent content, conveys flexibility and openness to change and difference, suggests client–therapist similarity of experience with intention to be empowering, is appropriately apologetic or acknowledging of therapeutic mistakes as needed, furthers and deepens here-and-now discussions of therapist-client relationship dynamics, or clarifies the therapeutic contract and limitations of treatment. Thus, helpful TSDs most frequently affirm the therapist's role and boundaries, rather than suggesting a fully peer-oriented relationship. Helpful TSDs also convey the therapist's emotional accessibility and openness, draw the client out of his or her isolation and inflexible and self-critical thinking, into a more egalitarian, self-accepting, and other-responsive way of participating in two-person relationships. TSD should convey to clients the therapist's acceptance and understanding of their emotional movement *toward and away* from therapeutic connection. Clients may then become incrementally more aware and insightful about how they use binging, purging, and food restriction to distract themselves form their authentic selves, decrease conflict and rejection in relationships, and thereby maintain inauthentic connections. For these reasons, TSD during client periods of disconnection and avoidance can help to re-establish emotional connection, prevent re-enactment of earlier life disconnections, and may be corrective when clients have not previously had their disconnection responded to with empathy.

In addition, Tantillo (2004) offers specific recommendations regarding what should be therapists' major clinical and relational considerations when considering whether or not to self-disclose to ED clients. TSDs must be authentic, and put forth at a pace and level of intimacy that is safe, appropriate, and responsive to the client's needs from the relationship. ED therapists considering TSD should reflect upon the client's unique and relevant history factors, level of functioning and associated ability to make use of the TSD, history of ED, and readiness for change. Therapists should also consider and formulate the treatment aim of their disclosure, as well as their comfort with the content, hopes and expectations regarding client response, power dynamics in the relationship, history and strength of the therapeutic relationship, and the amount of time remaining in session that would allow for client processing of the aftereffects (of TSD). Thus, Tantillo's (2004) recommendations are also consistent with recommendations in Chapter 5 on general TSD timing and decision-making, as well as Chapter 9 on TSD in cross-cultural contexts.

Per Tantillo (2004), and consistent with recommendations set forth in Chapter 3 of this text, TSD in cases of eating disorder would be contra-indicated when it meets the therapist's unconscious or conscious needs for acceptance or validation, or helps to address or resolve the therapist's personal problems. Additionally, TSD is contra-indicated when (a) helping the therapist and client avoid working through conflicts or painful emotions; (b) manipulating, controlling, or intruding on the client's experiences; (c) is overly confrontational rather than validating; (d) disregards or disputes the client's relational images, meanings, or patterns; or (e) would be followed by the therapist being unwilling/unable to participate in further dialogue initiated by client response. Also consistent with general guidelines discussed previously, ED therapists should generally refrain from disclosure in response to direct client inquiries, and instead decline in an authentic way (i.e., "I'm not comfortable sharing that").

Research Findings on Client and Therapist Perspectives

Extant client survey research related to ED-TSD (i.e., self-disclosure of personal history of eating disorder), as well as TSD in contexts of ED treatment, is summarized as follows, and offers confirmation of the prior theories. Stone's (2014) dissertation involved the showing of a simulated therapy video of TSD to 138 participants who met criteria for being diagnosed with an ED. Observers rated therapists who disclosed their personal histories of ED recovery as significantly more credible, trustworthy, and intervening in an appropriate manner, yet not more likeable nor likely to put forth a more beneficial treatment. Stone (2014) concluded that TSD of personal ED recovery was marginally associated with more positive client perceptions of treatment.

Oyer, O'Halloran, and Christoe-Frazier (2016) conducted a qualitative study of 15 ED clients and seven therapists to explore how the therapeutic relationship was built with ED populations, with attention to the potentially differential impact of TSD in contexts of ED treatment and ED-TSD as discussed in Stone (2014). Seven clients and six therapists in Oyer et al.'s (2016) study reported that TSD tended to strengthen therapeutic relationships, was frequently helpful when of lower intimacy (e.g., the therapist's vacation plans or experiences), and *did not* include the therapist's ED history. Additionally, clients consistently noted that general TSDs were helpful when promoting bonding, normalizing client experiences, and in the form of therapists acknowledging their lack of knowledge in at least some areas. These findings were somewhat affirmative of Tantillo's (2004) previously discussed theories, and were also identified in Chapter 5 on general TSD timing/decision-making and Chapter 10 on LGBTQ sexuality (i.e., a strategy for working through therapeutic ruptures). Interestingly, more than half of participants in Oyer et al.'s (2016, p. 129) study reported that their therapist having "a 'no fooling around attitude' helped to instill feelings of trust and safety."

Consistent with Stones' (2014) findings, Tantillo's (2004) advisement, and prior points made in Chapters 3 and 4 of this text, therapists and clients in Oyer et al.'s (2016) study consistently indicated that therapeutic relationships were negatively affected by TSDs that were irrelevant and/or poorly attuned to the client's individual needs. Negatively impactful TSDs, sometimes, were in the forms of therapists overly championing the client's recovery, pushing for hospitalization/coercive interventions, or showing a judgmental attitude. Six clients emphasized the need for some out-of-therapy contact, three clients reported a failure to individualize treatment as unhelpful, and all seven therapists reported that their self-perceived helpfulness was tied to awareness of personal reactions to clients and remaining objective. Therapists and clients agreed that therapist competence and confidence were helpful, with indications that this was somewhat more important to clients than therapists.

Simonds and Spokes (2017) conducted a study of 120 ED clients, 95% of whom were women, and all of whom were 16 years of age or older. As follows, Simonds and Spokes (2017) reported results that were consistent with results from both Stone's (2014) and Oyer et al.'s (2016) studies, as well as previously reviewed TSD research in general. Simonds and Spokes (2017) concluded that *when* TSD in contexts of ED (i.e., not necessarily ED-TSD) is perceived as helpful, the therapeutic alliance tends to strengthen. In Simonds and Spokes' (2017) study, most TSDs were rated by clients as affecting them and the therapeutic relationship in either a positive or neutral way, rather than being negative. The most helpful types of disclosures, from the client perspective, were of the therapist's positive feelings about the client, which was also consistent with previously discussed research on positive emotion TSDs, as discussed in Chapter 6 of this text, and Tantillo's (2004) theories of how TSD often fits into ED treatment. This consistency of findings is important in light of major risk factors associated with dropout from ED treatment, as well as prior research (reviewed by Simons & Spokes [2017]) indicating that the strength of therapeutic relationships with ED clients is associated with positive outcomes. As such, consistently positive results of ED-TSD and more general TSD in contexts of ED suggest that TSD may indeed deserve greater priority in ED interventional and treatment planning.

Research findings on ED *non-disclosure*, both from therapists to colleagues, and from clients to therapists, were consistent with prior theoretical discussions about ED clients and earlier precautions against non-disclosure in general. Williams and Haverkamp (2015) conducted an in-depth interview study of 11 therapists with personal histories of ED. Although therapists tended to acknowledge potential benefits of ED-TSD, and in a manner consistent with prior points, therapists also indicated a reluctance to disclose their personal histories *to colleagues* due to personal shame and stigma. Similarly, Swan and

Andrews (2003) studied a group of 68 female clients with eating disorders, 29 of whom reported not disclosing a high amount of information about their ED to their therapists, with non-disclosure correlated with higher levels of shame and vulnerability to depression. These results from both Williams and Haverkamp's (2015) and Swan and Andrews' (2003) studies were consistent with prior discussions regarding the nature of ED psychopathology. In prior chapters of this text, shame and stigma factors were also identified as impacting *therapists and clients* in TSD contexts of mental illness and personality disorder, trauma, and LGBTQ identity. In effect, non-disclosure may not only be harmful to clients with a range of trauma, illness, identity, and vulnerability factors, but may also have parallel negative effects on therapists when rooted in embarrassment, rather than a more conscious, well-thought-out, and clinically focused showing of personal restraint. As the known and available research has yet to broach the intentionality of TSD and non-disclosure, the prior statement is presented as a hypothesis warranting follow-up study.

Rabinor and Nye's (2003) case study illustrates how the prior theories of TSD in ED treatment, as well as research findings in support and converging with those theories, may apply in practice. As discussed within Rabinor and Nye (2003), Nye's client was a 34-year-old mother of three and was a clearly obsessive exerciser who experienced related health complications and refused intensive ED treatment. At the time of the therapy, Nye described herself as then-recently losing her hair due to an auto-immune disease, and going through understandable and severe distress, anger, and difficulty accepting her need to wear a wig. Nye noted her struggles with control, powerlessness, self-image, and the impossibility of living without her hair.

Nye self-disclosed to the 34-year-old compulsive exerciser that she initially thought living without her hair would be impossible, though over time she became more able to accept her loss and adjust. She elaborated to the client that the client, too, may be able to live without compulsive and unhealthy exercise, albeit with periods of difficulty, and intellectual awareness at times exceeding emotionally-rooted acceptance. As an indicator of outcome, and likely/reasonably at least partially related to a disclosure-permitting therapy, Nye noted that about three months after the prior disclosure, her client accepted residential ED treatment, reported her intention/commitment to give up her compulsive forms of exercise, and had been in ED treatment for eight weeks up to the time that the case study was submitted for publication.

Consistent with prior discussions in Chapter 3 of this text, Rabinor and Nye (2003) framed TSD through a feminist-empowerment perspective, while Nye's own therapist, an analyst, advised her against such a disclosure. In illustration of prior recommendations to explore possible countertransference, Nye acknowledged needing to process her feelings and perspectives as a necessary antecedent to TSD of her illness. She explained her uncertainty about disclosing content from an area of life she had not yet fully come to terms with or reconciled, as well as concern that she might be exhibiting poor role modeling to ED clients by being so concerned about her own physicality. Nye's reflections suggested she decided in favor of TSD based on relevance to treatment, attunement to client needs, and intention to necessarily shift the client's perspective on what was otherwise a deeply ingrained, enduring, and negative self-image persistently driving her need to exercise relentlessly.

De Vos et al. (2016) conducted a survey study of 205 clients with ED and 32 therapists who all had a personal history of ED, worked in an agency that specifically hired therapists based on them being in a more mature stage of recovery, and to see how experiential knowledge impacted therapeutic processes and outcomes. Among the respondents, 97% of clients and 100% of therapists indicated that experiential knowledge had advantages, 82% of clients and 77% of therapists reported higher therapist empathy, 26% of clients and 54% of therapists reported enhanced therapist knowledge and insight into ED, 20% of clients reported therapist accessibility, openness, and honesty, and 17% of clients and 42% of therapists reported an increased sense of hope for recovery. In response to a question on whether therapist personal history of ED has disadvantages, 11% of clients and 42% of therapists answered yes, with 2% of clients reporting the possibility of a negative comparison with the therapist, 2% of clients reporting the relationship might become too personal, 81% of therapists expressing concern about projection/over-identification, and 50% noting over-involvement. Among therapists, 54% reported what content to share with clients depends on the individual client, 46% reported not talking about their symptoms, 31% reported not discussing their weight, and 19% reported not discussing overly personal details. Also among therapists, 100% reported positive client reactions to therapist expressions of experiential knowledge (including tension relief, head nodding, or crying), reactions showing openness (e.g., making more eye contact or disclosing more), and clients saying directly that they felt more hopeful.

These results suggested therapists considered their lived experience, in and of itself, a therapeutic intervention with a specific therapeutic focus or goal, and was most helpful to treatment when used in an empathic and intuitive way. Thus, de Vos et al.'s (2016) findings could be said to have affirmed previously discussed quantitate research findings, offered an illustration of potential benefits, noted some of the benefits therapists and clients agreed on, and some of the benefits more frequently mentioned by ED therapists than clients. Differential perspectives will be elaborated upon and synthesized in Chapter 29, 'Therapists and Clients Agree on Most Aspects of TSD, But Not All.'

Conclusions

ED clients often enter treatment with high levels of interpersonal avoidance, uncertainty, and disconnection. In such cases, TSDs may be at least somewhat corrective when intended to emotionally reach out and communicate to clients their emotional impacts on the therapist as a symbolic other. TSD would then be relevant to the client's needs from treatment, and may be particularly potent when flowing from therapist's lived experience with ED.

The consistency of research findings suggests to practitioners that TSD should in many cases be one of the major interventional choices with ED populations and may even warrant a more formal level of consideration in treatment planning. While prior precautions against scripted, excessive, and disingenuine disorders certainly apply, it is reasonable to expect that at least marginally greater usage of brief, relevant, well-attuned, relationally-focused, and appropriately timed TSDs (as discussed in prior/general TSD chapters) may be among the strategies that help to improve retention for ED clients otherwise at heightened risk for dropout and mortality. Thus, TSDs may be beneficial to ED clients when demonstrating and modeling qualities at odds with the treatment-interfering facets of the disorder, just as a more non-disclosive stance may, indirectly, be reinforcing, damaging, and re-traumatizing.

While TSD may warrant greater consideration in many ED dyads, it may be that at least marginally higher frequency, higher activity, *and not higher intimacy* is most advisable. This may encourage the client to see the therapist as an emotionally accessible and responsive professional, though not fully a peer and to a level that would lead to negative reactions such as those summarized previously in the research. At the same time, Nye's case example (Rabinor & Nye, 2003) and de Vos et al.'s (2016) research illustrated some of the ways in which a more generally disclosive stance can inspire hope and communicate empathy, understanding, and expertise when put forth in appropriate treatment and clinical contexts. Accordingly, a major difference between TSD in contexts of ED (and in other vulnerability contexts) is that there seems to be more room to consider higher intimacy TSDs of personal history, and at times when doing so may strengthen the relationship, encourage client insights, solidify client commitment to treatment, and inspire client hope for personal recovery.

It was of interest that helpful TSDs with ED populations sometimes though not always conveyed a therapist's similar personal history. There was no clear or consistent indication that therapists' divulging their history of ED was necessary to establish client perception of qualification to treat. This should be encouraging or at least acknowledging to ED therapists without personal experience with ED. In addition, from the research it is reasonable to conclude that rules about whether or not therapists with personal histories of ED and at what stage of recovery should or should not treat ED clients are probably arbitrary. Instead, therapist self-awareness, willingness to seek supervision, client prioritization, relevant knowledge of ED, training, and a more reflective mindset should be primary determinates of competency.

Among the major limitations of this research was that intersectionality variables, such as race, gender, age, and sexual orientation, could not be analyzed reliably. Studies of TSD with ED populations were few in number and with sample sizes generally too small to explore between-group differences. While the delivery and effects of TSD in contexts of ED necessarily depend (primarily) on the dyad and specific clinical circumstances at hand, it is also reasonable to expect that how an ED client receives a TSD of a particular timing, type, content, frequency, and intentionality, may also depend not only on individual differences, and the individual client's way of expressing general ED psychopathology, but also gender, cultural, and identity factors. Indeed, most studies reviewed in this chapter were comprised nearly entirely of Caucasian female therapists and clients. Therefore, intersectionality considerations deserve greater priority in future ED and treatment research.

References

Basile, B. (2004). Self-disclosure in eating disorders. *Eating Weight Disorders, 9*(3), 217–23.

Bloomgarden, A., Gerstein, F., & Moss, C. (2003). The last word: A 'recovered enough' therapist. *Eating Disorders, 11*(2), 163–7.

Costin, C., & Johnson, C. (2002). Been there, done that: Clinicians' use of personal recovery in the treatment of eating disorders. *Eating Disorders, 10*(4), 293–303.

de Vos, J., Netten, C., & Noordenbos, G. (2016). Recovered eating disorder therapists using their experiential knowledge in therapy: A qualitative examination of the therapist's and the patients' view. *Eating Disorders, 24*(3), 207–23.

Oyer, L., O'Halloran, M., & Christoe-Frazier, L. (2016). Understanding the working alliance with clients diagnosed with anorexia nervosa. *Eating Disorders, 24*(2), 121–37.

Rabinor, J., & Nye, S. (2003). Healing through connection: Self-disclosure in psychotherapy. *Eating Disorders, 11*(3), 235–40.

Simonds, L., & Spokes, N. (2017). Therapist self-disclosure and the therapeutic alliance in the treatment of eating problems. *Eating Disorders, 25*(2), 151–64.

Stone, M. (2011). Psychotherapist self-disclosure of personal recovery in treatment of clients with eating disorders: Effects on predicted treatment outcome (Doctoral dissertation). Retrieved from ProQuest Dissertations and Theses database (UMI No. 3643897).

Swan, S., & Andrews, B. (2003). The relationship between shame, eating disorders and disclosure in treatment. *British Journal of Clinical Psychology, 42*(4), 367–78.

Tantillo, M. (2004). The therapist's use of self-disclosure in a relational therapy approach for eating disorders. *Eating Disorders, 12*(1), 51–73.

Williams, M., & Haverkamp, B. (2015). Eating disorder therapists' personal eating disorder history and professional ethics: An interpretive description. *Eating Disorders, 23*(5), 393–410.

CHAPTER 13

Religion and Spirituality

Graham S. Danzer, PsyD

Therapeutic self-disclosure (TSD of religious affiliation/non-affiliation is an under-discussed issue within the larger scholarly body of psychology and spirituality literature. This is of concern because a conjecture of research findings regarding religion and mental health, and research on TSD, converge in a manner suggesting that religious TSDs may, in at least some cases, be of benefit to clients. A lack of scholarly research on the topic of religious TSDs warrants further discussion and exploration as follows.

Background Research

Findings on religion and mental health are summarized via meta-analyses of 24 studies by Bergin (1983), 34 studies by Hackney and Sanders (2003), and 49 studies by Ano and Vasconcelles (2005), as well as a confirming study in recent history by Pargament (2013). Contrary to the presumptions and murmurings of many religion-disillusioned practitioners, it has long been established that religious identification does not associate with greater psychopathology, and in fact, consistently associates with at least marginally more positive mental health (Bergin, 1983). More recent meta-analyses (Ano & Vasconcelles, 2005; Pargament, 2013) clarified this association to depend (at least in part) on the extent to which religious coping strategies were positive (i.e., pro-adjustment conceptualization of after-life and increased participation in church-related services or activities) or negative (i.e., clearly and overly self-critical ways of conceptualizing stressful situations). At least some extent of discrepant findings in this research is attributable to researchers having different definitions of religiosity and mental health (Hackney & Sanders, 2003). Additionally, and as discussed throughout this text, research has roundly supported the benefits of TSD on the whole, in at least some circumstances, and with benefits based on the extent to which TSD supports the development of the therapeutic relationship and addresses the client's immediate emotional needs in a helpful and treatment/recovery-focused way (Audet, 2011; Henretty & Levitt, 2010; Levitt et al., 2016; Simonds & Spokes, 2017). Thus, it is reasonable to infer the potential benefit of religiously oriented TSDs, though necessary to more fully explore this subject and formulate implications and recommendations for the research-informed practitioner.

Avoidance of the Topic?

Offering a partial explanation for why religious TSDs haven't received adequate scholarly attention, recent survey data of 258 members of the American Psychological Association (APA) indicated that psychology practitioners, as compared to the general population, were/are significantly less likely to be Catholic or Protestant and were/are nearly seven times more likely to be formerly religious individuals who disaffiliated from organized religious entities (Delaney, Miller, & Bisonó, 2007). It is also not uncommon for clients to be significantly more religious than practitioners, to want to discuss spiritual issues or conflicts in therapy, and nevertheless avoid those topics based on perceived practitioner discomfort (Bourg, 2013). It is informative to consider that Sigmund Freud, as one of the most influential clinical figures, was a notorious and outspoken opponent of organized religion, while the strongest contemporary cautions against religious TSD continue to be formulated within psychodynamic theories (Tillman, 1998).

With the intention to ensure maximally ethical and efficacious care for clients, it is important to explore the deeper meanings and implications of religious TSDs *and non-disclosures*, both to similarly or differently affiliated clients. This exploration is important in light of the growing understanding of client religion and spirituality as an issue of diversity and even cultural competency (Hook, 2016). Moreover, this exploration is important because surveyed psychologists (and probably those from other clinical disciplines as well) overwhelmingly concede that religion tends to be beneficial to the mental health of most clients (Delaney et al., 2007), in a manner consistent with the general research reviewed previously, and in spite of what may be discomfort or even subtly avoidant tendencies to the contrary.

Clinical Discussions

In her review of psychoanalytic perspectives, Tillman (1998) noted that clients may inquire about a therapist's religious beliefs early in treatment in attempt to establish whether their deeply held beliefs will be understood and taken seriously. Ethically, the therapist's religious beliefs or background may therefore and at least on some occasions be an issue of informed consent (Thomas, 2008), and in a manner fundamentally consistent with the feminist perspective on leveling political and power imbalances in psychotherapy (Dean, 2010). Clinically, this position is also reminiscent of discussions of TSD in other contexts of vulnerability whereby clients may in some cases consider the therapist having a similar personal history (for example, of eating disorder or substance abuse disorder) to be an indication of benchmark competency (LaPorte, Sweifach, & Linzer, 2010; Sturges, 2012; Williams & Haverkamp, 2015). Early client inquiries about a therapist's religious beliefs may also suggest a rigid expectation that only sameness and perfect mirroring will predict positive outcomes (Tillman, 1998).

In response, therapeutic pull to "surrender" to client inquiries about the therapist's religiosity may suggest countertransference (Tillman, 1998, p. 282). Psychotherapists may reconcile these dilemmas by refraining from TSD so that subsequent client responses inform an understanding of the client's style of negotiating conflicts, frustration tolerance, and perhaps appropriateness for therapy (Tillman, 1998). In turn, these positions are consistent with prior therapist writer perspectives on TSD in general, in which it was recommended that TSD be purposeful and related to treatment, rather than being spontaneous, impulsive, and without sufficient consideration of the client's needs and prior relationship history (D'Aniello & Nguyen, 2017). From this consistency in the conceptual literature, and therapist writer perspectives on religious TSDs, the current author infers and supports a general caution against therapists quickly and directly answering a client's early religious inquiry in-kind, a possibility that will be followed up on in more detail in the implications for practice section of this chapter.

Conceptual and theoretical writings note various ethical dilemmas associated with intentional or unintentional TSDs of religiosity. Unintentional disclosures may occur when religious practitioners unknowingly attend the same religious service as a client (Gutheil & Gabbard, 1993). Researchers consistently acknowledge that intentional TSD *of similar religious affiliation* is likely to be beneficial to the therapeutic relationship, again, as among the most stable and reliable predictors of positive outcomes (Hanson, 2005; Horvath, 2000; LaPorte et al., 2010). At the same time, direct disclosures of a particular religious affiliation may also be interpreted by clients as disallowing their potentially divergent perspectives and thereby inhibiting their therapeutic processing (Chesner & Baumeister, 1985).

Therapists who feel unable to proceed with treatment on grounds of moral or religious solidarity should consider cautiously, appropriately, and tactfully addressing such issues early in treatment and consider referring the client out (Bernstein, 2000). Dilemmas may be reconciled through usage of an ethical decision-making model, consideration of diversity factors, and ongoing assessment of how the client may benefit from maintaining or changing the moment-to-moment balance of gratification and frustration tolerance (Denney, Aten, & Gingrich, 2008; Tillman, 1998). From the current author's perspective, prior research on (1) therapists more or less acknowledging the widespread benefits of religiosity to mental health, (2) at times avoiding the issue or imposing it on clients, and (3) a likelihood of being at least somewhat influenced by personal *affiliation or disaffiliation* should factor into this process.

A therapist should first determine through supervision/consultation that a decision to self-disclose affiliation (whether similar or different) *or* refer a client out (primarily due to religious reasons) was not based on discriminatory motivation. In turn, open exploration of the therapist's personal motives, pulls, and recall of specific manifestations in the particular therapeutic dyad would be an exercise in cultural competency. Additionally, such open exploration is likely to assist a therapist seeking, as conceptualized by D'Aniello and Nguyen (2017), to build a *therapeutic* relationship by optimizing the balance between meeting the client's needs for connection and reciprocity *and* meeting the client's simultaneous needs for therapist professionalism and restraint.

Denney et al. (2008) constructed a perspective paper in which appropriate and inappropriate clinical contexts for TSD of religious affiliation were identified. Such TSDs may be contra-indicated for clients with poor boundaries, insufficient identity formation, personality disorders, hostility towards religion, high levels of self-absorption, low capacities for intimacy, and psychotic disorders showing vulnerability to incorporating religious TSD content into hallucinations or delusions. Clients may benefit from learning how therapists experienced and worked through their own spiritual/religious conflicts. Clients may also benefit from interventions that contain spiritual metaphors, facilitate perspective taking or spiritually oriented referrals, normalize client experiences, or evidence the humanity of the therapist.

Research on Religious Self-Disclosure

Research on religiously oriented TSD efficacy is mostly of an analogue nature with student volunteers. Chesner and Baumeister (1985) conducted an analogue study of 78 undergraduate psychology students in order to determine the perceived impact of TSDs of religious affiliations on the intimacy of client disclosures. Therapists wore either Jewish or Christian insignia in order to self-identify (if not proclaim) religiosity to clients at the onset of treatment. Findings suggested that intimacy of client disclosures tended to be somewhat inhibited by the therapist's open affiliation with either religion, and by differences in client and therapist religious beliefs. Findings also indicated that stronger religious affiliation among therapy clients in both the treatment and control groups correlated with higher intimacy of client disclosures. Chesner and Baumeister (1985) interpreted their findings as suggesting a level of confirmation for the theory that religious TSD may lower the intimacy of client disclosure.

The current author more cautiously interprets that therapist bannering of religious affiliation (in a manner that may usually be considered atypical in professional clinical work) may not be well received even by openly religious clients. The current author also interprets Chesner and Baumeister's (1985) findings as suggesting the need for further study to determine the impacts of TSD of similar/different affiliation, with attention to content, timing, type, brevity-length, intentionality, and theoretical orientations, as noted in prior chapters of this text.

Young (2011) conducted an analogue study in which simulated religious (and financial) self-disclosure/non-disclosure scenarios were video-taped and presented to 673 student research volunteers, 457 (or 66.8%) of whom identified as Catholic or Protestant. Each student was asked to rate the impact of disclosure/non-disclosure on the therapeutic alliance. Student-participants in Young's (2011) study tended to perceive that therapists disclosing similar religious affiliations appeared to display more accurate empathy, appropriate transparency, and develop stronger therapeutic alliances as compared to therapists disclosing dissimilar religious affiliations. The latter finding is in turn consistent with prior research indicating that TSDs conveying similarity rather than difference tend to be better received by clients, likely based on a sense of conveying empathy. Young's (2011) findings are also somewhat in conflict with Chesner and Baumeister's (1985) interpretation of their findings.

Among the limitations of Young's (2011) study were that most student participant-observers identified as Christian and Caucasian, and all were simulated clients. Previously reviewed and general research suggests (1) important differences between college student-simulated clients and real clients, (2) TSD often has significantly different meanings and impacts depending on client culture of origin, and (3) non-religiously affiliated individuals may be at least somewhat more apprehensive about the introduction of religious content in psychotherapy. Thus, it is not clear whether Young's (2011) positive findings may or may not generalize to non-Christian and/or ethnically diverse populations.

Conclusions

Whether or not therapists should or should not self-disclose their similar or divergent religious affiliations *or non-affiliations* to which clients at what point in the therapeutic relationship and under what circumstances is inherently complex, multi-layered, and may have significant ramifications related to treatment ethics and helpfulness to clients. There is indication in an admittedly small literature base that the nature of client inquiries (about practitioner religiosity), as well as the manner in which practitioners immediately and emotionally respond, may be diagnostic of both the client and practitioner alike.

Decisions to self-disclose or not to self-disclose necessarily depend on the individual clinical situation at hand, as should be informed by a deeper understanding of the practitioner's personal and religious history and how personal history may have been influenced or informed by the history of the profession. It may even be helpful for practitioners facing something of a religious inquiry or tension with a client to consider whether the dyad may be enacting a broader and historical-religious context, paradoxically, as among the most life-saving (i.e., positive research findings, not to mention the promise of salvation) and life-threatening (e.g., wars and genocide) throughout human existence. Considerations of enactment may not only aid in the soothing of tense therapeutic moments, but may also inform a scholarly understanding of why spiritual and religious issues, including but not limited to TSD of affiliation/non-affiliation, may be so deeply discomforting for so many practitioners, and how that discomfort may be affecting the client's therapeutic processing.

In this manner, client inquiries and TSDs/non-disclosures may not be singularly motivated. Rather, clients may request if not demand to know the practitioner's religiosity as (1) a symptom of a demanding and rigid personality,

(2) fantasy of sameness, twinship or transferential omnipotence, (3) as a matter of credentialing and assessing qualification, *and/or* (4) anticipated fear of discomfort, judgment, rejection, dismissal, or ridicule. In turn, practitioners may or may not self-disclose religious affiliation based on inappropriate impulses and countertransference, self-serving motivations paralleling the aforementioned client fantasies, *and/or* sense of ethical obligation depending on which principle is clearly at issue if not pulling the hardest as the therapist decides what to do.

While it was indicated that non-disclosure in response to client inquiries may lead to informative client reactions, it is also reasonable to infer that well-thought-out and well-formulated TSDs of religious affiliation/non-affiliation may stimulate similarly productive and informative client reactions to disclosure of affiliation as a use-of-self intervention. If religious clients requested/demanded to know the therapist's religious beliefs, and were informed of the therapist being similarly identified, how the client proceeded in the relationship may be informative about his or her capacity for intimacy, relational behavior in more intimate contexts, and the extent to which morals about relationships and behavior in relationships are consistent or a source of dissonance. Contrastingly, if therapists responded to client inquiries by acknowledging non- or former affiliation, client responses are likely to be reticent if not overtly negative, though perhaps informative about their behavior in contexts of disagreement, difference, and tension in relationships. In such circumstances, and in a manner consistent with the previous review of therapeutic orientation perspectives, it should be remembered that therapeutic relationships are built through a tripartite balance of support, conflict, and transparent humanity. In example of an imbalanced approach, impulsive disclosures of religious similarity may be self-gratifying just as impulsive disclosures of difference may be oppositional.

What determines the ethical appropriateness and helpfulness of decisions to or not to self-disclose *similar or divergent* religiosity may be the extent to which client motives guiding their inquiries as well as therapist's motives guiding their answer are reciprocally open, humble, social, and curious. When client inquiries are rigid and indicate difficulty negotiating social relationships, non-disclosure followed by exploration of motives and perhaps social deficits may help to establish boundaries, generate insights, and/or establish client ability/inability to proceed with treatment. When client inquiries appear sincere and exploratory, it is reasonable to hypothesize that brief and well-thought-out TSDs may be experienced by the client as promoting egalitarianism, permitting deeper therapeutic exploration, and appropriately reinforcing tempered sharing and emotional expression. This need for balance and reciprocity in relational contexts may have particular implications for therapists paired with clients who demand to know their religiosity and in a manner that the therapist has a parallel, negative, and potentially moralistic reaction to.

Ethical arguments for and against therapists referring clients out based on moral solidarity should also apply when non- or formerly religious therapists feel put off by religious client inquiries, when religious therapists feel a reluctance to treat LGBTQ clients, and feel comforted at the thought of referring out. In such circumstances, referral may be necessary to prevent harm in the relationship, though may also be considered a micro-aggression, experienced by clients as a form of abandonment, and discourage re-engagement in psychotherapy in the future. Supporting this position, clinical disciplines including but not limited to psychology are ultimately professions of modulated self-sacrifice, whereby standards of practice demand a de-prioritization of personal needs and issues, as well as awareness of how those personal needs and issues may influence, contribute to, or interfere with client recovery. In effect, refusing to see a client due to the therapist's or the client's religious affiliation and expression may be considered unethical and, in many cases, is probably discriminatory.

It is noteworthy and informative that the current author found no scholarly literature broaching the subtopic of self-disclosure or non-disclosure of non- or former religious affiliation. This gap is concerning in light of research suggesting that non- or former affiliation among practitioners (particularly psychologists?) is fairly common and to a greater extent than what is common among surveyed client populations. The lack of scholarly attention may be attributable to spirituality and religion only recently beginning to be understood as a treatment variable and not necessarily a confound or source of interference. Additionally, this lack of research may be considered reminiscent of wider spread discomfort and avoidance of the issue altogether. To further address these possibilities, further study on precipitating circumstances of therapists disclosure or non-disclosure, of similar or different religious affiliation/non-affiliation, is clearly needed, and will therefore be the subject of Gerald Nissley's upcoming direct inquiry chapter (Chapter 16), entitled, 'Are You a Christian?'

References

Ano, G., & Vasconcelles, E. (2005). Religious coping and psychological adjustment to stress: A meta-analysis. *Journal of Clinical Psychology*, *61*(4), 461–80.

Audet, C. (2011). Client perspectives of therapist self-disclosure: Violating boundaries or removing boundaries? *Counselling Psychology Quarterly*, *24*(2), 85–100.

Bergin, A. (1983). Religiosity and mental health: A critical reevaluation. *Professional Psychology: Research and Practice*, *9*(3), 5–22.

Bernstein, A. (2000). Straight therapists working with lesbians and gays in family therapy. *Journal of Marriage and Family Therapy*, *26*(4), 443–54.

Bourg, E. (2013). Spirituality in psychotherapy (in-class lecture at Alliant International University), San Francisco, CA.

Chesner, S., & Baumeister, C. (1985). Effects of therapists' disclosure of religious beliefs on the intimacy of client self-disclosure. *Journal of Social and Clinical Psychology*, *3*(1), 97–105.

D'Aniello, C., & Nguyen, H. (2017). Considerations for intentional use of self-disclosure for family therapists. *Journal of Family Psychotherapy*, *28*(1), 23–37.

Dean, B. (2010). Therapist self-disclosure: Heterosexuals' perceptions of sexual minority therapists (Doctoral dissertation). Retrieved from the University Digital Conservancy database.

Delaney, H., Miller, W., & Bisonó, A. (2007). Religiosity and spirituality among psychologists: A survey of clinician members of the American Psychological Association. *Professional Psychology: Research and Practice*, *38*(5), 538–46.

Denney, R., Aten, J., & Gingrich, F. (2008). Using spiritual self-disclosure in psychotherapy. *Journal of Psychology and Theology, 36*(4), 294–302.

Gutheil, T., & Gabbard, G. (1993). The concept of boundaries in clinical practice: Theoretical and risk-management dimensions. *American Journal of Psychiatry, 150*(2), 188–96.

Hackney, C., & Sanders, G. (2003). Religiosity and mental health: A meta-analysis of recent studies. *Journal for the Scientific Study of Religion, 42*(1), 43–55.

Hanson, J. (2005). Should your lips be zipped? How therapist self-disclosure and non-disclosure affects clients. *Counselling & Psychotherapy Research, 5*(2), 96–104.

Henretty, J., & Levitt, H. (2010). The role of therapist self-disclosure in psychotherapy: A qualitative review. *Clinical Psychology Review, 30*(1), 63–77.

Hook, J. (2016, May). Cultural humility and spirituality/religion. Paper presented as part of a spirituality symposium at the annual meeting of the American Psychological Association, Denver, CO.

Horvath, A. (2000). The therapeutic relationship: From transference to alliance. *Journal of Clinical Psychology, 56*(2), 163–73.

LaPorte, H., Sweifach, J., & Linzer, N. (2010). Sharing the trauma: Guidelines for therapist self-disclosure following a catastrophic event. *Best Practices in Mental Health, 6*(2), 39–56.

Levitt, H., Minami, T., Greenspan, S., Puckett, J., Henretty, J., Reich, C., & Berman, J. (2016). How therapist self-disclosure relates to alliance and outcomes: A naturalistic study. *Counselling Psychology Quarterly, 29*(1), 7–28.

Pargament, K. (2013). *What role do religion and spirituality play in mental health?* American Psychological Association: Washington, DC. Retrieved from www.apa.org/news/press/releases/2013/03/religion-spirituality.aspx.

Simonds, L., & Spokes, N. (2017). Therapist self-disclosure and the therapeutic alliance in the treatment of eating problems. *Eating Disorders, 25*(2), 151–64.

Sturges, J. (2012). Use of therapist self-disclosure and self-involving statements. *The Behavior Therapist, 35*(5), 90–3.

Thomas, M. (2008). Shades of gray: Lesbian therapists explore the complexities of self-disclosure to heterosexual clients (Doctoral dissertation). Retrieved from Smith College Theses, Dissertations, and Projects.

Tillman, J. (1998). Psychodynamic psychotherapy, religious beliefs, and self-disclosure. *American Journal of Psychotherapy, 52*(3), 273–86.

Williams, M., & Haverkamp, B. (2015) Eating disorder therapists' personal eating disorder history and professional ethics: An interpretive description. *Eating Disorders, 23*(5), 393–410.

Young, S. (2011). Effects of an analogue counselor's religious or financial self-disclosure and observer characteristics on therapeutic processes (Doctoral dissertation). Retrieved from Psych INFO database (UMI Number: 3473295).

CHAPTER 14

Children and Adolescents

Graham S. Danzer, PsyD and David Sugarbaker, MS MPH

Therapeutic self-disclosure (TSD) to children and adolescent clients may strike the reader as a subtopic of particular curiosity. TSD is already a complex clinical issue, let alone with the added layer of children and adolescents being inherently vulnerable, impressionable, and trying to find their ever-growing and changing sense of belonging and identity. Most writings on TSD were organized around adult case examples, discussed treatment with a more adult-relevant conceptualization of transference, therapeutic contracting, and mature level of cognitive intervention, and therefore appear to have been put forth with adult populations in mind. These limitations, the particular and fairly nuanced challenges of engaging younger clients, and prior research indicating the benefits of TSD in many other psychotherapeutic contexts and with many other populations suggest that further review and discussion of TSD specifically to younger clients is warranted. As in prior chapters, the current chapter will begin with a review of the conceptual literature, follow with a summary of admittedly limited research, and conclude with implications for the research-informed practitioner.

Positions in the Developmental Psychotherapy Literature

TSD from a caring adult, including but not limited to a therapist, can offer young people something of a window or viewing into more advanced stages of psychosocial maturation and identity (Erikson, 1959; Rachman, 1996). Applying this theory first to the treatment of children, TSD often takes the form of the therapist's regressing to an earlier and more relatable state of humor, play, and exploration as a method of validating and encouraging engagement (Barish, 2004; Gaines, 2003). Less verbal approaches are often necessary with young children given their cognitive limitations, with Piagetian theories of preoperational and concrete operational thinking suggesting traditional forms of talk therapy are better suited for adolescents and beyond (Grave & Blissett, 2004). With children, therapists must frequently permit and participate in a greater-than-usual level of informal dialogue, play games during therapy, and reveal aspects of their personality they might ordinarily modulate to greater degrees when paired with adults (Gaines, 2003). Thus, while direct disclosures of the therapist's past and real-time revelations of reactions and feelings are probably beyond the maturity level of children, less direct and more implicit and expressive forms of TSD may be of potential benefit to therapeutic engagement with child clients less likely to respond favorably to traditional neutrality. Non-disclosure may not only damage rapport, but may also result in missed opportunities for children to grow in their awareness of self, other, and reality (Gibson, 2012; Peterson, 2002).

Applying developmental theory to practice with adolescents, Bolton, Oetzel, and Scherer (2003) emphasized that therapeutic engagement is often difficult with this population because many models of therapy and interventions that work well for adults are not so transferable. Treatments that work well for adults may fail with adolescents due to their presumably lower levels of maturity, limitations in insight and capacity for perspective taking, differential stigma associated with being in therapy, and often being forced into therapy by their parents. For these reasons, engaging adolescents and preventing early dropout most often requires greater than usual and proactive engagement, authenticity, and transparency, as also discussed as essential common factors with other vulnerable and hard-to-engage populations. Further, it is not uncommon for adolescents to push therapists to relate genuinely and be more direct and disclosive than they might ordinarily be (Rachman, 1996).

Conceptual/therapist writings on helpful TSDs are internally consistent with previous discussions of common factors, and are congruent with developmental theories of adolescent-adult relations. Commensurate with growing adolescent maturation and desires for independence, TSD may be beneficial when helping adolescents to relate on a more mutual and reciprocal level, show appropriate vulnerability, differentiate from others, accept responsibility for their behavior, and understand that adults must also accept responsibility for theirs (Capobianco & Farber, 2005; Papouchis, 1990; Rachman, 1996). It may be helpful to tell a child or adolescent's parent that the therapist is also a parent, while it may be unhelpful or inappropriate to tell a child or adolescent overly personal details such as the therapist's prior experiences with depression, past drug use, or marital/relationship problems (Capobianco & Farber, 2005; Felloney, 2010; Patrizio, 1990).

Whereas forms of regression to an earlier developmental state were somewhat recommended in the prior review of child-TSD literature, using adolescent language or trying to relate to adolescents in-kind is unlikely to be well received, and is likely to hurt rather than further engagement (Bolton et al., 2003). When younger clients reveal painful parts of their history, the therapist may at times feel pulled to reciprocate with a similar experience, with an underlying likelihood of motivation to relieve tension and pressure, self-gratify, and/or distract the therapist and/or client from a more intense transference-projective process (Schmukler, Atkeson,

Keable, & Dahl, 2011). Consistent with the prior chapters on personality considerations with adult clients, TSD may be contra-indicated for youth who are highly suspicious, self-absorbed, or unable to tolerate/receive empathy (Gaines, 2003).

Research Findings

Limited research on this subject was predominantly in the forms of unpublished dissertations and smaller qualitative interview studies. Studies tended to conclude with indications *either* of general support or contra-indication, as was likely and at least partially due to the inherent controversy of crossing boundaries with younger and inherently vulnerable populations. Results and connections to prior research are summarized as follows.

Studies on adolescents' perspectives generally supported the use of lower intimacy disclosures. Fotinos' (1996) dissertation was an analogue study in which 90 adolescents receiving special education services watched simulated therapy videos. Adolescents significantly preferred disclosing therapists to non-disclosing therapists and more favorably regarded solicited therapist disclosures, rather than unsolicited. Consistent with prior mentions of the cognitive limitations of younger adults, as well as prior positions on candor and transparency, these findings also suggested the possibility that a more neutral and process-oriented response to adolescent client inquiries may be beyond the maturity level of adolescents and therefore best reserved for adult clients. Consistent with theories of gender difference (as discussed in Chapter 24 in the upcoming 'clinical challenges' section of this text), findings from Carlton's (1993) dissertation study of 60 mixed gender adolescents suggested adolescent girls may negatively react to limits of confidentiality, while boys may regard these limits more favorably. Eyrich-Garg's (2008) focus group study of five adolescent girls living in a homeless shelter revealed that girls under study were often interested in the therapist's professional expertise, qualifications, experience, basic personal details including marital status and number of children, and would feel more inclined to disclose if they felt treated as equals.

Multiple studies and dissertations, both on therapist and adolescent perspectives, reported findings with respect to TSD on the whole and in comparison of TSD to non-disclosure. Capobianco and Farber (2005) surveyed 126 child therapists, 120 of whom were psychologists, all of whom were Caucasian. Capobianco and Farber (2005) developed and used the Therapist-to-Child Disclosure Inventory (TCDI), a 42-item Likert-type measure, for the purposes of this study. Specific ages of child populations served by the surveyed therapists were not mentioned. Therapists in Capobianco and Farber's (2005) study tended to report that TSD rarely seemed to advance treatment aims for children, and that children almost never solicited disclosures. Consistent with Capobianco and Farber's (2005) findings, and as a showing of congruence between therapist and client perspectives, Carlton's (1993) dissertation research on 60 adolescents as well as Patrizio's (1990) dissertation research on

300 adolescents both concluded that non-disclosing therapists were perceived as more of an expert, albeit with some indication that adolescents compared non-disclosing therapists to over-disclosing therapists.

Felloney's (2010) dissertation explored 14 Caucasian school-based mental health professionals' views on TSD and humor, included 8 psychologists and 6 social workers, with levels of experience in school-based mental health services ranging from 4–20 years. Of the 14 participants, three were in elementary and middle schools, three were in middle schools only, and five were in high schools. Participants were generally reserved about TSD with child and adolescent populations, and in a manner generally consistent with mentions in previous studies. Interestingly, there were multiple indications that use of humor could often serve as an alternative to TSD in many clinical scenarios and was often a helpful alternative with severely emotionally disturbed and acting-out youth.

When interviewees in Felloney's (2010) dissertation felt that TSD was appropriate, it was most often put forth with intention to convey to youth clients their humanity, accessibility, and client–therapist similarity. Other common intentions of TSD were to impart helpful information to students or shift their perspectives, positively affect their mood (though humor was regarded more favorably than TSD for this purpose), increase student motivation and hope (by sharing relevant struggles and methods of working through those struggles), or encourage students to change their behavior (which was positively and consistently impacted by *either* humor or TSD).

Consistent with prior mentions of the differences between adult and child/adolescent therapy, participants in Felloney's (2010) dissertation indicated that higher frequency of lower intimacy disclosures was often necessary to build relationships with younger populations. School-based mental health professionals identified their weekend activities and hobbies as content of lower intimacy TSD they at times put forth to build rapport. This area of content was also mentioned in therapist perspective papers summarized in Chapter 5 of this text (on timing and decision-making), as a potentially helpful, early, and non-threatening form of disclosure, which in turn suggests another area/content of TSD that therapists tend to regard favorably in many cases.

Participants at times reported sharing with students their similar and relevant struggles when they were that age, as well as how they worked through struggles. Higher intimacy content of TSDs that school-based mental health professionals described as helpful in some cases included that therapists too, and around the age of the particular client, had been bullied, taken psychiatric medication, struggled with body image and self-esteem issues, had difficulty learning English after immigration, and had academic and adjustment issues masked via similar forms of disruptive behavior. Participants indicated that when TSDs were not well received, it was usually because of student misinterpretation of counselor intention, and would be contraindicated when counselors might seem to be agreeing with students in ways that undermined teacher authority.

Conclusions

The general idea of therapeutic self-disclosure (TSD) to child and adolescent populations likely brings the research-informed practitioner both reservations and intrigue alike. While there is an immediate concern about boundaries and relevance to treatment, there should be equal consideration with respect to the common challenges of getting children and adolescents more fully engaged in therapy. Engagement is difficult because of their expectably adverse reactions to therapeutic neutrality, limitations in cognition and maturity, and so often being forced to attend therapy by parents, teachers, or other authorities they are likely in opposition to. In such cases, practitioners are challenged to maintain boundaries, practice in accordance with ethical standards of clinical professions, and somehow build relationships with younger populations in spite of barriers and generally lower receptivity to counseling as usual. Thus, while TSD with young clients may seem controversial if not contraindicated, it may at times be advantageous and even necessary.

Given prior chapter discussions of TSD ethics, types, timing, content, and delivery, the multi-layered question for practitioners then becomes: What forms of TSD are appropriate for which child and adolescent age groups, at what point in the development of relationships, for what purposes, and at what level of frequency and intimacy? Admittedly research on TSD to child and adolescent populations is generally consistent with TSD research on adult populations in this respect, with a level of convergence between therapist and child/adolescent client perspectives. Specifically, the research suggests that infrequent, lower intimacy, age-appropriate, sincerely motivated, and treatment-relevant forms of TSD are most likely to be well received. In turn, impulsive and therapist-gratifying disclosures are likely to interrupt young clients' processing and damage relationships.

Implications regarding content and intimacy of TSD are as follows. With younger children, therapists may facilitate engagement by at times regressing to a younger stage of relating and playing. With older children and adolescents, helpful and well-received TSDs are likely to be of a more direct and verbal nature, as a showing of respect for growing adolescent maturity. TSDs should be clearly relevant to the child/adolescent's treatment needs, sincere in terms of content and intention, and of a conversational nature. Content should generally be of a lower intimacy and biographical nature. Specifics may include the therapist's ideas about the treatment of children, or the therapist having children him or herself. Higher intimacy disclosures about the therapist's own adolescent years was at times regarded favorably by practitioners, though would require further research to determine adolescent client agreement. In particular, a cautionary approach with respect to higher intimacy TSD content is advised because mentions in the literature of negative adolescent reaction were often in regards to higher intimacy TSDs.

Theoretically and clinically, it is questionable how a child or adolescent verbalizing a particular challenge or life struggle and with inherently limited maturation and capacity for true forms of insight would benefit from (or even care) that the therapist too had similar issues. It may be more likely that a reciprocal TSD would interrupt the adolescent's processing or be experienced as the therapist changing the subject. Adolescents are likely to be annoyed or possibly experience the therapist as another self-absorbed, presumptive, or intrusive adult trying near-desperately to be young again. As suggested in multiple research studies and perspective papers, youth are unlikely to be highly interested in the earlier life of a strange and nebulous professional they were likely to be pressured if not outright forced to see.

As an alternative, youth can reasonably be expected to ask therapists personal questions as they become relevant and as they become interested. Given positive responses noted in limited client survey studies, it is reasonable to infer that when adolescents make age-appropriate and relevant inquiries of the therapist, it may at times be helpful to answer in kind, though on a limited basis. This contrasts with recurring therapist perspectives on the advantages of adopting a more process approach in response to adult client inquiries. A more process-style of responding may in many cases be beyond an adolescent's level of maturity and reflective capacity. Judiciousness is important as it is among the factors that makes TSD potent, healing, and deepening of the relationship.

TSD content flowing from the literature that seems professional, appropriate, reasonable, and most likely to be generalizable are lower intimacy and even subtle TSDs flowing from conversational dialogue, communicating therapist emotional accessibility, and age-appropriate relations. These TSDs may be at least moderately less likely to be misinterpreted to a degree that damages the therapist–child/adolescent relationship. For example, it may be helpful for therapists to sincerely, briefly, and moderately share their positive emotions in response to a child or adolescent's accomplishments, concern in response to their struggles or frustrations, or actively problem solve and help them think through a problem based partially on the therapist's own cognitive process and more experienced history of working through similar circumstances (i.e., without necessarily sharing the content of the experience directly).

In such cases, a therapist may be less likely to be experienced as an adult with arrested development, and more likely to be experienced as a trustworthy, reliable, and respectful and respectable parental figure and mentor. From a developmental vantage point, this would theoretically help children and adolescents progress through their challenges, become gradually interested and receptive to more mature perspectives, and possibly apply their experience with the therapist to other trusting and caring relationships in the future. In effect, conversational, lower intimacy, sincere, judicious, age-appropriate/adjusted, and treatment-focused TSDs may be among the interventions that help practitioners to better and more appropriately connect with children and adolescents, work through expectable engagement barriers, and optimally balance mandates for professionalism with the need to build relationships.

References

Barish, K. (2004). The child therapist's generative use of self. *Journal of Infant, Child, and Adolescent Psychotherapy, 3*(2), 270–82.

Bolton Oetzel, K., & Scherer, D. (2003). Therapeutic engagement with adolescents in psychotherapy. *Psychotherapy: Theory, Research, Practice, Training, 40*(3), 215–25.

Capobianco, J., & Farber, B. (2005). Therapist self-disclosure to child patients. *American Journal of Psychotherapy, 59*(3), 199–212.

Carlton, C. (1993). The effect of therapist self-disclosure and explanation of confidentiality on adolescent clients' willingness to self-disclose and therapist preference (Doctoral dissertation). Retrieved from ProQuest Dissertations and Theses database (No UMI No.).

Erikson, R. (1959). *Identity and the life cycle.* New York: W.W. Norton & Co.

Eyrich-Garg, K. (2008). Strategies for engaging adolescent girls at an emergency shelter in a therapeutic relationship: Recommendations from the girls themselves. *Journal of Social Work Practice, 22*(3), 375–88.

Felloney, R. (2010). A qualitative analysis of school-based mental health professionals' views on the use of self-disclosure and humor (Doctoral dissertation). Retrieved from PCOM Psychology Dissertations and Theses Database.

Fotinos, K. (1996). The effects of therapist self-disclosure and clients' solicitation of self-disclosure on adolescent client willingness to self-disclose and therapist preference (Doctoral dissertation). Retrieved from ProQuest Dissertations and Theses database (No UMI No.).

Gaines, R. (2003). Therapist self-disclosure with children, adolescents, and their parents. *Journal of Clinical Psychology In Session, 59*(5), 589–80.

Gibson, M. (2012). Opening up: Therapist self-disclosure in theory, research, and practice. *Clinical Social Work Journal, 40*(3), 287–96.

Grave, J., & Blisset, J. (2004). Is cognitive behavior therapy developmentally appropriate for young children? A critical review of the evidence. *Clinical Psychology Review, 24*(4), 399–420.

Papouchis, N. (1990). Self-disclosure and psychotherapy with children and adolescents. In G. Stricker & M. Fisher, *Self-disclosure in the therapeutic relationship* (pp. 157–74). New York: Springer.

Patrizio, T. (1990). Effect of self-disclosure and interpersonal touch on high school students' perceptions of a school psychologist during an initial interview (Doctoral dissertation). Retrieved from ELibrary, Hofstra University.

Peterson, Z. (2002). More than a mirror: The ethics of self-disclosure. *Psychotherapy: Theory Research, Practice, Training, 39*(1), 21–31.

Rachman, A. (1996). Analyst self-disclosure in adolescent groups. In P. Kymissis & D. Halperin (Eds.), *Group therapy with children and adolescents* (pp. 155–73). Arlington, VA: American Psychiatric Association.

Schmukler, A., Atkeson, P., Keable, H., & Dahl, K. (2011). *Ethical practice in child and adolescent analysis and psychotherapy.* Lanham, MD: Jason Aronson.

Part IV

Responding to Direct Client Inquiries

CHAPTER 15

"So Why Did You Decide to Become a Therapist?"

Devlin Jackson, MA and Barry A. Farber, PhD

Fielding questions about one's choice to pursue a career in psychotherapy is par for the course. At one time or another, therapists have no doubt explained in some detail to significant others, immediate family members, distant relatives, fellow cocktail party guests, even the chatty person next to us on a long flight, why we chose to enter this field. The intrigue is understandable—people are curious to know what compels a person to choose a career that involves listening to others' difficulties, an activity that many seek to avoid. In all likelihood, therapists have developed a couple of responses that come naturally, spanning a scale of openness from perfunctory (e.g., "I've always liked helping people") to more wholehearted (e.g., "I was inspired by how a therapist once helped me").

However, despite perhaps extensive experience responding to this question in social settings, it is easy—even probable—to be thrown by the same query from a client in session. Even experienced therapists are often flummoxed by a personal question of this kind (Chakraborti, 2006), although therapy trainees are particularly likely to be caught off guard and feel unsure about how to respond (Edelstein & Waehler, 2011).

To be sure, there are a myriad of reasons one might pursue a career in psychotherapy, some of which might be easy to identify (e.g., enjoying one's undergraduate psychology classes, a penchant for understanding others, etc.), while others may remain undiscovered. A 1958 study by Holt and Luborsky revealed that psychotherapists get to the heart of this question themselves after many years in practice or in their own psychotherapy. A 2005 issue of the *Journal of Clinical Psychology: In Session* featured eight autobiographical essays by a group of psychotherapists, diverse in background, career trajectory, and theoretical orientation, reflecting on their own reasons for becoming psychotherapists. In his essay, Albert Ellis (2005, p. 945), creator of Rational Emotive Behavior Therapy (REBT), reflected on his decision to become a therapist, stating:

> In a word, because I primarily wanted to help myself become a much less anxious and much happier individual. Oh, yes, I wanted to help other people, too, and I wanted to help the world be a better place, with healthier and

happier people who fought like hell to create better conditions. But I *really* and *primarily* wanted to help me, me, me!

In a similar vein, feminist psychotherapist Laura Brown (2005) described her path to a career in psychotherapy as beginning with familial strife in her early childhood. She recalled, "That misery was extremely formative of my interests in human behavior, as well as of the development of the self-capacities that have made me the particular therapist that I have become" (p. 950), adding, "I was also left with a compelling sense that my own safety and well-being were intimately linked to soothing the distress of others" (p. 951). Experiential therapist Alvin R. Mahrer (2005, p. 960) recalled,

> Psychotherapy was a fine tool in a noble profession, a helping profession. But this aspect of psychotherapy was not especially what inspired me. From the first meeting, psychotherapy seemed to have an inspirational wallop in two ways that were better than drugs or anything else. One was that psychotherapy offered the magical promise of letting go of the person I was and becoming a person I could become, an intoxicating invitation to become a radically new person.

These courageous and genuine reflections offer good insight to the many and complex reasons for becoming a psychotherapist—for many, to help heal others and, on some level, help heal the self as well. However, the question at hand goes beyond how to truthfully and thoughtfully explain to another what led to one's choice of psychotherapy as a career; rather, how does one best respond to this question when asked by a client in session? While the above reflections are no doubt true and thoughtful, therapists must focus fundamentally on the question of what is in the client's best interest. In an attempt to be genuine, even a skilled practitioner may run the risk of over-sharing—of making the session, or even part of the session, about him or herself. Even the most honest reflection on the therapist's past hardships or process of self-discovery may disorient the therapy, allowing the client to consider the notion that the therapy is not his or hers alone, but rather, part of the therapist's personal journey. While the therapist will almost inevitably find the work personally fulfilling and meaningful, the means to this should not be through extensive personal disclosure; specifically, a detailed account of the therapist's career path is quite unlikely to be in the client's best interest.

So, how should the question be approached? As discussed in Chapter 2 on self-disclosure ethics, recent literature advises that one should be clear about the intention of the disclosure (LaPorte et al., 2010; Sturges, 2012) and keep the disclosure brief (Audet & Everall, 2003; Bottrill, Pistran, Barker, & Worrell 2010; Henretty & Levitt, 2010; Kelly & Rodriguez, 2007; Sturges, 2012). However, even after applying these guidelines when considering responses to this particular question, it is still not immediately obvious what—if any—degree of self-disclosure regarding reasons for getting into the field is appropriate in this situation. How much, if anything, should be shared?

The difficult task, of course, is putting together a response that appropriately balances disclosure and non-disclosure, and one that aligns with the goals of psychotherapy broadly, as well as the individual goals for the client at a particular time. It is important to appreciate that this balance of disclosure and non-disclosure will vary not only from one client to another, but from one therapist to another, and furthermore, will differ for every client–therapist pair. Moreover, the therapist's task revolves not just around making decisions about frequency of disclosure but on content as well. These are related though distinct tasks discussed in more detail in Chapters 5 and 6 of this text on self-disclosure decision-making and types of disclosure.

Completely honest disclosures in response to this question—as evidenced by the examples from Ellis (2005), Brown (2005), and Mahrer (2005) at the beginning of this chapter—risk exposing the less-than-completely altruistic motives that influenced most, if not all, of us as we pursued careers in this field. On the one hand, sharing that one's interest in psychotherapy was to some degree self-serving or related to healing one's own wounds may have the effect of diminishing the client's idealization of you as therapist, including perhaps one's potential influence as a respected authority (see Chapters 4 and 30 of this text on self-disclosure efficacy research and expertness). On the other hand, as Wachtel (2008, p. 257) has noted,

> In some respects, this is in itself of value, since the tendency to idealize others who are seen as authorities is one part of what keeps many patients locked into the experience that they are not up to par. [. . .] Most of us, in essence, need a *mix* of attitudes toward those we admire or depend on, a combination of idealization and readiness to learn from them, freedom to compete with them, freedom to see their flaws without the danger of toppling or losing them, and so on.

As with all matters of fielding questions from clients, the method of response depends in large part on the modality in which one is currently practicing (e.g., a more indirect, neutral response typical of a psychodynamic approach versus a more direct CBT approach), as well as one's own stylistic preferences—or, for trainees, the adopted stylistic preferences of their supervisors. However, every good response will take into account a handful of important factors, including, among others, the context of the treatment (e.g., is this a new client trying to determine whether the therapist is a good match for them, or someone in treatment with this therapist for years?), the nature of the therapy (e.g., is this short- or long-term therapy?), the client's diagnosis (e.g., are trust or boundaries an issue?), and the extent to which the client has any prior familiarity with the traditional nature of psychotherapy. A consideration of these factors, when developing a response to this question, allows for an attunement to the needs of the individual client for whom this question has arisen.

For example, hearing this question from an inquisitive client in a college counseling center, as they consider a similar line of work, might elicit a different response than if the inquiry came from a distraught client in the middle of a tearful account of difficult interactions with her son. Similarly, hearing this question from a new client in the first session would likely warrant a different (and perhaps more forthcoming) response. In this regard, McWilliams (2004) suggests that therapists, particularly beginning therapists, should be conservative about their self-disclosures, with the exception of the initial sessions, "when clients deserve answers to questions that for them are prerequisites to hiring a particular mental health professional," (p. 188).

Inherent to considering these contextual factors is an attempt to better understand what is arguably the most important piece of information needed to develop a response appropriate to the client and the situation—what prompted the client's question in the first place? As such, the current authors suggest beginning with the following response, as appropriate for most clinical situations: a simple, warm, and inquisitive, "Why do you ask?" For therapists who are comfortable opening the door to some self-disclosure regarding this question, one might augment, "This is an interesting question, and I am happy to answer it, but first I'd like to know why this might be of interest to you."

The client may offer that he or she is "just wondering," or that he or she is curious to know what motivates you to "listen to people's problems all day." Asking the client what brought this question to mind, or even—per classic psychodynamic technique—asking the client to express why he or she imagines you might have become a therapist, might provide some insight into their unconscious and object relations. In response, some clients may resist exploring their reasons for asking, and some may express frustration that you don't "just answer the question."

Keeping in mind points made in the Introduction and Chapter 3 of this text, that non-disclosure may result in clients feeling that the therapist is inaccessible (Goldstein, 1994) or even hostile (Henretty & Levitt, 2010), a useful tactic, one originally situated within a psychodynamic paradigm, would be to explain that both the client and therapist are here to explore what is going on for the client, and everything discussed in session has meaning and can help them gain understanding together, even the questions that come up. It may also be helpful to reiterate the uniqueness of the relationship and the ways in which it differs from other relationships, wherein the back-and-forth question-and-answer conversations one experiences in typical social interactions do not apply. These responses help reestablish the frame and boundaries of the relationship, highlighting the fact that boundaries do not limit the relationship, but rather support its uniqueness that, in turn, allows for the work to be done (see Chapter 3 and 6 on theoretical perspectives and types of disclosure for further explanation).

Most often, the client who asks this question wants to know that the therapist is "in it for the right reasons." Thus, asking the client to talk with you about what brought this question to mind is likely to lead to a clinically productive conversation—is he or she worried that you are only here for a paycheck, that you don't genuinely care for him or her, that you somehow enjoy listening to the woes of others, or, perhaps worse, that you might have grown sick of hearing people's problems day after day? Opening up the conversation in this way is, importantly, not a deflection of the question, but a reorientation to the purpose and goals of therapy. However, this approach does not diminish the importance of being aware of one's reasons for pursuing a career in psychotherapy, nor offering the client a reasonably accurate and relatively brief response.

The authors contend, too, that the tone in which this question is posed by the client should affect greatly the answer given. That is, if the client poses this question more in the way of a challenge, the therapist's answer would more appropriately reflect the underlying affect (e.g., "It feels to me that you're wondering whether I can do this work effectively, that is, whether I can be helpful to you"). Conversely, if it feels that this is a relatively simple question of inquiry, it might well be answered by a short phrase or two (e.g., "I've always been interested in helping people with their problems"; "I've been doing this kind of work for many years and found that I enjoy it a good deal and that others have felt helped and supported by me"). Third, if it feels like it's a mild form of resistance to beginning the work, the therapist's answer might be in the form of,

> Here's the short answer to your question—I've always liked doing this work and found I was reasonably good at it—and I'd be willing to give you a bit of a longer answer to this question at another time, but now I'd like to hear more about what's on your mind and what it is we should be working on.

The authors imagine that some therapists might add another phrase in this latter situation—especially if it was a new client beginning treatment for the first time—"It's hard to actually begin the work of therapy, isn't it?"

Conclusions

Like most matters of therapeutic self-disclosure, this question does not lend well to the adoption of a single catchall technique. In line with the three facilitative conditions that Rogers (1957) hypothesized to be necessary and sufficient for effective psychotherapy, the authors would generally aim to be genuine (i.e., providing only truthful responses), empathic (i.e., reflecting awareness of the client's current emotional state and motives for asking), and affirming (i.e., demonstrating caring and overall positive regard). The authors emphasize that a genuine, empathic, and affirming approach can look very different from one client–therapist pair to the next and encourage highly individualized approaches, some of which may rely more on non-verbal responses such as smiling or nodding one's head (Suzuki & Farber, 2016).

While 'hard' questions like this one force therapists to confront the limits of their ability or willingness to self-disclose, these questions can also signal that there is an important opportunity for a client's growth. Wachtel (2008, p. 251) explained,

> Depending on the therapist's theoretical orientation and her assessment of the key issues and conflicts for the patient, questions such as these [that request therapist disclosure] may be experienced by her as more an *opportunity* or a welcome sign of progress by the patient than as a dilemma or invasion.

This, of course, assumes that the question at hand—why did you decide to become a therapist—has occurred at a point in therapy beyond the first session or two (see Chapter 5 on therapeutic timing). In a similar vein, Feldman (2002) posited that questions like this one can supply important information about the client's internal world, present an opportunity to deepen the therapeutic relationship, and encourage curiosity for the client about his or her own thoughts and feelings in session. In short, it is important to remember the goal in responding to a client's question about one's motives for becoming a therapist is not simply to expound on one's career choice, but develop a greater understanding of and connection to one's client.

References

Audet, C., & Everall, R. (2003). Counsellor self-disclosure: Client-informed implications for practice. *Counselling and Psychotherapy Research, 3*(3), 223–31.

Bottrill, S., Pistrang, N., Barker, C., & Worrell, M. (2010). The use of therapist self-disclosure: Clinical psychology trainees' experiences. *Psychotherapy Research, 20*(2), 165–80.

Brown, L. (2005). Don't be a sheep: How this eldest daughter became a feminist therapist. *Journal of Clinical Psychology, 61*(8), 949–56.

Chakraborti, A. (2006). Did you ever suffer from any mental illness? *British Medical Journal, 333,* 708–9.

Edelstein, L., & Waehler, C. (2011). *What do I say? The therapist's guide to answering client questions.* Hoboken, NJ: John Wiley & Sons.

Ellis, A. (2004). Why I (really) became a therapist. *Journal of Rational-Emotive and Cognitive Behavior Therapy, 22*(2), 73–7.

Ellis, A. (2005). Why I (really) became a therapist. *Journal of Clinical Psychology: In Session, 61*(8), 945–8.

Feldman, T. (2002). Technical considerations when handling questions in the initial phases of psychotherapy. *Journal of Contemporary Psychotherapy, 32*(2–3), 213–27.

Goldstein, E. (1994). Self-disclosure in treatment: What therapists do and don't talk about. *Clinical Social Work Journal, 22*(4), 417–33.

Henretty, J., & Levitt, H. (2010). The role of therapist self-disclosure in psychotherapy: A qualitative review. *Clinical Psychology Review, 30*(1), 63–77.

Holt, R., & Luborsky, L. (1958). *Personality patterns of psychiatrists: A study of methods for selecting residents* (Vol. 1). New York: Basic Books.

Kelly, A., & Rodriguez, R. (2007). Do therapists self-disclose more to clients with greater symptomology? *Psychotherapy: Theory, Research, Practice, Training, 44*(4), 470–5.

LaPorte, H., Sweifach, J., & Linzer, N. (2010). Sharing the trauma: Guidelines for therapist self-disclosure following a catastrophic event. *Best Practices in Mental Health, 6*(2), 39–56.

Mahrer, A. (2005). What inspired me to become a psychotherapist? *Journal of Clinical Psychology, 61*(8), 957–64.

McWilliams, N. (2004). *Psychoanalytic psychotherapy: A practitioner's guide.* New York: Guilford Press.

Rogers, C. (1957). The necessary and sufficient conditions of therapeutic personality change. *Journal of Consulting Psychology, 21*(2), 95–103.

Sturges, J. (2012). Use of therapist self-disclosure and self-involving statements. *The Behavior Therapist, 35*(5), 90–3.

Suzuki, J., & Farber, B. (2016). Towards greater specificity of the concept of positive regard. *Person-Centered and Experiential Psychotherapies, 15*(4), 263–84.

Wachtel, P. (2008). *Relational theory and the practice of psychotherapy.* New York: Guilford Press.

CHAPTER 16

"Are You a Christian?"

Gerald E. Nissley, Jr., PsyD

It seems like such an innocuous question. However, questions related to integration of faith into clinical work have been heatedly debated ever since the days of Sigmund Freud (as discussed in more detail in Chapter 13 of this text). When the current author trained in psychology at a faith-based university, he was instructed by Christian professors to avoid self-disclosure of religious orientation and refrain from deeper discussion of faith-based considerations based on concerns about scope of practice.

How clients make existential meaning relates in part to their beliefs, behaviors, and feelings about everyday experiences and 'big picture' matters (Park & Ai, 2006). For many clients, their experience of religion and spirituality provide a relational frame and narrative for meaning-making. It becomes the language they use to adapt, grow, and increase if not create coherence in the world.

However, in the area of religious therapist self-disclosure, the research (reviewed in Chapter 13) is limited. Thus, professional commentary may be informative to the reader seeking to navigate the client query "Are you a Christian?" as helpfully and appropriately as possible. Therapists must in some way respond to and not invalidate client desires to explore their psychological dynamics within a spiritual frame. However, therapists must also figure out how to do this in a way that is maximally beneficial to the therapeutic alliance and the client's mental health. When asked of their religious orientation, many therapists struggle to answer. While therapist's conflicted identities may make choosing a response difficult, a lack of guidance in this form of disclosure also contributes to the challenge (Magaldi-Dopman, Park-Taylor, & Ponterotto, 2011). Henceforth, what will be discussed are the potential benefits and risks associated with different ways of fielding the client inquiry that is the topic of this chapter. Guidelines for therapist self-disclosure in this context will be shared. Prior research on religious non-disclosure will be elaborated upon.

A Blessing: Possible Benefits of Therapist Self-Disclosure

As clients seek to make meaning, both globally and situationally in their spiritual and religious language, there is evidence that therapist self-disclosure of religious orientation can be beneficial. Research has shown that process variables—those related to the establishment and maintenance of therapeutic alliance—can be as important as interventions selected. Therapist self-disclosure can model for the client how to courageously and authentically express deeper internal states, conflicts, and inquiries within the safety and frame of the relationship (Henretty & Levitt, 2010). Over 75% want to explore existential matters in therapy and want to use their religious and spiritual language as the infrastructure (Worthington, Jr., Johnson, Hook, & Aten, 2013).

An important message is communicated when clients experience therapists responding to their questions about religious and spiritual orientation with authenticity, genuineness, and empathy, regardless of the content of their answer. Therapists answering client queries in this manner express to the clients that their presentation in session, and indeed their personhood, is of worth and esteem. Religiosity and spirituality serve both as risk and protective factors for resilience, as one's existential worldview can either aid them or inhibit them in their efforts to flexibly and capably respond to challenges. Clients being permitted, in some cases via self-disclosure, to openly discuss how spirituality and religion promote or inhibit adaptive functioning are often paramount in treatment. However, many clients do not know that. Clients are often taught in other social and professional contexts not to discuss sensitive and potentially offensive topics such as religion or politics. As mentioned Chapter 13, subtle or not so subtle therapist discouragement is often driven by the therapist's own discomfort with the topic, as may in turn be driven their own earlier religious conflicts and separation from religious entities, and may be considered an unethical form of self-prioritization.

Given the potential benefit of establishing bidirectional, authentic communication between client and therapist, it seems intuitive that therapist self-disclosure could improve rapport. Young's (2011) dissertation was an analogue study exploring the effects of religious self-disclosures on process variables in therapy. This study was also reviewed in Chapter 13, though with attention to common factors across studies, and will here be reviewed with attention to clinical factors and implications. Young (2011) found that therapist disclosures of similar religious identification were regarded favorably by student observers, most of whom identified as either Catholic or Protestant. From this study can be inferred that disclosure of similar religious affiliation is likely to be regarded favorably by inquiring clients, may build rapport, and communicate a level of understanding, relevant experience, and realer empathy.

Applications to Trauma and Sexual Orientation

The benefits of disclosing similar religious identifications are akin to what was described in prior chapters as among the benefits of therapist disclosures of similar/shared trauma history or sexual orientation. While this application may seem like a stretch to some, it should be remembered that religion is often at the root of clients' stories of trauma and recovery, as it has also been at the root of some of the greatest stories of trauma, recovery, and redemption throughout history.

This author does a lot of clinical work with Christians who also identify as LGBTQ. When those clients ask about this author's religious orientation, they are often trying to assess the likelihood that therapy will yield the relief and reward they are looking for. A case example comes to mind. The gay male client informed this author in the intake session that he was asking "Are you a Christian?" because he did not want to self-disclose intimate details with yet another person who would view him as inherently bad or misguided. Particularly, because he wanted to explore the relationship between his sexual identity, his faith identity, and relevant personal experiences.

In this author's experience, this client's concerns are not unusual. In such a context, individuals who identify as Christians have often learned that merely identifying as Christian does not guarantee that rapport is likely. Many of these folk have also been actively hurt by self-disclosing either their sexual or religious identification and enter therapy actively processing their referral questions within the context of their faith. Thus, they often want to know that (a) they can talk about faith and same-sex orientation in-session, and (b) the therapist is likely capable of understanding their relational frame and spiritual language, without an aversion to either or a presumption that one is inherently more worthwhile or deserving of greater priority. Indeed, therapist self-disclosure of religious and spiritual dynamics can be very beneficial for rapport development in such cases and at times may communicate to the client the therapist's qualification to treat.

The Curse: Risks of Religious Self-Disclosure

Although some research suggests that therapist self-disclosure of religious and spiritual orientation can be beneficial (Young, 2011), other research has suggested otherwise. In a classic study comparing therapist and client self-disclosure, it was found that more overt forms disclosure of religious affiliation (i.e., wearing religious insignia) can reduce the intimacy of client self-disclosures generally, albeit with limitations and implications discussed in more detail in Chapter 13 (Chesner & Baumeister, 1985). Interestingly, while one would expect that non-matching religious orientations might result in reduced therapeutic intimacy, Chesner and Baumeister (1985) also found that wearing religious insignia as a form of disclosure, to similarly affiliated clients, still yielded less intimacy (as compared to non-disclosure, e.g., not wearing religious insignia). Thus, early research into therapist self-disclosure of religious orientation suggested that the best advice might be to refrain.

While Chesner and Baumeister (1985) explain the direction given by this author's mentors, mediating variables were eventually discovered in additional research that represent associated obstacles: competency and countertransference. Clinical competence essentially involves having the appropriate knowledge, skills, and awareness to perform a task effectively. In a qualitative study, a number of experienced psychologists were interviewed regarding their use of self-disclosure regarding religious and spiritual variables (Magaldi-Dopman et al., 2011). Those psychologists expressed conflict both regarding their own spiritual and religious identities. Moreover, they struggled to determine when and how to disclose (a finding that is explored more fully in Chapter 5 on disclosure timing and decision-making). A common theme in Magaldi-Dopman et al.'s (2011) results was that psychologists reported receiving no significant training regarding the integration of religious and spiritual dynamics into their clinical work. Psychologists under study reported receiving minimal if any supervisory/training program feedback on whether or not to disclose their religious orientations. As ethical codes at the national and state level typically obligate therapists to work within the scope of their training in non-emergent situations, the absence of training on this form of self-disclosure presents an ethical quandary for the therapist. As it is not a given that a therapist cannot process spiritual variables in psychological terms, client inquiries to the tune of "Are you a Christian?" may present competency questions for therapists.

As an example of this last point, the current author was previously working with a devout Christian client at a time when this author was strongly questioning his own religious identity. The client expressed the security of her religious orientation in the intake session before asking the author about his own affiliation. The client was likely asking in an effort to assess the likelihood this author would accept and appreciate her contextual lens for how she made/makes meaning out of experience. Immediately, this author found himself conceptualizing the client as simple, psychologically rigid, and unsophisticated because of her certainty of identity. The author was tempted, before reflecting on his own countertransference, to answer the client in a snarky, intellectual, dismissing, and therapeutically contraindicated manner.

Guidelines for Self-Disclosure of Religious Orientation

If one's goal is to competently make decisions on whether or not to self-disclose religious and spiritual orientation for a client's benefit, the therapist must engage in appropriate assessment before directly and intentionally responding (which should be recalled as a general precaution in all self-disclosure scenarios, as mentioned previously in Chapter 6 on the different types of self-disclosure). Notice that a lack of response cannot reasonably be considered a therapeutically viable option. The therapist may choose not to disclose certain religious and spiritual variables/identifications, but some form of direct response and acknowledgment should nonetheless occur. Regardless of how the therapist responds to the client's question "Are you a Christian?" the goal should be to competently progress the relationship and the therapy.

The first aspect in an effective therapist self-disclosure along religious and spiritual lines involves assessment of why the client is asking in the first place. For sure, the client is not merely taking a survey! However, clients may have varied purposes for asking (Tillman, 1998). For example, some clients are seeking to discern a therapist's 'goodness of fit.' Others are seeking to explore the connection between religious, spiritual, social, and lifestyle variables within the boundaries of their psyche and therapeutic frame. Still others are seeking spiritual direction that is overtly about their religious and spiritual journey. In cases where clients are more clearly and truly in search of pastoral counseling, limited disclosure and referral may be warranted.

This author does answer client religious queries (because he values open exchange with the client and seeks to honor the client's disclosure in asking), but also seeks to know more about why the client is asking in the first place. Essentially, this author answers and also asks why it matters, as a form of compromise between ethical precautions and relationship building strategies noted in chapters in Part I of this text. This strategy is further supported by research findings and positions noted in Young (2011) and Worthington et al. (2013).

The amount of information shared by this author, in response to the client query, necessarily matches the nature of the question. If the client merely wants to know out of curiosity, then the disclosure may be rather basic. On the other hand, the author's self-disclosure of religious identity may be an insight intervention. For example, this author's identification as an Anabaptist has often resulted in clients reporting forms of existential conflict between their experiences and their 'theology of origin.' In such dialogues, clients sometimes become more able to see more heterogeneity in theological models available for helping them to develop adaptive responses to life.

When Clients' Inquiries Are Hostile or Divisive

Other clients may be rigid, hostile, and using religious content to unconsciously recreate problematic early family dynamics. In such cases, it is possible that the client's religious identifications, queries of the therapist, and problematic style of engaging may or may not be related, and may be indicative of either a longer lasting personality trait or a more malleable expression of recent stressors. In cases where clients' inquiries early in the relationship are of a more demanding and off-putting nature, it may be helpful to conceptualize the occurrence *as a symptom* and answer in ways that balance boundaries and rapport.

So doing may begin with: "I don't usually talk about my private life in therapy, but I really do want to get to know you, understand what brings you to therapy, and be helpful to you." From a more client-centered/relational direction, the therapist may smile curiously and say: "That being said, why do you ask?" Or in psychodynamic direction: "What do you imagine my answer will be?" Or in a cognitive behavioral direction: "What would my answer mean to you? What if I say yes and what if I say no?" Or possibly with a more daring self-involving disclosure: "I feel the need to be honest and tell you I find your question intrusive." From different vantage points, these responses to the client query "Are you a Christian?" err toward restraint, therapeutic exploration, and offer alternatives to therapists unintentionally revealing a lot about themselves in cases where they answer quickly and without forethought.

When Therapists and Clients Are of Similar Religious Identifications

As was noted in previously discussed research, therapist-client matching of religious orientation can impact how therapist self-disclosure is received by clients and treatment outcomes. Research shows that matching can be particularly beneficial when the client and/or the therapist is fundamentalist in his/her/their religious orientation. However, therapist capacity for empathy and provision of unconditional regard has been noted to be more important, clinically, than religious/spiritual matching (Aten, McMinn, & Worthington, Jr., 2011). Thus, while matching may offer a benefit, a lack of close match of religious orientation can be addressed through general client-centered process interventions.

As an Anabaptist Christian, this author currently lives in the 'Baptist Belt' in the southern United States. The author's Baptist clients are often more deterministic, nationalistic, and fundamentalist. While the author and his clients' religious identities are different in ways that are very important to clients, the author can build therapeutic rapport with them through traditional humanistic dynamics, such as acceptance, empathic reflection, and respectful questions about their worldview and expressions of it.

A particular risk is that therapist self-disclosure in cases of therapist-client matching can be driven by fusion and countertransference. When client and therapist match closely in religious and spiritual orientation, it is easy to conceptualize the other through one's own lens and assume sameness of belief, values, and lifestyle. Thus, and with particular attention to self-disclosing, it is important that the therapist remain intentional in exploring such dynamics through the client's relational frame and attends to his or her own reactions.

The possibility of 'religious overshadowing' can have significant implications. Sometimes, when clients ask this author about his spiritual orientation, they are trying to assess the likelihood that it is permissible to share religious and spiritual struggles (as an indication of capacity to be empathic, as discussed in Chapters 10 and 13 on TSD in contexts of religion and LGBTQ identity). In the author's experience, and somewhat contrary to previously discussed analogue research findings, when there is a perceived match in religious orientation, it often impacts the intimacy of disclosure.

It is also worth stating that if the client does not ask the therapist's religious or spiritual orientation, it may be prudent not to offer. Probing the client on religious and spiritual variables during assessment would still work to establish rapport and inform them that such topics are acceptable to discuss in therapy. As mentioned in prior research chapters, it has been suspected that clients may not broach the subject of religion for fear of the therapist's discomfort. In such cases, clients may require assurance or queuing to ask the question "Are you a Christian?" and possibly for underlying and clinically informative reasons.

When the Therapist's and Client's Religious Identifications Differ

For the therapist whose religious orientation does not match that of the client's, it is encouraging to know that use of other process-oriented interventions can work as well or better than disclosure. This is particularly important for those who do not espouse a religious or spiritual identity (i.e., atheists, agnostics). In the rural small town this author lives in, he is well known both as a Christian and a psychologist. Interestingly, he is the only local mental health professional whose office is open on Wednesday night (a 'church night' in many calendars for Christians). He keeps these hours of operation because many atheists and agnostics feel very isolated on Wednesday nights in the area.

When the author and non-Christian identified client work together in therapy, they often ask about the author's experience of Christianity and explore how the author's identity as both a Christian and a psychologist may affect the therapeutic alliance and essentially whether the author can be empathic and understanding. As the author responds and tries to gather information about the client's worldview and relevant prior experiences, the author looks for opportunities to express unconditional positive regard and show basic dignity and genuine respect for differing perspectives. Moreover, many atheists and agnostic folks come to therapy due to injuries or even traumas related to their prior religious and spiritual experiences, so that the author's empathy, respect, and genuineness may have something of a corrective effect.

Conclusions

With all clinical interventions, it is important to intentionally select tools based on assessment of client–therapist dynamics and client-desired outcomes. How to answer the client query "Are you a Christian?" is no different in that regard. Therapists must make decisions on whether or not to disclose based on their intention to improve the therapeutic alliance and advance the work together. To do so, therapists must also be aware of their own and the client's personal dynamics and match the decision on disclosure to the client's reason for asking. Personal dynamics include but are not limited to the extent of congruence between the worldview of the client and therapist.

References

Aten, J., McMinn, M., & Worthington, Jr., E. (Eds.). (2011). *Spiritually oriented interventions for counseling and psychotherapy*. Washington, DC: American Psychological Association.

Chesner, S., & Baumeister, R. (1985). Effect of therapists' disclosure of religious beliefs on the intimacy of client self-disclosure. *Journal of Social and Clinical Psychology*, 3(1), 97–105.

Henretty, J., & Levitt, H. (2010). The role of therapist self-disclosure in psychotherapy: A qualitative review. *Clinical Psychology Review*, 30(1), 63–77.

Magaldi-Dopman, D., Park-Taylor, J., & Ponterotto, J. (2011). Psychotherapist's spiritual, religious, atheist or agnostic identity and their practice of psychotherapy: A grounded theory study. *Psychotherapy Research*, 21(3), 286–303.

Park, C., & Ai, A. (2006). Meaning making and growth: New directions for research on survivors of trauma. *Journal of Loss & Trauma*, 11(5), 389–407.

Tillman, J. (1998). Psychodynamic psychotherapy, religious belief, and self-disclosure. *American Journal of Psychotherapy*, 52(3), 273–86.

Worthington Jr., E., Johnson, E., Hook, J., & Aten, J. (Eds.). (2013). *Evidence-based practices in counseling and psychotherapy.* Downers Grove, IL: IVP Academic.

Young, S. (2011). Effects of an analogue counselor's religious or financial self-disclosure and observer characteristics on therapeutic processes (Doctoral dissertation). Retrieved from ProQuest Dissertations and Theses database (No UMI No.).

CHAPTER 17

"Are You in Recovery?"

Graham S. Danzer, PsyD

Clients with substance abuse histories present some unique challenges to therapists, one of which is their common desire to know if the therapist too is in recovery. This question is challenging to answer both for therapists in substance abuse recovery and for therapists without such a personal history. It is not uncommon for substance abusing clients *not* to ask the therapist directly, but rather to make statements showing a presumption either way and almost baiting a disclosure opportunity. Whether the therapist's personal recovery or lack thereof is addressed directly or indirectly by clients, it is reasonable to assume that the therapist's response may be of some importance and impact, albeit for different reasons and in different clinical circumstances that are largely the subject of this chapter and indeed the larger framework and recurring acknowledgment of this text. As mentioned by guest authors of prior chapters, "Are you in recovery?" and other direct client inquiries may have different meanings and implications, with respect to the nature and goals of treatment, the time and manner in which the client's inquiry is made, and whether the therapeutic relationship at the time of client inquiry was just beginning to grow, was already strong, or was precarious or damaged.

Clients with substance abuse histories frequently have substance abuse as a necessary focus of treatment, not necessarily because it is what they want to talk about, but often because they are involuntarily mandated by the courts and/or pressured to come to therapy by a loved one. Even in cases where a substance abusing client may seem voluntary, it is often the case that the therapist learns over time that initial pressures/coercion from frustrated family members, spouses, housing authorities, or employers may have been the true referral source. In such cases, it is common (in the current author's experience) for such clients to feel that mandates for treatment are unnecessary, inconvenient, and indeed an unfair exertion of control over their lives. It is also not uncommon for such clients to report histories of alcohol and drug abuse, related consequences, and court involvement in a manner that at face value may seem relatively minor and inconsistent with the patterns and facts of their lives not so readily made clear, particularly to a therapist without a similar history of addiction, denial, and self-interested story telling. In these cases, addicted clients may have been involuntarily pressured or mandated to treatment several times, had far more addiction-related consequences and intrusions in their lives than they are willing to admit, and to make considerable and not wholly conscious efforts to change the focus away from their addiction and to other individuals or situations they see as blameworthy.

When Clients Ask Early in Treatment

One way that addicted clients (and particularly those who are involuntarily referred or pressured to come to treatment) may demonstrate the prior defense strategy is to make the inquiry "Are you in recovery?", in a more defensive and even demanding manner likely to engender similar anxieties, irritation, resentment, and frustration in the therapist. Although difficult to navigate in the moment, such feelings brought out in a self-aware therapist may be clinically productive, informative, and useful. A less mindful therapist may retaliate by asking the intrusive client, "Why do you ask?" or "How would that be helpful for you to know?", "Yes" and with a quick and poorly thought-out sharing of personal history details, or "No" with a fairly desperate attempt to demonstrate qualification in some other way. As discussed in Chapter 6 on types of therapeutic self-disclosure (TSD), such impulsive gratifications of client inquiries permit the addicted or substance abusing client to succeed in altering the focus and frame of therapy, just as they have probably succeeded in keeping attention off of them and instead on (who they consider to be) blameworthy spouses, authority figures, and family members. This dynamic also highlights prior ethical discussions about how a therapist's ability to appropriately and helpfully disclose, paradoxically, requires the ability to exercise restraint and forethought, particularly in the more tense and testy moments of therapy.

With such considerations in mind, it may be more helpful for the therapist to (not overtly) interpret the client inquiry/demand as if the client might really be saying "You don't know what I'm talking about," or "You don't understand me," as discussed in Chapter 19 of this text. It is likely that the involuntary substance abuse client's inquiry, on an unconscious level, is at least partially intended to determine whether the therapist can be empathic. Although the inquiry may seem hostile or uncooperative, the client may on some level really want to know whether the therapist can begin a healing relationship by hearing and understanding his or her helplessness, depression, and frustration about having been forced (on multiple occasions) to attend undesired treatment, endure considerable expense, and while necessarily confronting a very sensitive issue.

Reflecting on such possibilities, a more mindful therapist might respond in an inquisitive manner: "That's a fair question and I will answer, but what will my answer mean to you? What I say yes? What if I say no?" So doing may help a client reflect upon what they asked, what his or her real intentions are, and perhaps refocus. These treatment goals, if actualized upon, would likely be instrumental in relapse prevention because the client would be helped to analyze and potentially second-guess their impulsive thoughts (i.e., to return to active using in the future). With a client who gives indication of greater capacity for reflection, a therapist might answer, "I feel like talking about my personal history in your therapy would not really be a good use of your time." This response, in many cases, will lead a client to agree, and progress onward. A particularly disordered client may resist the empathy by stating that his or her being forced to come to therapy is also not a good use of their time or money. Such an answer would open the door to motivational interviewing interventions intended to explore ambivalence, address dissonance, and progress towards resolution of conflicting thoughts about ongoing addiction versus recovery often plaguing substance abusers on a daily basis.

Paradoxically, many substance abusers of hardened and impoverished lifestyles may have more respect and appreciation for a treatment approach that is still relational, though confrontational in a tough love kind of way that may not be what most therapists are accustomed to. It is frequently the case that such clients presume to very quickly know a lot about individuals' (including but not limited to the therapist's) backgrounds and personal circumstances, based on limited personal interactions, projections, and in ways that maintain higher likelihood of interpersonal conflicts both in and out of therapy. In interactions, presumption and personality-driven conflicts are frequently excuses for ongoing substance abuse, may be reminiscent of early family dynamics, and again help substance abusers keep the attentional focus away from them and their addiction, and instead on others attempting to take care of them and becoming equally sick by proxy. Thus, a more hardened substance abusing client may ask/demand to know if the therapist 'is in recovery,' with the potential to recreate a dynamic reminiscent of how their addiction may have originated and may be maintained in recent history.

Based on a deeper and more clinical line of thinking, the possibility that the client may respond favorably to a more confrontational treatment, and with at least fleeting periods of rapport up to the point of inquiry, the therapist may smile invitingly but coily, and say, "Throw some odds at me, what are the odds I say yes and what are the odds I say no?" It is possible and perhaps even likely (in the current author's experience) that the client may revel in the therapist's game, unwittingly open the door for motivational interviewing as described previously, and hopefully progress towards a more helpful understanding of how they presume to know much about people they have just met and ask intrusive questions early in relationships, and in an off-putting way. A goal would be to explore whether this style of relating to the therapist as symbolic other is a style they desire to maintain, or may want to address in an effort to make their mandatory therapy useful and potentially change their addiction-characteristic ways of relating to others and avoiding intimacy through confrontation and disagreement.

What Does the Research Say?

There is controversy within the field of psychotherapy about whether therapists with personal histories of addiction and recovery should self-disclose a similar history to similarly afflicted clients. This area of TSD is controversial because of the vulnerability and high risk nature of substance abuse, as well as the widespread successes of 12-step approaches wherein self-disclosure from more senior participants in recovery to newer members is *the* primary intervention (Galanter, 2014; Krentzman, Cranford, & Robinson, 2013). Higher usage of disclosure is common in treatment centers where daily interactions are peer-driven, significantly more directive, and confrontational as described previously. So much, in fact, that it may be helpful for therapists to keep in mind that there are and should be distinctions though also overlap between therapeutic interventions and substance abuse treatment, with particular respect to how the client inquiry "Are you in recovery?" should be handled.

Supporting the efficacy of 12-step approaches, Project MATCH (Matching Alcoholism Treatments to Client Heterogeneity), a regression study of 952 alcoholics, as well as several subsequent longitudinal studies conducted on this data set, have consistently found that Alcoholics Anonymous program participation predicted significant decreases in alcohol consumption and higher rates of abstinence, as well as decreased problematic behavior and improved coping and sociability (Blonigan, Timko, Finney, Moos, & Moos, 2011; Magura, Cleland, & Tonigan, 2013; Pagano, White, Stout, & Tonigan, 2013; Young, 2013). Thus, 12-step programmatic methods should be considered (though not necessarily adopted whole-heartedly) by therapists interested in achieving similar outcomes, and with more severely compromised substance abusing populations that (a) roundly benefit from 12-step (when willing to attend and participate fully), and (b) are frequently resistant and, at best, marginally responsive to therapeutic treatment as usual.

Supporting the benefits of adding therapy to substance abuse treatment as usual, McHugh, Hearon, and Otto (2010) conducted a meta-analytic review of 34 randomized control studies of cognitive behavioral therapy for 2,340 total clients with substance abuse and dependence histories. Consistent with older meta-analyses reviewed in their paper, McHugh et al. (2010) reported small–large effect sizes depending largely on participant drug of choice. Marijuana abusers had the most positive results, followed by abusers of cocaine and opioids, and polysubstance abusers. Consistent with prior discussions of treatment approach, the efficacy of CBT for substance abuse was discussed by McHugh et al. (2011) as rooted in the inclusion of motivational approaches, contingencies, integrating individual, group, and family treatments, and teaching relapse prevention strategies, with generally less benefit from medication interventions.

The reader is also encouraged to consider that the latter CBT strategies/approaches and goals are also detailed (albeit in different terminology and in a peer-peer form of delivery) in 'The Big Book' of Alcoholics Anonymous (2001), which was constructed in its original form in 1912, and was at the source of widely reported results long before cognitive behavioral therapies gained mass popularity. Additionally, it should be considered (as mentioned in Chapter 3 on theoretical perspectives), that CBT permits in some circumstances therapist disclosures of coping and problem-solving strategies in similar fashion to recurring themes in the 'Big Book' stories of peer-helping, mentoring, and personal growth. Put another way, research on cognitive behavioral therapies and 12-step programs suggests self-disclosure has similar aims under each model, albeit with different frequencies and intimacies of disclosure, as is to be expected and appropriate relative to the nature of the relationship.

While peer and professional interventions are necessarily of different boundaries and forms of delivery, the 12-step research suggests that professionals unilaterally discounting 12-step programs may be doing a disservice to clients. Further, discounting of 12-step may be unethical when rooted less in a research-informed understanding of the client's issues and needs from treatment, and/or rooted more in a therapist's personal aversion to religion/spirituality. The latter possibility was discussed in Chapter 10 on religious TSDs as a common source of countertransference.

When the Answer Is "Yes," the Therapist Is in Recovery

It has been estimated that between 37% and 57% of addiction treatment providers have personal histories of addiction (de Vos, Netten, & Noordenbos, 2016). Consistent with previously stated advantages of general TSD in theory, formerly addicted therapists sharing aspects of their addiction history (with addicted clients) may at times be a helpful strategy for building therapeutic relationships (LaPorte, Sweifach, & Linzer, 2010). Moreover, substance abuse clients may at least partially base their perception of therapist competency on knowledge of the therapist having similar personal experiences (LaPorte et al., 2010; Sturges, 2012).

In illustration of this point, as well as prior discussions of what is often referred to in the substance abuse treatment field as 'addict thinking,' Knox, Hess, Peterson, and Hill (1997) conducted a qualitative interview study of 13 clients. This study included one client who was primarily in therapy due to substance abuse issues. The client (a woman) also had a history of chronic depression and borderline personality disorder. She was documented as presuming her therapist (a man) had never tried street drugs, and questioned him directly in effort to determine whether he would be able to understand her addiction history. She was surprised when he responded yes, he had tried street drugs. It was indicated that this interchange led the client to reflect upon if not reconsider her presumptive thinking and behavior, both in the therapeutic relationship and in other personal relationships, to the tune of:

> It snapped me right out of that self-righteous thing, you know, that "How would you know?" . . . like I was different than him. At that moment it made him a lot more human than I was feeling at the time . . . and changed the whole perspective immediately . . . it made him sort of a kindred spirit in a way.
>
> (Knox et al., 1997, p. 381)

In cases where the therapist and client are both addicted, it must be remembered that 12-step programs are peer-driven and non-professional. Thus, additional precautions are aptly noted in the research. Unlike 12-step members, addicted therapists should refrain from prolonged and overly detailed disclosures of their addiction histories (Sturges, 2012). Clients who learn of their therapist's addiction history may become worried about triggering their therapist to return to active addiction, or develop an anti-therapeutic sense of competition (Henretty & Levitt, 2010). Additionally, it is reasonable to assume that addicted clients probably do not want to know nor would benefit from hearing extensive details of the therapist's personal history, and may in some cases be susceptible to following with more inquiry until role reversal is fully achieved.

When the Answer Is "No," the Therapist Is Not in Recovery

Frequently, voluntary therapy clients who are in personal recovery are actively involved in 12-step programs and desire to have their 12-step programs in some way incorporated in their therapy, or at least feel a sense of therapist receptivity to discussion of 12-step program involvement and effects. In a way that is often difficult for non-addicted therapists to understand, beyond a more superficial and intellectual level, 12-step programs are frequently experienced by fully invested clients as a more comprehensive system of personal support, life management, problem solving, existential direction, connection, social commitment, and helping of others. In such cases where the therapist feels an aversion to 12-step (and likely the spirituality component), a lack of firsthand knowledge and thorough understanding is likely. It may be advantageous for the therapist to transparently acknowledge this form of shortcoming to the client, attend a 12-step meeting that is open to the public, discuss how the program works with other members after the meeting is over, and re-engage with the client in a better-informed, more competent, inquisitive, and less presumptive manner.

When clients ask "Are you in recovery?" and the therapist's honest answer would be "No," the relevant research may be informative. There is limited research specifically regarding substance abuser inquiries, though research in other areas of TSD suggests that non-disclosure or disclosure of difference is unlikely to be significantly more or less impactful on outcomes (Henretty & Levitt, 2010). Thus, therapists need not anguish over whether or not to disclose, because either answering in the negative or not answering directly is unlikely (in most cases) to be differentially impactful. Supporting this point, Reeh's (2010) dissertation involved 132 adult men in residential treatment centers and shown hypothetical treatment scenarios of intake workers who did and did not self-disclose. Participants were not significantly more or less likely to report willingness to return for further treatment depending on the presence/absence of disclosure.

Although there are ethical arguments of clients' rights to know aspects of the therapist's qualification (McWilliams, 2004), there are also questions of how far these arguments extend. In particular, precautions may be necessary and even advantageous in cases where clients' presenting conditions suggest a likelihood of problematic boundaries, including substance abuse, and as also applied in other chapter discussions of TSD in contexts of client eating disorders (Chapter 12) and severe mental illnesses (Chapter 11). Whereas TSD may appease these clients' curiosities and help to build a relationship quickly, professional restraint, boundary maintenance, and responsive probing may be uncomfortable for the client, though potentially corrective. Moreover, if a client's inquiry of "Are you in recovery?" is not quickly and directly answered, and the therapeutic relationship is already ruptured, his or her suitability for therapy is questionable. In addition, a therapist should feel free in some cases to answer a client inquiry with an affirmative "No," without presuming that further discussion or elaboration is inherently necessary.

Conclusions

How the therapist responds to the client inquiry about whether or not the therapist is in recovery should depend in part on the strength of the relationship at the time, whether the client is voluntary or involuntary, and whether or not the inquiry is rooted in the client's 12-step affiliation. Additional considerations relate to whether the client is asking in a more curious way and thereby suggesting effort to determine the therapist's qualification to treat, or if the client is more hostile and hardened. In the latter case, the client may be paradoxically asking whether the therapist can be empathic and/or suggesting his or her need for a more confrontive approach.

Although answers to the question "Are you in recovery?" will of course differ based on the individual and clinical circumstances at hand, the mindful and reflective therapist will most often not answer directly, immediately, and without momentary reflection on implications of the question. Rather, the therapist will consider how the question was asked, at what point in the development of the relationship, based on what apparent client motivation, and in what ways this client behavior may be informative about their current emotional state and longer standing addiction and family history. With such thoughts in mind, the therapist may answer in a way that is primarily considerate of both the therapeutic relationship and the therapeutic process at play, more than just the literal content. This therapist is maximally likely to acknowledge, inquire, and either self-disclose directly or indirectly, or not disclose, in a way that will be most helpful to the client. Specifically, this more mindful and addiction-knowledgeable therapist would be helpful by going beyond the provision of unnecessary personal information, and instead providing information to the client about themselves, as should be among the major goals of all therapies.

References

Alcoholics Anonymous. (2001). *Alcoholics Anonymous* (4th ed.). New York: A. A. World Services.

Blonigan, D., Timko C., Finney, J., Moos, B., & Moos, R. (2011). Alcoholics Anonymous attendance, decreases in impulsivity and drinking and psychosocial outcomes over 16 years: Moderated-mediation from a developmental perspective. *Journal of Addictions, 106*(12), 2167–77.

de Vos, J., Netten, C., & Noordenbos, G. (2016). Recovered eating disorder therapists using their experiential knowledge in therapy: A qualitative examination of the therapist's and the patients' view. *Eating Disorders*, 24(3), 207–23.

Galanter, M. (2014). Alcoholics Anonymous and twelve-step recovery: A model based on social and cognitive neuroscience. *American Journal on Addictions*, 23(3), 300–7.

Henretty, J., & Levitt, H. (2010). The role of therapist self-disclosure in psychotherapy: A qualitative review. *Clinical Psychology Review*, 30(1), 63–77.

Knox, S., Hess, S., Peterson, D., & Hill, C. (1997). A qualitative analysis of client perceptions of the effects of helpful therapist self-disclosure in long-term therapy. In C. Hill (Ed.), *Helping skills: The empirical foundation* (pp. 369–87). Washington, DC: American Psychological Association.

Krentzman, A., Cranford, J., & Robinson, R. (2013). Multiple dimensions of spirituality in recovery: A lagged meditational analysis of Alcoholics Anonymous' principal theoretical mechanism of behavior change. *Journal of Substance Abuse*, 34(1), 20–32.

LaPorte, H., Sweifach, J., & Linzer, N. (2010). Sharing the trauma: Guidelines for therapist self-disclosure following a catastrophic event. *Best Practices in Mental Health*, 6(2), 39–56.

Magura, S., Cleland, C., & Tonigan, J. (2013). Evaluating Alcoholics Anonymous' effect on drinking in Project MATCH using cross-lagged regression panel analysis. *Journal of Studies on Alcohol and Drugs, May 2013*, 378–85.

McHugh, R., Hearon, B., & Otto, M. (2010). Cognitive-behavioral therapy for substance use disorders. *Psychiatric Clinics of North America*, 33(3), 511–25.

McWilliams, N. (2004). *Psychoanalytic psychotherapy: A practitioner's guide*. New York: Guilford Press.

Pagano, M., White, W., Stout, R., & Tonigan, J. (2013). The 10-year course of Alcoholics Anonymous participation and long-term outcomes: A follow-up study of outpatient subjects in Project MATCH. *Journal of Substance Abuse*, 34(1), 51–9.

Reeh, H. (2010). The relationships between perceived therapeutic alliance, therapist self-disclosure, and dropout expectancy among male substance abuse treatment participants (Doctoral dissertation). Retrieved from ProQuest Dissertations and Theses database (UMI No. 3433371).

Sturges, J. (2012). Use of therapist self-disclosure and self-involving statements. *The Behavior Therapist*, 35(5), 90–3.

Young, L. (2013). Characteristics and practices of sponsored members of Alcoholics Anonymous. *Journal of Groups in Addiction & Recovery*, 8(2), 149–64.

CHAPTER 18

"Are You Gay?"

Apryl A. Alexander, PsyD

Members of the gay, lesbian, bisexual, transgender, and queer community (LGBTQ) community face a number of challenges related to the homophobia, discrimination, and acts of violence they encounter. LGBTQ therapists are not immune from these challenges. Although research in Chapter 10 on LGBTQ disclosure indicates that disclosures are frequently beneficial to clients, the therapist's safety concerns cannot be ignored (as also mentioned in Chapter 10 on self-disclosure ethics/therapist self-care). Per Rees-Turyn (2007), LGBTQ therapists must "negotiate an intricate balancing act between self and client welfare in an ethical manner" (p. 8).

There is some (albeit limited) research on lesbian client disclosure of same-sex orientation that speaks to the prior negotiation for balance, and can reasonably be inferred to apply both ways. Lesbian disclosure of sexuality is affirmative of her self-esteem and personhood, though is also necessarily conscious of risk and personal safety (Daley, 2012). Based on their interviews of lesbian women, Hitchcock and Skodol Wilson (1992) developed a theory that lesbians considering self-disclosure of sexuality progress through two phases of a "personal risking process" (p. 179). First, lesbian women go through a phase of anticipation in which they assess the risk for self-disclosure by anticipating, imagining what might happen, and assessing for signs of threat, acceptance, or safety. Next comes an interactional phase in which a decision is made to passively disclose, passively not disclose, actively disclose, or actively not disclose. Factors shaping the women's decision-making process are personal attributes, including relative comfort with same-sex orientation, relationship status, attitudes about health care, aspects of the client–provider relationship and context, and relevance to the treatment at hand.

Negotiating the aforementioned balance may be further difficult in light of under-emphasis of LGBTQ issues in graduate education and training (Hearn & West-Olatunji, 2015). It is therefore unsurprising that therapists-in-training consistently acknowledge feeling somewhat under-prepared to work competently with individuals from LGBTQ backgrounds (Fassinger & Richie, 1997; Phillips & Fischer, 1998). Additionally, Hearn and West-Olatunji (2015) report that LGBTQ therapists-in-training frequently experience considerable anxiety during the training process and particularly when they are selecting practicum and internship sites, which is at least partially related to insufficient attention to this community-specific issues in training.

Thus, it is important for LGBTQ therapists to consider safety, helpfulness, and training factors during their process of deciding whether or not to intentionally disclose their sexual orientation or gender identity, and to clients of either similar or different identities. This chapter will provide three case scenarios and discuss self-disclosure of sexual orientation in each context. The discussion will include potential implications of disclosing or not in each vignette.

Case Study #1: "Are You Gay?"

Antonio, a 36-year-old White gay male therapist, is having his initial session with a 21-year-old White male client who presents with depressive symptoms. During the course of the intake, the client is engaged, but appears to be cautious and withholding information. Toward the end of the session, Antonio asks the client if he has any questions about his credentials, experiences, or the therapeutic process. The client hesitantly asks, "Are you gay?"

Discussion

The previous research chapter discusses how therapists and researchers are somewhat divided, conflicted, or even reserved on how to address this question from clients. In the current scenario, Antonio must respond and in a manner that will be directly or indirectly informative about him, to his client.

Many therapeutic and training models prompt the therapist to query the client on why this would be important for them to know this information. Again, some psychoanalytic therapists adopt a 'don't ask don't tell' policy (Cole & Drescher, 2006). The focus remains on the client's process rather than their content. For instance, Bernstein (2000) warns that sexual and gender minority therapists may be placing themselves at risk professionally (e.g., loss of referrals, client termination) by discussing their sexual or gender identity during initial phone screenings with inquisitive others. Additionally, disclosure of same-sex orientation over the phone may pose legitimate threats to therapist safety, particularly if they are practicing in less progressive, more conservative, or highly religious communities. Thus, these therapists may approach self-disclosure more cautiously.

When therapists do not disclose same-sex orientation to a same-sex oriented client at the onset of treatment, and then disclose later in the treatment, it is not uncommon for the therapist to be perceived by the client as lying, deceiving, or betraying their trust (Hearn & West-Olatunji, 2015). Although disclosing sexual identity poses risk for the therapist, not disclosing their identity may also lead to a growing anxiety and even fear of the client (Hearn & West-Olatunji, 2015). In studies reviewed in Chapter 10 on sexual orientation, gay male therapists openly worried about how their decision to or not to disclose might impact a client's treatment and focus. However, in the vignette described above, we do not know the client's motives for asking this question, so we cannot properly assess the potential negative consequences of self-disclosure and expand upon its meaning beyond the research and into a more clinical realm. The client may want to reciprocate the dialogue early in treatment (Jeffrey & Tweed, 2015), which may in turn improve their engagement.

Researchers have noted another factor that has impacted the practice of disclosure: technology. With the era of social media, clients may learn or make assumptions about their therapist's sexual orientation even when the therapist did not disclose (Farber, 2014, p. 174). Therefore, facts about a therapist personal life, such as advocacy or involvement in social organizations may be known prior to the client coming into the office. There may be increased/perceived pressure for therapists to self-disclose 'today' and indeed before it may be helpful and/or before the therapist is comfortable. Clients may also ask about the therapist's sexual orientation while already/unknowingly being armed with outside information as a form of a test. Although this may present safety concerns, social media profiles mentioning sexual identity may also help clients determine qualification to treat and alleviate the therapist's anticipatory anxiety related to their impending decision on whether or not they should disclose sexual identity (Hearn & West-Olatunji, 2015).

Case Study #2: Gay Male Client

A gay 38-year-old male therapist, Eric, has a new 31-year-old gay male client, Marc, who recently began treatment for romantic relationship problems. Marc has also been discussing discrimination he's faced in both his work and personal life. He struggles with coworkers using offensive language in meetings. Marc is having trouble finding a LGBTQ community in the small, rural town in which he lives, which would otherwise provide him with affirmation and encourage resilience. Eric does not openly advertise his sexual orientation, so it is reasonable to assume that Marc does not know it. Marc's gendered language in sessions suggests he assumes his therapist, Eric, is heterosexual.

Discussion

Much of the literature on self-disclosure of sexual orientation by therapists supports disclosures to sexual minority clients, and will be applied to the prior case study. Sexual minority clients often seek therapists who self-identify as a sexual minority due to the presumption of safety, trust, and a more relatable/understanding/therapeutic environment (Haldeman, 2010; Kronner, 2005). For these reasons, studies of gay male clients offer a recommendation for gay male therapists to self-disclose *at the onset* of treatment (Satterly, 2006), as a form of establishing qualification to treat. In a study of heterosexual undergraduate students, 129 of whom were female and 55 of whom were male, therapists who disclosed same-sex orientation were viewed by student observers as more trustworthy and, surprisingly, as more of an expert, as compared to therapists who did not disclose (Carroll, Gauler, Relph, & Hutchinson, 2011). This finding on differential views of expertness conflicts with research reviewed in Chapter 4 on disclosure research efficacy and outcomes, whereby therapists often worry that disclosure may lower the client's impression of expertness (Henretty & Levitt, 2010). As a broader form of advocacy, several researchers remark on the importance of self-disclosure of sexual orientation to sexual minority clients given the relative lack of openly LGBTQ professionals and role models in society, and particularly in less affirming sections of society (Brown & Walker, 1990; Kooden, 1991; Kronner, 2005; Perlman, 1991).

Is there potential for negative consequences not self-disclosing at this point in treatment? Perhaps. Farber (2014, p. 173) suggested that the implications of non-disclosure of personal sexual orientation may be profound for gay or lesbian patients. In the prior case example, if Marc were to find out later that Eric was also gay, and did not volunteer this information initially, would he be upset? Feel abandoned? Particularly, given the concerns Mark has expressed in previous sessions? However, it would also still be possible for Eric to provide Marc with the resources he needs, as a lower intimacy form of disclosing knowledge. In this case, needs for community and connection could be addressed without self-disclosure and while maintaining professional restraint, so that Eric could better understand any deeper potential implications and motives behind Marc's inquiry.

Case Study #3: Homophobic Statements

A 30-year-old Caucasian gay male therapist is conducting an assessment on a 15-year-old African American boy in order to make treatment suggestions for the child's behavioral problems at home and school. The boy has been diagnosed with Oppositional Defiant Disorder on the basis of a history of illegal behavior (e.g., interpersonal violence). Rapport between the client and therapist was established relatively easily during the initial interview. However, the boy boastfully and frequently expressed hyper-masculine attitudes. He spewed several misogynistic, victim-blaming, homophobic, and hostile verbiages (not directly targeting the therapist) throughout the assessment process. From his behavior it is inferred that the adolescent male likely assumes that the therapist is also heterosexual.

Discussion

One might read this scenario and question whether self-disclosure is needed. As a clinical supervisor, the current author has witnessed such a scenario several times with trainees. Trainees (both gay/lesbian and heterosexual) usually remain silent and avoid—neither validating nor negating the client's remarks. However, in supervision, it is common to process such experiences in the aftermath with trainees. Many gay and lesbian trainees remark on their ability to 'pass' as heterosexual and describe feelings of sadness, frustration, anger, and/or passive understanding of homophobic statements such as those made by the youth in the prior case example as an example of youthful immaturity. These experiences are consistent with Hearn and West-Olatunji's (2015) concern that more graduate training focus and individual mentoring on LGBTQ issues is particularly necessary to help LGBTQ students work through prejudicial/discriminatory experiences in ways that contribute to the consolidation, growth, and resilience of their personal and professional identities (Hearn & West-Olatunji, 2015). The ultimate question is: When should a therapist comment on these remarks and/or self-disclose? In such cases, what is the extent and indeed motivation behind the decision to or not to disclose?

As an assessor, the therapist may not think it is necessary to engage in a more *in vivo* dialogue at this earlier juncture. In conducting his or her initial clinical assessment, the therapist is to remain objective and gather information. Thus, the boy's comments are data about his earlier life, worldview, and perhaps needs from treatment.

Does age of the client matter in this scenario? Probably. Self-disclosure could serve as a 'teachable moment' by having the boy reflect on his comments, identify how those comments might affect others (especially a person he has built rapport with), and better address his perceptions of gay males as an indication of a discriminatory attitude he too may have endured. It must be acknowledged that adolescents are navigating their own sense of identity development and may be receptive to caring and patient adults helping them progress in a socially appropriate and validating way. To this end, it should be remembered that adolescent males often face considerable family and peer/social pressure to adopt popularized and discriminatory attitudes and behaviors that they may in turn verbalize to a far greater degree than they truly believe.

Cultural and Gender Minority Considerations

Much of the literature on self-disclosure of sexual orientation centers on gay males. Lesbian, bisexual, non-binary individuals, and those of various gender identities (e.g., transgender) face both similar and unique challenges. For instance, if a therapist is transitioning (or affirming) genders during treatment, self-disclosure may be visible/inevitable and also more impactful on the therapeutic process. Further, there has been a lack of self-disclosure research concerning intersectionality (as noted in Crenshaw [1989] and Cole [2009]) and multiple minority statuses (e.g., LGBTQ Latino therapist). Thus, more qualitative and quantitative research is clearly needed in order to represent the range of narratives and experiences. The Cass (1979) model of LGBTQ identity development (as summarized in Walz, Bleuer, & Yep [2015]) conceptualizes the most mature stage as integrating sexual identity into other identities, rather than being distinct or paramount.

From a personal vantage point, the current author would like to acknowledge experiences and differences as a Black, heterosexual, cisgender woman. The author wants to acknowledge there may be critical lapses in her assessment of this clinical challenge. Although the author's Blackness and gender have been addressed in sessions, the author has never directly revealed heterosexual identity. Visible differences (i.e., some disabilities) between client and therapist (i.e., race, ethnicity, gender, disability) are more commonly discussed in the literature and clinical training; however, this chapter and the larger text offer discussion of how to navigate self-disclosure of the more invisible differences. In several of the case scenarios above, there are other demographic differences between therapist and client, including age/generational differences and race/ethnicity. Thus, additional client–therapist dynamics aside from sexual orientation may impact the therapeutic environment and need to be addressed—providing a more intersectional approach to decision-making of self-disclosure.

Conclusions

The aim of the chapter was to address the pros and cons of self-disclosing sexual orientation with clients. Research has mostly focused on self-disclosure of gay male sexual orientation, yields largely positive findings, but does not discount reservations to the contrary. While some gay and lesbian therapists value transparency and authenticity, others may understandably be concerned about personal safety and thereby refrain from disclosure in a manner consistent with prior ethical chapter discussions of self-care and indeed self-preservation. The current chapter begins the dialogue necessary to assist therapists and trainees to navigate their decision-making process regarding self-disclosure opportunities, particularly, in novel situations.

References

Bernstein, A. (2000). Straight counselors working with lesbians and gays in family therapy. *Journal of Marital and Family Therapy*, *26*(4), 443–54.

Brown, L., & Walker, L. (1990). Feminist therapy perspectives on self-disclosure. In G. Stricker & G. Fisher (Eds.), *Self-disclosure in the therapeutic relationship* (pp. 135–54). New York: Plenum Press.

Carroll, L., Gauler, A., Relph, J., & Hutchinson, K. (2011). Counselor self-disclosure: Does sexual orientation matter to straight clients? *International Journal for the Advancement of Counselling*, *33*(2), 139–48.

Cass, V. (1979). Homosexual identity formation: A theoretical model. *Journal of Homosexuality*, *4*, 219–235.

Cole, E. (2009). Intersectionality and research in psychology. *American Psychologist*, *64*(3), 170–80.

Cole, G., & Drescher, J. (2006). Do tell: Queer perspectives on therapist self-disclosure introduction. *Journal of Gay and Lesbian Psychotherapy*, *10*(1), 1–6.

Crenshaw, K. (1989). Demarginalizing the intersection of race and sex: A black feminist critique of antidiscrimination doctrine, feminist theory, and antiracist politics. *University of Chicago Legal Forum*, *1*(8), 139–67.

Daley, A. (2012). Becoming seen, becoming known: Lesbian women's self-disclosures of sexual orientation to mental health service providers. *Journal of Gay and Lesbian Mental Health*, *16*(3), 215–34.

Farber, B. (2014). *Self-disclosure in psychotherapy*. New York: Guilford Press.

Fassinger, R., & Richie, B. (1997). Sex matters: Gender and sexual orientation in training for multicultural counseling competency. In D. Pope-Davis & H. Coleman (Eds.), *Multicultural counseling competencies: Assessment, education and training, and supervision* (pp. 83–110). Thousand Oaks, CA: Sage.

Haldeman, D. (2010). Reflections of a gay male psychotherapist. *Psychotherapy Theory, Research, Practice, Training, 47*(2), 177–85.

Hearn, B., & West-Olatunji, C. (2015). Deciding to disclose: The LGBTQ counselor's unique challenge. *VISTAS Online, 74*, 1–8.

Henretty, J., & Levitt, H. (2010). The role of therapist self-disclosure in psychotherapy: A qualitative review. *Clinical Psychology Review, 30*(1), 63–77.

Hitchcock, J., & Skodol Wilson, H. (1992). Personal risking: Lesbian self-disclosure of sexual orientation to professional health care providers. *Nursing Research, 41*(3), 178–183.

Jeffrey, M., & Tweed, A. (2015). Clinician self-disclosure or clinician self-concealment? Lesbian, gay, and bisexual mental health practitioners' experiences of disclosure in therapeutic relationships. *Counselling and Psychotherapy Research, 15*(1), 41–49.

Kooden, H. (1991). Self-disclosure: The gay male counselor as agent of social change. In C. Silverstein (Ed.), *Gays, lesbians, and their counselors: Studies in psychotherapy* (pp. 143–54). New York: W. W. Norton & Co.

Kronner, H. (2005). The importance of counselor self-disclosure in the therapeutic relationship as perceived by gay male patients in treatment with gay male counselors: A mixed methods approach (Doctoral dissertation). Retrieved from ProQuest Dissertations and Theses database (UMI No. 3174247).

Perlman, G. (1991). The question of counselor self-disclosure in the treatment of a married gay man. In C. Silverstein (Ed.), *Gays, lesbians, and their counselors: Studies in psychotherapy* (pp. 201–9). New York: W. W. Norton & Co.

Phillips, J., & Fischer, A. (1998). Graduate students' training experiences with lesbian, gay, and bisexual issues. *The Counseling Psychologist, 26*, 712–34.

Rees-Turyn, A. (2007). Coming out and being out as activism: Challenges and opportunities for mental health professionals in red and blue states. *Journal of Gay and Lesbian Psychotherapy, 11*(3–4), 155–72.

Satterly, B. (2006). Counselor self-disclosure from a gay male perspective. *Families in Society, 87*(2), 240–7.

Walz, G. R., Bleuer, S. C., & Yep, R. K. (2015). *Compelling counseling images: The best of VISTAS 2009*. Alexandria, VA: American Counseling Association.

CHAPTER 19

"You Don't Know What I'm Talking About"

Barry A. Farber, PhD and Devlin Jackson, MA

What is a therapist to do when a client accuses him or her of ignorance of something (assumedly important to the client) that the client is talking about? How should the therapist respond? To what extent should he or she self-disclose, i.e., acknowledge (or dispute) the validity of the client's accusation? The authors address these questions from the dual vantage points of therapists and researchers interested in the issue of self-disclosures to clients.

The authors' initial clinical inclination, born of a primarily psychodynamic-relational perspective, would be to respond with something on the order of, "I'm sorry it seems that way to you, are you willing to fill me in, help me understand?" Or, because this response includes a phrase ("it seems that way to you") that could feel invalidating to the client—that is, it could imply a questioning of the client's judgment or perception—we could also envision a response like, "You're right, I don't understand a good deal of what you're trying to tell me, can you help me with this?" Or perhaps, this same phrase without the second half, a response that would allow the client to stay with the feeling of being misunderstood rather than being implicitly asked to let go of the feeling and proceed with a narrative more tailored to the therapist's worldview. Or another possibility, a response that speaks even more directly to the client's sense of not being understood: "OK, let's talk more about that, about what's going on here between us. What's your sense of what's happening?" Or, finally, a response that combines an empathic awareness of the client's feelings and the therapist's acknowledgment of his or her role in this event: "That must be so frustrating for you, I'm sorry that I'm missing so much of what's important to you."

In considering which of the above responses may be appropriate in any given scenario, the authors' immediate thought was, "it depends." In fact, a good clinical response here (and in virtually every other clinical situation) is dependent on so many client, therapist, and treatment factors discussed in the first two major sections of this text. Among the details/considerations the authors would want to know in order to respond in the most clinically sensitive manner are the following:

1 **Demographics** of both client and therapist, including age, gender, ethnicity, nationality, religion, SES (while growing up and currently), relationship status, immigration status (if relevant), level of education, and sexual orientation. How different—at least on these basic variables—are these two individuals? Importantly, too: To what extent have these putative differences been acknowledged and discussed?

2 **Nature of therapy**: What is the theoretical orientation of this therapy? Is this a short-term or long-term model? And relatedly, what are the client's treatment goals at this time? Problem solving? Symptom reduction? Self-awareness?

3 **Previous treatment(s)**: Has the client been in therapy previously? When? For how long? With whom? For the same or different issues?

4 **Diagnosis**: What are the current working diagnoses and level of character organization for this client? And what are his or her predominant defense mechanisms?

5 **Social support system**: With whom is this client close and supported by? With whom, if anyone, does he or she disclose experiences fully and in turn feel understood?

6 **Context (treatment)**: At what point in the treatment was the comment "You don't know what I'm talking about" made? During the first session? Early in treatment? After six months or longer? Was this the first time this subject was broached? The tenth time? If spoken about before, what was the tone of the conversation previously? Did the client make similar remarks at earlier points in the therapy? That is, was this client's 'accusation' the first of its kind? Or does it fall into a pattern wherein the client has been repeatedly suggesting that the therapist is incapable of understanding the problems or experiences presented in treatment? If this subject was discussed at a previous point in treatment, how did the therapist react then—with questions? Comments? Requests for clarification? Acknowledgment of not fully understanding? Acknowledgment of difficulty stemming from the fact that they come from different backgrounds or have different cultural worldviews or living situations? And at what point during this particular session was this client's comment made? Was it as the session began, as the session was ending (doorknob comment), or some time in-between? And for how long did the client speak about this subject in this session before he or she reported this sense that the therapist was not capable of understanding what he or she was discussing? And what were they discussing, and with what tone, right before this subject came up? And what was the previous session like, and how did it end?

7 **The client's tone of voice**: with what affect was this client's statement of being misunderstood, or rather not capable of being understood by his or her therapist, conveyed? Was he or she angry? Frustrated? Bemused? Disappointed? Resolute? Sad? Frightened? Ashamed? Although the words might have sounded angry, this needs to be confirmed. In this

regard, too: Imagine how different the phrase used—"You don't know what I'm talking about"—would feel if the client rephrased it slightly to, "I'm not sure you know what I'm talking about." What emotions did the actual words spoken seem to reflect?

8   **Context (life outside treatment):** What was going on for this client at that time outside of treatment? Was he or she feeling misunderstood, alone, or badly treated outside of therapy? Was there a crisis in his or her life?

9   **The therapeutic relationship:** What is the general and current state of the therapeutic alliance—in terms of the bond, agreement on goals, and agreement on tasks? Have there been any noticeable ruptures in the alliance? If so, how were they negotiated? Have there been any boundary violations (e.g., in terms of fees, scheduling, lateness to or cancellation of sessions)? And what was the nature of the feelings each seemed to have toward each other, i.e., from a psychodynamic perspective, what were the transference and countertransference patterns?

10   **Importance of this topic to this client:** Why was he or she discussing this issue at that particular time? With what level of urgency?

Only after understanding more fully the nature of the client, the therapist, their relationship, and multiple treatment factors could the authors craft a response more likely to reflect the clinical exigencies of that moment. And even then, the authors' status as outside observers of this moment can, at best, only approximate the experience of the actual therapist hearing this statement, at that particular moment, and at that particular junction in that particular therapy. A term that reflects a good deal of what the authors are arguing here is that of 'responsiveness' (Stiles, Honos-Webb, & Surko, 1998), which can be defined as

> behavior that is affected by emerging context, including emerging perceptions of others' characteristics and behavior. Insofar as therapist and client respond to each other, responsiveness implies a dynamic relationship between variables, involving bidirectional causation and feedback loops . . . in psychotherapy, responsiveness may include . . . the timing and phrasing of interventions based on client's level of understanding and emotional state.
>
> (Stiles et al., 1998, p. 439)

The authors don't know the basic contextual details of this client's statement and thus crafting a definitive, responsive reply is unachievable. What the authors can say, though, is that prior the research on types of therapist disclosure (see Chapter 6), while far from definitive, can offer some useful direction. To review, statements that reflect a therapist's own feelings about what is transpiring clinically in the moment in the relationship, and statements that include both an empathic and positively regarding flavor, have the greatest potential for making clients feel less personally vulnerable, strengthening the therapeutic bond, modeling new ways of thinking and acting, and generally furthering clinical work (Farber, 2006; Hill & Knox, 2002). Importantly, too,

Lane, Farber, and Geller (2001) found that among the most frequent therapist disclosures was acknowledgment of a clinical mistake, an admission likely to make the client feel respected by and closer to the therapist.

Application to Practice

How might we translate these findings into a clinically sensitive and helpful response to this client's sense that the therapist just doesn't get what he or she is talking about? If we incorporate elements of self-involvement (including the acknowledgment of a mistake or instance of insensitivity), reassurance, and empathy—and if we avoid challenges (in this case, therapist excuses or defensiveness or alternative, client-based reasons for this perceived lack of therapist understanding)—we might wind up with a statement along these lines:

> Yes, it's clear that I don't fully understand what you're saying and I feel badly about that and imagine how frustrating that must be to you. But I do appreciate our work together and hope we can find a way for me to be more helpful and for us to do our work more effectively.

That may be a few too many words and it may also be a bit too 'relational' or Rogerian for some, but this statement is intended to help clients to feel understood and respected and also lets them know that their therapist is still committed to them and to their work.

It's possible too that the therapist (let's assume a man, for the moment) has made a mistake in this case, perhaps one of omission, i.e., not noting earlier in the client's narrative that he does not understand some or even much of what she (let's assume a female client) is telling him and would like her to please clarify or provide more details so that he might better grasp what she is trying explain. Similarly, he might have failed to note a burgeoning sense of frustration on her part and preemptively asked about that—"I'm wondering," he might have said, "whether it's difficult or frustrating to you to have to explain this to me so carefully when others might understand what you're talking about so much more easily." And if the authors are right in this presumption, then the therapist might have added a clause to the words we suggested in the previous paragraph, something to the effect of, "I'm sorry for not asking you about this earlier, about whether explaining this to me was hard for you." Or, in a related vein, "I'm sorry for not letting you know earlier that I was struggling to understand what you were trying to explain to me." Or, from a more relational perspective, "Though I can't help being who I am, I'm still sorry that I can't understand this more easily."

These kinds of immediacy disclosures are also reminiscent of the kind of intervention called for when therapists become aware of an impending or ongoing alliance rupture (see Chapter 5 on therapeutic timing). That is, to the extent that this client's statement to the therapist—"You don't know what I'm talking about"—comes quite close to fitting the criteria for a therapeutic rupture, a therapist's immediacy response becomes even more appropriate and necessary.

As Safran and Muran (1996, 2000) have pointed out, strong negative affect (e.g., anger, resentment, or dissatisfaction) directed at the therapist is typically indicative of a therapeutic rupture—that is, of a deterioration in the relationship. They suggest, in this situation, the therapist's responses should acknowledge (a) the client's experience in the here-and-now, (b) the possibility of a rift in the relationship, (c) the therapist's role in this situation, and (d) the need to discuss feelings in the here-and-now and the relationship in general. They warn against therapist defensiveness, suggesting that such responses could only exacerbate the situation: "Ruptures often emerge when therapists unwittingly participate in maladaptive interpersonal cycles that resembles those characteristic of patient's other interactions, thus confirming their patient's dysfunctional . . . representations of self-other interactions" (Safran & Muran, 1996, p. 447). An example they use is that of the therapist who responds to a client's hostility with his or her own hostility, in essence confirming the client's sense of a mutually hostile interpersonal world. Thus, in the case of the misunderstood or non-understood client discussed in this chapter, one task of the therapist would be to avoid being drawn into a dialogue rife with dueling accusations, one that could start with the therapist's use of the word 'but' and proceeding to suggest that the client has not done a particularly good job of making him or herself understandable.

Theoretical Considerations

To return to an earlier point: the nature of a therapist's response to this client will be determined by many factors, including the primary theoretical orientation of the clinician. Although the authors believe that the basics of an appropriate response—empathy, acknowledgment of the therapist's part in this situation, and openness to discussing the relationship—are well outlined by researchers in the areas of therapist disclosure and alliance ruptures, the way that these elements are emphasized and expressed is likely to vary considerably across theoretical perspectives. The authors offer some examples below, though it's important to keep in mind that (a) there are significant 'within-cell' variations among therapists within the same orientation, (b) many therapists are eclectic or integrative in their therapeutic approach, and (c) these examples do not include the possibility of significant age, racial, religious, cultural, gender, or sexual orientation differences between therapist and client, any or all of which would almost certainly affect these responses. Although these hypothetical responses may seem stereotyped, the authors believe they embody the basic stance that therapists within these categories would convey to a client who says, "You don't know what I'm talking about."

Client:	You don't know what I'm talking about.
CBT therapist:	That may be, but what parts in particular do you feel I don't understand? . . . Can we look at the evidence for that—for my not knowing what you're talking about?

Client:	You don't know what I'm talking about.
Client-centered therapist:	You seem frustrated that I seem unable to get you're talking about. I want you to know though that I do want to understand what you're trying to tell me.
Client:	You don't know what I'm talking about.
Experiential (EFT) therapist:	OK, that's a strong feeling you have. Can you make that even stronger? Really get into that feeling?
Client:	You don't know what I'm talking about.
Interpersonal (IPT) therapist:	Has anyone been able to understand this? I'm wondering what kind of support you have in your life, who's close to you, who really does get what you're trying to tell me.
Client:	You don't know what I'm talking about.
Contemporary relational psychodynamic therapist:	What just happened here? I clearly haven't given you what you need here—let's figure this out.
Client:	You don't know what I'm talking about.
Rational-emotive behavior (REBT) therapist:	OK, but no one can understand everything all the time. Why don't you take some responsibility and try harder to let me know more about what you're talking about?
Client:	You don't know what I'm talking about.
Dialectical behavior (DBT) therapist:	Can we replay what just happened? It's true I didn't understand, but it also feels to me that you overreacted. Rather than asking whether I followed what you were saying, or rather than seeing me puzzled and trying again in a somewhat different way to help me understand, you became angry. It's a pattern that gets you in trouble.

Other Dyadic Considerations

The authors just speculated as to how responses to this client's statement might vary as a function of the therapist's theoretical orientation. Among the many other factors that could affect a therapist's response in this situation, one deserves particular attention: the 'match' between therapist and client on significant demographic variables including age, gender, race, SES, and sexual orientation. Depending on how many categories one assigns to each of these five variables, there are well over 100,000 combinations to be potentially reckoned with—and that without entering the therapist's theoretical orientation, the client's diagnosis, the strength of the therapeutic alliance, or the length of current treatment. But let's imagine at least a few combinations—in the context of a few specific therapeutic topics—that might encourage re-thinking or revising previously hypothesized responses:

1 A 20-something single, African American female client is describing her experience growing up in an inner city in a racially segregated high school to her white, middle-aged male therapist.

2 A 20-something single, African American female client is describing her experience growing up in an inner city in a racially segregated high school to her 30-something African American female therapist.

3 An 18-year-old white female client who self-identifies as gender fluid is describing her sexual experiences to her white, 70-something, seemingly married (wearing a wedding ring) male therapist.

4 An 18-year-old white female client who self-identifies as gender fluid is describing her sexual experiences to her white, 30-something, female therapist whose relational status is unknown (to the client).

5 A 50-something Hispanic man is describing his legal problems regarding his immigration status to his 24-year-old white, female therapist.

6 A 50-something Hispanic man is describing his legal problems regarding his immigration status to his 50-something Hispanic male therapist.

How, then, might we imagine the therapist in one of these cases responding to the client's charge that he or she does not understand, attempting a response that reflects the particular dynamics or demographics of this case? In the first case noted above, the therapist could ask the client what has prompted her to say that. She may express her assumption that he has not encountered any of the experiences she is describing to him, thus she believes he cannot fully understand what she has been through. Here, an opportunity arises for the two to discuss in what ways their differences have affected the therapy to date and how they might proceed in the future when their differences once again become salient. The therapist might suggest that his understanding of the client's experiences arises through what she shares with him—what it was like for her, what she has taken with her from those experiences, and what she feels when she discusses it now. The therapist might also offer an affirming prompt of sorts: that even if he has not experienced firsthand what she is describing, her courage in sharing her experiences helps him understand what it was like for her.

Contained in each of these scenarios is another potentially significant variable: whether or not the therapist actually has knowledge of this situation despite the client's insistence otherwise. While there are undoubtedly therapists whose adherence to a strict theoretical orientation, say classical psychoanalysis, would mandate their assuming an unvarying clinical stance regardless of circumstances, the authors imagine that most therapists would alter their response in each of these situations and, moreover, that most supervisors (including peer supervisors) would modify their suggestions to supervisees as clinical context changes—and here, clinical context includes the possibility that the therapist has knowledge, albeit unspoken to this point, of this particular aspect of the client's life. Should gay therapists let clients know of their sexual orientation when the client begins to speak about his or her sexual orientation, while 'accusing' the therapist of ignorance of this? Should a therapist who was sexually abused as a child acknowledge this when his or her client speaks of that experience and claims that the therapist knows nothing of this experience? Should a therapist with a history of depression let the client disclose this information when the client insists that the therapist knows nothing about the sadness or suicidal feelings he or she is currently experiencing? In regard to this last example: in fact, Carl Rogers (1967) once disclosed to a quite depressed, nearly silent client that he himself had once "been there"—although Rogers offered this information spontaneously, not in response to his client's statement that Rogers was incapable of understanding depression.

Conclusions

While the literature on therapist disclosure continues to grow and expand awareness that such responses clearly have a place in virtually every therapist's repertoire, there are clear limits to our being able to specify with any degree of confidence what words spoken by what kind of therapist with what kind of client under what circumstances with what tone and with what degree of culpability such responses should take. The authors believe this client's statement—"You don't know what I'm talking about"— clearly deserves recognition. The authors also believe that it most likely demands empathy and inquiry as well. And it may also require some degree of therapist acknowledgment of culpability in terms of not being able to understand or of not listening well enough to have understood. But even with more and better research into the area of therapist disclosure, no therapist is likely to know exactly what the best response is to most client needs.

References

Farber, B. (2006). *Self-disclosure in psychotherapy*. New York: Guilford Press.

Hill, C., & Knox, S. (2002). Self-disclosure. In J. Norcross (Ed.), *Psychotherapy relationships that work: Therapist contributions and responsiveness to patients* (pp. 255–65). New York: Oxford University Press.

Lane, J., Farber, B., & Geller, J. (2001, June). What therapists do and don't disclose to their patients. Paper presented at the annual conference, Society for Psychotherapy Research, Montevideo, Uruguay.

Rogers, C. (1967). A silent young man. In C. Rogers, C. Gendlin, D. Kiesler, & C. Truax (Eds.), *The therapeutic relationship with schizophrenics* (pp. 184–256). Madison, WI: University of Wisconsin Press.

Safran, J., & Muran, J. (1996). The resolution of ruptures in the therapeutic alliance. *Journal of Consulting and Clinical Psychology, 64*(3), 447–58.

Safran, J., & Muran, J. (2000). *Negotiating the therapeutic alliance: A relational treatment guide*. New York: Guilford Press.

Stiles, W., Honos-Webb, L., & Surko, M. (1998). Responsiveness in psychotherapy. *Clinical Psychology: Science and Practice, 5*(4), 439–58.

Part V
Clinical Challenges

CHAPTER 20

Chronically Traumatized Clients

Tyson D. Bailey, PsyD

Traumatized clients entering therapy can be expected to have vastly different experiences/reactions to the use of self-disclosure depending on myriad factors, including the nature of the event(s), chronicity and complexity of symptoms, level of betrayal (e.g., Freyd, 1996), and how many different types of trauma have been experienced (Briere, Dietrich, & Semple, 2016; Briere, Kaltman, & Greene, 2008). Terr (1991) discussed the difference between Type I (single incident) and Type II (repetitive/complex/attachment-based); while both have the potential to create distress, Type II traumas tend to have a cumulative impact on overall functioning and significantly increase symptom complexity (Briere et al., 2016; Briere et al., 2008; Courtois & Ford, 2013; Terr, 1991). While self-disclosure may be helpful in both types, many argue that certain forms of self-disclosure become a *necessary* part of treatment when working with individuals who have experienced repeated harm (e.g., Courtois & Ford, 2013; Dalenberg, 2000; Herman, 1997; Terr, 1991).

Self-Disclosure as a Weapon

Much like in therapy in general, moments of self-disclosure in a family context are supposed to foster a deeper sense of connection. However, for those who have experienced chronic attachment disruptions or other repeated trauma, self-disclosure in families is often used as a method of control or other tactic for perpetuating abuse (Herman, 1997; Liotti, 1992; Lyons-Ruth, 2008). For instance, many of the clients this author has worked with have only experienced moments of self-disclosure within their personal/family relationships, either prior, during, or most after an experience of physical, sexual, or emotional abuse. Given the confusion experienced by clients in these moments, inter-familial disclosure may momentarily increase the sense of connection (e.g., Schore, 2009), yet also signal danger was on the horizon.

Therapists working with chronically traumatized populations must be acutely aware of the conflicting emotions that often arise within clients and may be re-enacted in and outside of therapy. Further, it is critical to validate all aspects of clients' experience of the self-disclosure in a nonjudgmental manner (Courtois & Ford, 2013; Dalenberg, 2000; Herman, 1997). The literature suggests that experiencing nonjudgmental self-disclosure from a person in an authority position who maintains appropriate boundaries is critical in healing from attachment-based traumatic experiences (Courtois & Ford, 2013; Dalenberg, 2000; Herman, 1997; Pearlman & Saakvitne, 1995). So doing can also have a corrective and balancing effect. Moreover, it may be a necessary precursor to the cognitive component of trauma therapy and also builds the necessary relationship foundation that has been discussed in prior chapters as highly predictive of self-disclosure impacts and efficacy.

Kinsler, Courtois, and Frankel (2009) noted that, "Victimized children are hurt in relationships," yet, paradoxically, "Relationships can be the core component of healing from these injuries" (p. 183). Pearlman and Saakvitne (1995) noted attachment trauma survivors often *need* a clinician who is willing to be genuine (including using self-disclosure). However, survivors are also sensitive and at times vigilant to potential boundary crossings and violations.

Therefore, a therapist's choice to utilize self-disclosure with complex trauma survivors poses an interesting conundrum: how does one utilize genuine, thoughtful self-disclosure to form a safe therapeutic relationship, which is considered one of the most important factors in successful treatment (Ellis, Simiola, Brown, Courtois, & Cook, 2017; Kinsler et al., 2009; Norcross & Wampold, 2011), when the client's entire history and bodily system suggests 'human relationships equal danger?' The following discussion will build upon the prior chapter summarizing research on self-disclosure in contexts of trauma and apply it more directly and thoroughly to real-world practice considerations.

What Information Is Most Beneficial to Disclose?

Consistent with prior research on self-disclosure types and efficacy, chronically traumatized clients do not generally consider therapist personal information as important as the therapist's emotional reactions (particularly anger) or other here-and-now experiences in therapy (Dalenberg, 2000). It is critical to remember that individuals who have experienced repeated trauma throughout childhood often develop a keen eye for reading the body language of others, which develops as a method for attempting to maintain safety (Courtois & Ford, 2013; Herman, 1997). For example, many clients who report a history of being subjected to physical violence will discuss how certain facial expressions or other somatic cues would suggest the perpetrator was likely to engage in abusive behavior.

As also discussed in Chapter 6 on the different types of self-disclosure, body language can be a particularly impactful form of unavoidable self-disclosure within the context of therapy with traumatized populations (e.g., Russell, 2006). Because survivors are more likely to notice subtle changes or possibly interpret an ambiguous/benign therapist behavior as indicative of danger, it is critical for therapists to monitor and reflect upon their visceral reactions *as an unintentional self-disclosure* and consider how they may impact the therapeutic relationship (Dalenberg, 2000; Herman, 1997; Pearlman & Saakvitne, 1995). Dalenberg (2000) purports that therapist reactions can pose significant danger to the therapeutic process, as traumatized clients frequently spend more time wondering about the therapist's reactions than focusing on their own personal change process. In addition to decisions about self-disclosure, monitoring personal reactions is imperative for reducing the likelihood of developing vicarious trauma, which can lead to inappropriate or damaging use of counter-transferential self-disclosure within session (Pearlman & Saakvitne, 1995).

The Need for Therapists to Own and Use Countertransference

Traditionally, therapists were encouraged to be a 'blank screen,' though individuals who have experienced attachment-based trauma often report difficulties forming and maintaining a connection with a therapist who they do not experience as genuine (Courtois & Ford, 2013; Ellis et al., 2017; Pearlman & Saakvitne, 1995). Dalenberg (2000) defined "traumatic countertransference" (p. 11) as including attachment behaviors within the therapy room (demonstrated by both therapist and client), therapist's emotional reactions, interventions applied that increase emotions for either person in the therapeutic dyad, and the process for repairing ruptures or other difficult moments in trauma therapy. Given the difficulties chronically traumatized clients have with self-perception, interpreting relational behavior, and meaning-making, Dalenberg (2000) argues that therapists disclosing information that arises from traumatic countertransference is indeed an integral part of the healing process, a position that was supported consistently in research reviewed in previous chapters on self-disclosure in contexts of shared environmental traumas. This discussion also builds on prior chapter discussions of how traditional therapeutic boundaries and neutrality were neither developed nor advanced with contexts of trauma in mind.

Clients harmed through attachment relationships often have significant difficulties understanding and evaluating their personal experiences, which are often shaped by explicit or implicit messages from their perpetrator(s) (e.g., "you're bad," "your experiences are wrong," "good children don't act that way") (Courtois & Ford, 2013; Dalenberg, 2000; Pearlman & Saakvitne, 1995). Dalenberg (2000) noted that self-disclosure can help establish and reinforce clients' reality testing abilities, increase self-trust and confidence in their personal experiences, and help them to learn it is acceptable to have a differing opinion or experience from others.

Further, and as discussed in research on self-disclosure in cognitive behavioral therapies, self-disclosure can serve as a model for effectively interacting with and communicating about emotional experiences. Whereas neutralist models of therapy may discuss self-disclosure as crossing boundaries and promoting fusion, contemporary trauma perspectives discuss disclosure as advancing individuation, differentiation, self-determination, and adulthood.

An Evolutionary Perspective

From an evolutionary perspective (e.g., LeDoux, 1998; Schore, 1994), emotions continue to be present in our lives because they serve an adaptive function. While we may want to increase happiness and decrease shame, it is critical for us to determine whether, in fact, the emotion and intensity we are experiencing is consistent with the context at hand (e.g., Linehan, 2015). Clients who have experienced chronic traumatization frequently experience intense fear in regard to emotional expression, whether it is from someone else or themselves.

Therefore, utilization of self-disclosure can serve a dual function in regard to emotional growth and maturity when working with trauma survivors: (1) it provides a model for them to express emotions in a manner designed to maintain and increase connection, and (2) it can help clients strengthen their abilities to be present with and work through personal emotions (Dalenberg, 2000). Interestingly, many trauma survivors are also not used to people (i.e., self-disclosing therapists) expressing positive emotions (e.g., excitement, pride); therefore, it is critical not to make the assumption that disclosures of excitement or other positive experiences, in contexts of attachment trauma, are inherently less problematic than those emotions we label as negative (see Chapter 6 on types of therapist self-disclosure for general background on this point).

As an example of how this point can work in practice this author shared how proud he was with a particular female client's recent increase in mindful analysis, a form of positive reinforcement that she had previously only talked about experiencing in contexts of abuse. This utilization of self-disclosure resulted in a palpable fear response in the moment. Although this author had been working with the client for more than a year, and was aware of her history of severe attachment trauma (including daily physical, sexual, and emotional abuse by parents), her reaction caught the author completely off guard. When the author discussed with his supervisor the confusion he experienced, and the certainty with which he was not going to share positive emotions again, his supervisor gave a knowing smile and encouraged him to push forward.

Returning to the therapeutic room, the ensuing conversation about the disclosure was uncomfortable for both client and therapist, though the end result was the client experiencing self-disclosure as a profound method of connection. This interaction highlights the potential benefits of self-disclosure as a pathway to *in vivo* work, was referred to many times within future sessions of the therapy with the client in this example, and helped foster a connection that became "both context and container for interpersonal experimentation and learning" (Kinsler et al., 2009, p. 187). The prior case provides an example in practice of Dalenberg's (2000) discussion of the benefits of utilizing disclosure of traumatic countertransference experiences in trauma therapy, providing clients with the skills necessary to regulate their emotions in response to disclosure, disclosure not solely associated with a therapist's urge to discuss personal emotions, and with appropriate timing relative to the context at hand (e.g., appropriate time in session, proximity to experience).

Inter- and Intrapersonal Evaluation

As a trauma-informed feminist therapist, self-disclosure is a tool this author utilizes regularly with his clients. Although he is generally open with his clients, particularly about emotions that arise in session, self-disclosure is an intervention he mindfully evaluates every time. To this end, he has open discussions with clients about how his behavior affects them in attempt to reduce the likelihood of a moment of self-disclosure becoming a boundary violation. Although clinical and research evidence suggests that therapist disclosure is likely necessary in complex posttraumatic presentations (e.g., Courtois & Ford, 2013; Dalenberg, 2000; Herman, 1997), it is imperative clinicians do not make assumptions about what is helpful for the client nor assume that any intervention necessarily had the desired effect. Therefore, just as it is important to engage in self-analysis surrounding using self-disclosure in general, it is critical to maintain dialogue with traumatized clients about their reaction to disclosing therapists.

Case Example: Bringing It All Together

One client, a cisgender male in his fifties who experienced significant emotional neglect and abuse throughout his childhood, entered therapy and essentially yelled 'toward' this author throughout the entire first session. Although none of the emotion was directed personally at the therapist, it remained an unpleasant beginning to therapy.

During the following session, this author shared his experiences of being in the room with the client, which primarily included frustration and sadness. After the therapist/author utilized self-disclosure as an intervention, the client made a dismissive comment with a judgmental tone. Instead of the author allowing the frustration to grow into anger, the author paused and said to the client: "Would you be open to hearing how your comment just affected me?" Begrudgingly, the client agreed. The author shared the sinking sensation in his gut and frustration that arose after the comment, and then asked if the client realized how his tone impacted others.

This was the first moment in the two sessions the author and client had spent together that the client began to cry. As he expressed and showed his feelings, the author asked what it was like to get this feedback from another person, to which the client reported it was uncommon throughout his life and in fact one of the first times he had been told in a way that was not attacking or punitive. Under these circumstances, eliciting the client's experience of the self-disclosure seemed even more important than usual. This author does not commonly disclose frustration so early in the therapeutic process. However, the client continued to cite this and other similar moments as one of the more important components of his therapy, as a genuine effort to maintain and make real the relationship.

This case provides an example of how trauma survivors who lack real and authentic relationships can begin to mimic perpetrators of the abuse they suffered and also how therapeutic self-disclosure of real and even negative emotions can disrupt this cycle. This interaction is also an example of how prior research on self-involving disclosures and disclosures in contexts of trauma applies in practice.

Conclusions

In summary, self-disclosure when working with trauma survivors must be carefully considered based on the needs of the individual person and the development of the therapeutic relationship. While some form of self-disclosure is likely to be a necessary component of the therapy when there is a history of attachment-based trauma, research has suggested that most clients focus on the importance of therapists discussing present moment attachment/relational dynamics and emotions, rather than personal details about their lives (Dalenberg, 2000). Although there have been some classic texts written on using self-disclosure with trauma survivors (e.g., Dalenberg, 2000; Pearlman & Saakvitne, 1995) and there has been more research on variables in trauma therapy (e.g., Ellis et al., 2017), there remains a need for further research on disclosure with those who have experienced repeated, attachment-based abuse or neglect.

References

Briere, J., Dietrich, A., & Semple, R. (2016). Dissociative complexity: Antecedents and clinical correlates of a new construct. *Psychological Trauma: Theory, Research, Practice, and Policy, 8*(5), 577–84.

Briere, J., Kaltman, S., & Greene, R. (2008). Accumulated childhood trauma and symptom complexity. *Journal of Traumatic Stress, 21*(2), 223–6.

Courtois, C., & Ford, J. (2013). *Treatment of complex trauma: A sequenced, relationship-based approach.* New York: Guilford Press.

Dalenberg, C. (2000). *Countertransference and the treatment of trauma.* Washington, DC: American Psychological Association.

Ellis, A., Simiola, V., Brown, L., Courtois, C., & Cook, J. (2017). The role of evidence-based therapy relationships on treatment outcome for adults with trauma: A systematic review. *Journal of Trauma and Dissociation, 19*(2), 185–213.

Freyd, J. (1996). *Betrayal trauma: The logic of forgetting childhood abuse.* Cambridge, MA: Harvard University Press.

Herman, J. (1997). *Trauma and recovery: The aftermath of violence—from domestic abuse to political terror.* New York: Basic Books.

Kinsler, P., Courtois, C., & Frankel, A. (2009). Therapeutic alliance and risk management. In C. Courtois & J. Ford (Eds.), *Treating complex traumatic stress disorders: An evidence-based guide* (pp. 183–201). New York: Guilford Press.

LeDoux, J. (1998). Fear and the brain: Where have we been, and where are we going. *Biological Psychiatry, 44*(12), 1229–38.

Linehan, M. (2015). *DBT skills training manual* (2nd ed.). New York: Guilford Press.

Liotti, G. (1992). Disorganized/disoriented attachment in the etiology of the dissociative disorders. *Dissociation: Progress in the Dissociative Disorders, 5*(4), 196–204.

Lyons-Ruth, K. (2008). Contributions of the mother–infant relationship to dissociative, borderline, and conduct symptoms in young adulthood. *Infant Mental Health Journal, 29*(3), 203–18.

Norcross, J., & Wampold, B. (2011). Evidence-based therapy relationships: Research conclusions and clinical practices. *Psychotherapy, 48*(1), 98–102.

Pearlman, L., & Saakvitne, K. (1995). *Trauma and the therapist: Countertransference and vicarious traumatization in psychotherapy with incest survivors.* New York: W. W. Norton & Co.

Russell, G. (2006). Different ways of knowing: The complexities of therapist disclosure. *Journal of Gay and Lesbian Psychotherapy, 10*(1), 79–94.

Schore, A. (1994). *Affect regulation and the origin of the self: The neurobiology of emotional development.* Hillsdale, NJ: Lawrence Erlbaum Associates.

Schore, A. (2009). Attachment trauma and the developing right brain: Origins of pathological dissociation. In P. Dell. & J. O'Neil (Eds.), *Dissociation and the dissociative disorders: DSM-V and beyond* (pp. 107–41). New York: Routledge.

Terr, L. (1991). Childhood traumas: An outline and overview. *American Journal of Psychiatry, 148*(1), 10–20.

CHAPTER 21

Intellectual and Developmental Disabilities (IDD)

Gerald E. Nissley, Jr., PsyD

Two misconceptions exist in the collective consciousness of society that often impede the progress and prospects of individuals with IDDs. The first one is that individuals with IDDs are inherently incapable of generativity and reciprocity necessary for social integration and inclusion. The other is that applied behavior analytic interventions often used with this population must be reductionistic, sterilized, and devoid of humane character.

The appropriate and effective utilization of therapeutic self-disclosure can address both of these concerns and in a way that allows intervention to embrace the dignity of the client while improving treatment within the context of the client's experience of an IDD. Despite the intuitive promise of self-disclosure to embrace dignity and improve treatment, little research has been conducted on the topic for this population, which makes this chapter an essential contribution.

Even in Treatment of IDDs, It's About the Relationship

The provision of an IDD diagnosis has significant implications for an individual. In a manner akin to diagnostic overshadowing, other aspects of an individual's human dignity are often stripped when he or she is so labeled. While some individuals are relieved by the diagnosis, oppressive seizure of their autonomy by others is also common. Choices on how free time is spent, opportunities for achievement, and clothes and snacks are often structurally eliminated (i.e., made for them) due to the presumption that the individual is not capable of making their own choices. In a society where industry and generativity are highly valued (as psychosocial tasks of maturation), an individual diagnosed with an IDD—and therefore seen as incapable—is likely to be ostracized.

The IDD experience of social stigma and rejection can be addressed and somewhat mitigated in treatment through therapeutic self-disclosure. As discussed previously in the postmodern conceptualizations of self-disclosure in Chapter 3 of this text, self-disclosure has the potential to help the client diagnosed with an IDD avoid internalizing the false narratives and stigma that promote negative self-concept and self-esteem. Often, clients with IDDs—who may perceive themselves as qualitatively different and less capable than everyone around them—may also believe that they are the only one experiencing a particular daily concern *because they are flawed*. Case examples in the following sections of this chapter will show how therapeutic self-disclosure can be empowering in this respect.

This author has often seen in his work with clients that therapist self-disclosure can help to normalize the prior experience in a way that allows the concern to be less internally localized. Moreover, when the client views the therapist as capable and positive, he or she grows in his or her sense that he or she is capable of handling normal human concern. In addition to communicating the inherent dignity of folks with IDDs, self-disclosure is important for improving outcomes generally, advancing them in a *socially valid* manner, and modeling how to speak of one's experience in a way that is self-affirming in spite of vulnerability/limitations.

While Maslow argued for humanizing behaviorism as part of the Third Wave of psychology, applied behavior analysis was always meant to be a technology that improved the lives of clients and embraced their individual personality and context. A key aspect of the humanizing of intervention, for individuals who experience IDDs, is that of social validity. Wolf (1978) defined social validity as the conglomerate consideration of goals, appropriateness of interventions, and reflection on social context when identifying goals and interventions. Essentially, social validity involves assurance that goals, interventions, and implications appear as natural and practical as possible. When assessing social validity, one asks whether the intervention is acceptable, relevant, and useful to the individual in their context.

In the behaviorally oriented intervention experience of this author, tangible rewards are often utilized with clients with IDDs until satiation occurs or the reinforcement/reward values diminishes significantly. Often, therapists then throw up their hands and suggest there is nothing that motivates the client. However, within the lens of social validity, how does one typically change behavior of 'neurotypical' (i.e., non-IDD) youth? The forms of reinforcers are changed from tangible ones to social reinforcers. While the necessity of rapport with other client populations is well established, it is not only central in working with individuals with IDDs, but also a reinforcer and an establishing operation (i.e., any variable that increases the value of a reinforcer and typically increases the effectiveness of a reinforcer).

In this author's experience, many IDD clients did not engage in/respond to intervention because they believed it would work. In fact, they often believed the opposite. An example is the author's former client, who had IDD and also autism. He was over six feet tall, over 350 pounds, and was prone to anger outbursts when unable to manage his frustration. In an effort to teach him prosocial communication, which every therapist at the facility had previously tried, this author developed a 'social script' (i.e., prompting to expand the usage of a wider variety of social and appropriate communication) like other therapists before the author, only this time it worked. The frequency and the intensity of explosive outbursts decreased notably.

Why? The author asked the client why he tried his social script this time. He told me, "Because I like you, Mr. Gerald." He didn't believe in the intervention. Rather, he believed in his relationship with this author. McLaughlin and Carr (2005) found through functional behavioral analyses that strong rapport between interventionist and client resulted in increased task completion (i.e., compliance) and lowered frequencies of problem behavior. Of note, when McLaughlin and Carr (2005) operationally defined rapport, they discerned through research that rapport involved social communication and reciprocity as foundational variables. Thus, TSD has the ability to promote both of those dynamics in a socially valid manner, as described previously.

The Role of TSD in Promoting Self-Management

One of best embodiments of socially valid treatment paradigms/models is *self-management*. Self-disclosure can be effectively utilized within. Whether discussing typical development of infants into adults, or discussing the promotion of improved quality of life and well-being among treatment participants, a common desire is for individuals to transition from the requirement of extensive externalized prompting and regulation to increased self-regulation and functional independence. For individuals experiencing IDDs, the social validity gained through self-management is important for both consideration of less restrictive support and development of prosocial skills within their present context and lifestyle. Self-management includes a number of components: goal-setting, selection of support strategies, self-monitoring, self-evaluation, and self-reinforcement. Research summarized in the following paragraphs will demonstrate that the more components of self-management incorporated into a treatment regimen, often, the better the outcomes. Therapist self-disclosure can be useful in optimizing each aspect of self-management.

Self-Selection of Goals

Mogensen and Mason (2015) found that individuals with autism struggled with a sense of identity and autonomy, noting that such difficulties are often/ also present among individuals with IDDs due to absence of theory of mind and insufficient metacognition. Therapist self-disclosure can be utilized to challenge unhelpful self-attributions, model behaviors of goal selection, and provide a frame of reference for options. Self-disclosure also allows the therapist to use relatable language and concrete experiences to teach the client about the meanings of abstract concepts and how they can be applied in support of improved judgment and problem solving. The IDD client may struggle to follow the more abstract steps of problem solving, but they are more likely to remember the therapist's revelation of a problematic habit and how the therapist tried to fix it.

Sometimes, when working with clients, this author assists them in making lifestyle changes related to eating and weight management. With 'neurotypi-cal' patients, the author might abstractly and conceptually discuss making manageable short-term goals based on values. When working with clients with IDD, the author has told of his initial attempts to lose weight by setting the goal to go from being fat to skinny and failing. One client was told how set-ting smaller goals—losing five pounds by making smaller changes, because the author wanted to see his young kids grow up—eventually helped the author to lose 100 pounds. During their selection of goals, IDD clients often do not remember the abstract steps to selecting goals as overviewed in textbooks. Instead, they more often remember a story example and may use it as a guide to select value-based goals and make progress towards actualization.

Self-Selection of Strategies

As comorbid intellectual limitations for creative thinking may paradoxically create new problems and new solutions to problems, individuals with IDDs often struggle to develop an ample range of problem-solving methods. Often, strategies and solutions are initially chosen based on trial and error and are limited in their inspiration to previous experience. Moreover, given the expe-rience of a restrictive society, many folks with IDDs have been socialized to limit their autonomous consideration of strategies and are unduly encouraged to defer to others' thinking. Therapist self-disclosure can be an excellent way to concretely though subtly and non-instructively provide examples of addi-tional strategies that can expand the client's repertoire of options. Consistent with research on cognitive behavioral therapy summarized in Chapter 3 of this text, disclosure by the therapist of his or her personal challenges can encourage reciprocal disclosure of the client.

Self-Monitoring and Self-Reinforcement

While self-monitoring has been used frequently in other cognitive and behav-ioral contexts, it is often a forgotten tool with individuals with IDDs. However, research shows that self-monitoring can be effectively utilized with folks with a variety of IDDs, and consistently results in reduced problem behavior. As discussed in the introductory chapter of this text, some extent of intentional therapist self-disclosure is inevitable and even preferred. The self-disclosure of the author's personally used self-monitoring protocols has modeled self-monitoring strategies for IDD clients.

An adolescent male client with an early form of IDD taught this author an important lesson about the individualized experience of self-monitoring and reinforcement. This author was asked by a school he consulted with to observe the client in the classroom because he was having outbursts that placed other students in danger. The author set up a self-monitoring protocol to collect data. The self-monitoring form was simple. It used smiley faces and frowning faces to demarcate self-control versus engagement in the explosive behavior.

When teaching the client to use the protocol, this author detailed how he once broke an unwanted habit of biting fingernails by checking boxes on a chart when he/the author was doing it and then rewarded himself for not doing it. The author told the adolescent client how the checking of boxes on a similar chart helped the author become more aware he was biting his nails so he could learn to refrain from the behavior more often. Sometimes, the author was not very aware he was biting my nails until his fingers hurt.

This example from the author's personal experience helped the client to learn the interventional strategy, which he probably would not have been able to follow or make use of if it was only presented in the abstract. When the author/therapist came back to collect the data on the adolescent client, his major behavior problems had stopped completely! This author asked the client what happened. The client reported that every time he could mark that he did not have an outburst, he was able to figuratively give himself a pat on the back. He had been offered every other tangible reinforcer his teachers could think of . . . all he seemed to want was validation. This case provides an example of how therapist self-disclosure can help individuals with IDDs learn to communicate and assert their reinforcement preferences and diversity of preferences to family members/supportive others and also professionals in the future. Over time, they may grow more trusting of their personal perspectives and in turn grow in their *self-evaluation.*

Self-Evaluation

Mogensen and Mason (2015) determined that his therapeutic disclosure of his diagnosis of autism at times helped clients to evaluate and reflect upon their definition and application of normality more effectively. Thus, non-directive disclosures and revelations by others—in a broad sense—can be utilized by clients with IDDs to assist them to develop more accurate and helpful scripts and narratives that in turn allow them to evaluate their implementation strategies and personal outcomes. As has been mentioned previously in this chapter, therapist self-disclosure of evaluating personal choices can help the client to internalize new scripts, accommodate old ones, and expand skills for doing so. As a therapist, it is also important to self-disclose examples of perceived failure when helping individuals with IDD evaluate their different/possible choices in social situations. Whereas such disclosures have been affirmed and discouraged in prior chapters of this text, it should be recalled that such prior advisements were based on the presumption of neurotypical populations. Self-disclosures of failures or shortcomings to populations with IDD is important because it normalizes failure as part of problem solving and provides an opportunity to model concretely some different methods of addressing and rebounding from task failure.

The Implications of TSD on Behavioral Transfer

Behavior transfer refers to applied learning of the relationships between antecedents, behaviors, and consequences, and to contexts beyond the one where the learning took place. In the behavioral theories, two concepts are primarily discussed within this construct: generalization and discrimination. Generalization broadly refers to the application of a learned connection to a similar context. The similarity could be seen in the setting of the initial event (classically), the anticipated consequence (operantly), or both. In contrast, discrimination is the behavioral term for a learner's ability to differentiate contexts where the previously learned association was not yet applied, thereby having the potential to result in a different and potentially more optimal behavior in a newly developing context. Therapist self-disclosure—through verbalization or formal intervention—can be useful for promoting both.

As noted earlier, this author often helps IDD clients discern how to develop social scripts. One of the tasks is to teach scripts that can be used across contexts as well as those that are more situation-specific. When the author teaches scripts, he may self-disclose which ones he used across contexts—such as initiating discussions with unfamiliar people about the weather—and also ones that are situation-specific, such as conversations with friends. Clients with IDDs can often appreciate this concrete explanation of difference. Showing greater capability than some may assume, they often can identify places they have been told different rules for—school versus home, for example. Therapeutic self-disclosure makes the development of scripts for behavior easier to appreciate for many of this author's clients.

Individuals with IDDs tend to share less of their internal cognitions and personal narratives with others. In turn, and without encouragement, it is difficult for social interactions to shape their internal and frequently negative scripts. Therapist self-disclosure can be useful to teaching the generalization of positive and prosocial behavior. As has been noted in the introductory chapter of this text, every intervention selected by a therapist is a form of self-disclosure. In the development of social scripts, therapists utilize their own perspective to offer language to clients that they can use to understand and respond to their personal contexts. Self-disclosure is important for providing clients opportunities to revise their schemas so that they are more flexibly applied.

For example, this author was recently working with a 45-year-old female with an IDD who was raped by her boss. When the author and client began the therapy, the client/she was mad that her boss was going to be incarcerated and that she could not see him. She reported that her boss told her that people who like each other have sex, and so she engaged in unwanted intercourse. She reported a history of having sexual relations with a variety of more powerful individuals in her life based on this generalization.

In the therapy, the author used self-disclosure to tactfully and without detail explain how engaged in sexual activity with his wife, but did not engage in sexual activity with everyone he/the author liked. The client asked a lot of questions about how people decide to make the choice to engage in sexual relations in varied contexts, which allowed her then to expand her schemas about platonic and sexual relationships. The author also self-disclosed about a time that he experienced a painful end to an unhealthy relationship. As the author and client discussed the author's personal experience, the author told the client about the mixture of emotions experienced. The client reported not appreciating, prior to that conversation in therapy, that it was okay to be sad to not see the boss she liked, and also angry that he coerced her to have sex when she did not want to.

This interaction demonstrates how self-disclosure can be used to change social scripts, promote differentiation, self-management, and self-evaluation. As discussed in Chapters 3, 5, and 6 of this text, this interaction also provides an example of how higher intimacy and personal failure disclosures (ordinarily discouraged in other contexts) may be useful for IDD clients after a strong therapeutic relationship has been established.

Conclusions

The benefits, limits, and clinical/nuance factors of therapist self-disclosure have been extensively reviewed in the previous chapters of this text. In this chapter, the reader may have noticed that there was little research on the role of therapist self-disclosure in working specifically with individuals diagnosed with IDDs. There is an extensive gap in the literature, so that this chapter is intended to provide examples of interventions in practice and also serve as a conceptual call for more research to be done. Wisdom from practice and further research may further affirm how therapist self-disclosure may aid IDD population with living well, autonomously, and with dignity.

References

McLaughlin, D., & Carr, E. (2005). Quality of rapport as a setting event for problem behavior: Assessment and intervention. *Journal of Positive Behavior Intervention*, 7(2), 68–91.

Mogensen, L., & Mason, J. (2015). The meaning of a label for teenagers negotiating identity: Experiences with autism spectrum disorder. *Sociology of Health & Illness*, 37(2), 255–69.

Wolf, M. (1978). Social validity: The case for subjective measurement or how applied behavior analysis is finding its heart. *Journal of Applied Behavior Analysis*, 11(2), 203–14.

CHAPTER 22

Forensic Settings

Tobias Wasser, MD, Daniel Papapietro, PsyD,
and Reena Kapoor, MD

Since the deinstitutionalization movement of the 1960s, individuals with mental illness have transitioned in great numbers from psychiatric facilities into the criminal justice system. An estimated 16% of the 2 million prisoners in the United States have been diagnosed with a mental illness, which results in correctional facilities by de facto serving as some of the country's largest psychiatric treatment centers (Torrey, Kennard, Eslinger, Lamb, & Pavle, n.d.). In addition, as state hospital beds have been reduced by over 90% since the beginning of deinstitutionalization up to the recent present, a larger proportion of the remaining hospital beds are dedicated to forensic patients—those who are too sick and dangerous to be treated in less restrictive settings. As a result of these systemic shifts, hundreds of thousands of psychiatric patients now receive care in high-security forensic settings, including correctional facilities and psychiatric hospitals (Torrey et al., n.d.).

Correctional facilities and forensic psychiatric hospitals are unique environments. They are not exclusively devoted to treatment; safety and security are necessarily equally important considerations. Forensic settings typically restrict patients' movement, association with other people, and access to property. In order to enforce security, facilities maintain a visible law enforcement presence, typically with uniformed officers (either police, corrections, or private security officers) as part of the treatment milieu. Additional security measures are necessary because patients in forensic settings usually have significant histories of violence and other rule-breaking behavior. This history is an indication of their risk of future violence and sometimes elicits fear in the overburdened, highly stressed, and frequently undertrained staff tasked with caring for them. These interpersonal dynamics, combined with the isolated settings in which many forensic treatment facilities are located, can easily lead to boundary violations between patients and staff if not carefully monitored.

The purpose of this chapter is to examine the issue of therapeutic self-disclosure within the safety and treatment parameters of forensic settings. The authors first discuss boundaries, identifying ways in which the forensic setting differs from more 'traditional' therapeutic settings. The authors next identify several important clinical and boundary-related considerations for therapists considering self-disclosure. Finally, the authors present and discuss two case examples in which self-disclosure was used therapeutically to enhance the patients' treatment and distinguish these cases from circumstances in which boundary violations occurred.

Boundaries in the Forensic Setting

In any clinical setting, boundaries between psychotherapist and patient can be bent, broken, ignored, transgressed, or violated in a number of benign and serious ways. Certainly, some boundary crossings are likely to be harmless, such as when a therapist returns from vacation and shares briefly with the patient where he or she went. Indeed, such disclosures are referenced in Chapter 6 on disclosure types as often helping to build rapport and therapist humanization.

In locked, secure forensic settings, patients often accumulate a great deal of this kind of personal information about staff members over the years. It is common for forensic settings in rural environments to be a primary location for employment for entire communities, so that longer term, intergenerational, personal, and professional contacts are increasingly likely. The very nature of such settings, with patients and staff confined together for many years, is that staff members sometimes become so inured to the presence of patients (or the invisibility of patients) that they talk among themselves without remembering that patients are literally just around the corner. Often, patients may listen with benign, curious, intrusive, or antisocial and exploitative motivations. Patients learn about staff weekends, vacations, marriages, divorces, affairs, and many other personal tidbits of information just from going about their daily routines.

In secure forensic institutions, where the length of stay is typically measured in years instead of days, professional boundaries must be closely monitored. When treatment relationships with patients exceed two or three years, both patient and psychotherapist can achieve sufficient familiarity to create a potential for more casual interactions. As the therapist relaxes his or her guard over time, such casual interactions run the risk of becoming a slippery slope toward boundary violations. Patients may regularly attempt to cross boundaries by asking personal questions or making comments about the therapist's looks, demeanor, clothing, background, or gender. Thus, right from the start of the treatment relationship, the therapist must be prepared to manage and hold firm professional boundaries. Forensic patients often push boundaries subtly and persistently over time as a form of testing, seduction, and manipulation to achieve desired ends (e.g., developing a personal relationship, assistance with contraband, and recommendations for reduced length of confinement). With these possibilities in mind, how one responds to forensic patients' personal inquiries is critical for both treatment and liability's sake and cannot be left to spontaneity. The therapist's responses must be considered beforehand in training and supervision so that they are appropriately practiced and prepared.

It is important to note that in many forensic settings a therapist is seen as an outsider, both literally and figuratively. Some forensic hospitals employ therapists whose only work on a given housing unit is to see individual therapy patients. These therapists are often considered separate from the 'core' treatment team and security staff. Similarly, in correctional facilities, mental health professionals, including therapists, come and go on the cell blocks, with corrections officers and other professionals making up the permanent and more visible staff. Because of these systemic factors, patient and therapist never exist in isolation. They are always in contact with other staff members who make up what can be thought of as a 'therapeutic triad.' All members of the triad must consider and maintain the boundaries between them in order for a therapeutic relationship to be successful. From a theoretical vantage point, it is as if the therapist and treatment and correctional teams are the ego and superego trying to control the id (i.e., forensic patient), and to help it adapt and discharge in socially appropriate ways. This is also the way in which the triad is supposed to join, align, and collectively facilitate patient growth in the context of a necessarily adversarial system and involuntary confinement.

When therapists come on to a secure forensic unit to provide therapy to a patient, the dynamics of boundaries change. There is often an inclination for front-line staff to demonstrate a natural curiosity about this 'off-unit' colleague. Someone coming to a unit is often repeatedly questioned by staff members about who they are, why are they there, and where they come from. Over time, the visiting psychotherapist will often try to be casual and chatty, hoping to allay suspicions and become accepted by the on-unit staff. A casual familiarity may develop between the unit staff and the visiting therapist. As this transpires, private conversations among staff and therapist previously held in the 'back room' may eventually become conversation material for staff while walking down the hallway or sitting with patients. Thus, it is not unusual for patients to learn details of their therapist's life (e.g., recent vacations, work or relationship issues, or even relationship-damaging views of patients) simply by listening to conversations among on-unit staff members. Some patients later use this information to ask direct questions of their therapist (e.g., "So, Dr. P, I heard you've been to Asia, how was it?"). Determining how to answer such questions and unearth the motivation behind forensic patient inquiries is complex.

The Importance of Regular Training and Supervision

Boundary maintenance between therapist and patient is as important in a forensic setting as it can be difficult to accomplish. Many inmates/patients in prisons and secure hospitals had disturbed attachments with their primary caretakers in childhood. In such cases, their adult criminal behavior can be seen as a recapitulation of boundary violations enacted towards them during childhood. Patients will frequently try to reenact the same maladaptive interpersonal dynamics with the therapist who is tasked with treating them after the offense, either consciously or unconsciously.

Exploration of a patient's pathological childhood experiences, as well as a detailed exploration of the criminal offenses, can be an emotionally exhausting experience for the therapist. This task becomes even more draining if the therapist has an entire caseload of patients who have committed heinous crimes and/or an environment lacking an appropriate balance between treatment and security. For this reason, it is highly recommended that therapists in forensic settings be highly trained in forensic competencies, including the evaluation of response style and corroborating self-reports against objective records, and arrange regular peer supervision and support. Such peer supervision and support provides an opportunity for one's work to be openly and comfortably reviewed among trusted colleagues. Discussion of feelings described in the next section of this chapter is important so that therapists are increasingly aware of their potentially problematic feelings and reactions, which in turn may lower likelihood of boundary violations and possibly major security, safety, and liability issues.

Pay Attention to Urges to Self-Disclose

In the forensic setting, emotions that arise between therapist and patient are often heightened in the extent to which they are impactful. As the therapist listens to a patient disclose details of a criminal offense or deviant urges, he or she can feel revulsion, anger, fascination, seduction, or judgment. Sometimes the therapist may cope with these feelings by emotionally disengaging from the patient, but at other times an urge to self-disclose might arise. For example, the therapist may believe that disclosing his or her own deviant behavior might help to normalize the patient's experience. In another instance, when a patient is speaking about adverse childhood experiences and blaming his parents for his problems as an adult, the therapist may feel an urge to disclose his or her own history of childhood abuse in an effort to challenge the patient's conclusion that others are to blame for his criminal actions. These possibilities speak to the line of reasoning behind historical disclosures for the purpose of empathizing and shifting thinking patterns, as described in Chapters 3 and 6 on theory and types of disclosure.

As discussed in trauma-focused chapters of this text, paying attention to when these urges arise and related physiological sensations is the first step in managing them appropriately. Keeping notes and discussing such occurrences in supervision can be helpful in understanding why a patient evokes a particular response in the therapist. If urges to self-disclose are acted on indiscriminately, or if they are simply ignored, the therapist is at risk of committing a boundary violation.

For example, a forensic patient pleads with the therapist to bring a newspaper, saying things such as,

> You can pick one up at the front desk . . . the cops will let you bring it in . . . what's the harm in a newspaper? Come on, you're always telling me I should get out of my shell and pay attention to the world . . . besides, you brought a book for another patient, that's not fair.

The therapist may have difficulty refusing the patient's request because it is, on the surface, almost benign (patients are allowed to read the daily newspaper), but also because the therapist had (for appropriate reasons) one time brought a book for a different patient on a different unit. However, the present forensic patient asking for a newspaper is unimpaired by a psychotic or manic illness, but instead demonstrates a mixture of personality disordered traits (antisocial and narcissistic), and was clearly attempting to manipulate the therapist into doing something that is 'against the rules.' When the therapist crossed the line and conceded to this seemingly benign request, the patient 'wrote up' the therapist for breaking the rules. The more sociopathic the forensic patient is, the more often they observe, manipulate, and use an individual's behaviors against them—either for their own sadistic enjoyment or to gain some leverage and control over staff to compel future boundary violations.

Put the Patient's Needs First

Therapists strive to provide the patient a non-judgmental relationship in which the patient can safely express pain, anger, hate, sadism, and other difficult emotions. The moment the therapist feels compelled answer the patient's emotions or stories in kind, the focus is pulled away from the patient, potentially to the detriment of the therapeutic relationship, and likely due to patient projections and countertransference. Therefore, the general precaution noted Chapter 2 of this text, that self-disclosure should only be done when there is a clear benefit to the patient, and not just to gratify the needs of the therapist, is particularly applicable in forensic settings. As Olarte (2003, p. 599) notes,

> [Personal self-disclosure] . . . is specifically differentiated from a boundary violation, because the personal disclosure is brought to the patient's interactional awareness not for gratification of the therapist's sexual or narcissistic needs, but to provoke a response in the patient's conceptualization of a phenomenon being presented in the session and to actively influence the inter-subjective field.

In other words, a well-timed personal disclosure can reassure the patient that the psychotherapist has the necessary personal knowledge or experience to understand the patient, but more importantly, can help the patient to feel understood.

The Effects of Self-Disclosure in the Forensic Setting

Sharing personal information or reactions in a forensic setting is different from making the same disclosure in a more traditional psychotherapy setting. Forensic patients often struggle to maintain hope in the face of long periods of confinement. They sometimes have very few positive, non-superficial, and non-institutional goal-driven interactions with other human beings. A therapist who empathizes with their pain and sadness from personal experience can help the patient feel understood and can help foster trust in the therapeutic relationship. Self-disclosure might also help the patient feel hopeful that, no matter what crime they have committed, or how mentally unwell they might be, other people can still relate to their experiences.

However, this potential therapeutic benefit must be weighed against the heightened risks in the forensic setting. In a secure hospital or prison, the therapist must be prepared for the possibility that information disclosed to a patient may ultimately be known by others in the environment. Building on earlier points in this chapter, patients might share what they learned about the therapist with other members of the treatment team, other patients or inmates, or with security personnel. The therapist must be prepared for all members of the 'therapeutic triad' to know the information, given how easily such information can be spread as gossip. In addition, treatment in forensic settings often undergoes multiple layers of oversight from internal administrators and external agencies, not all of whom will be familiar with principles of boundaries in psychotherapy. Self-disclosure can easily be misinterpreted as a boundary violation by untrained overseers, so the therapist must be prepared to explain the therapeutic rationale for the disclosure easily and succinctly. See Chapter 24 in this text on gender and power dynamics for case illustrations of points made in this paragraph.

Of course, no discussion of disclosure in the forensic setting would be complete without acknowledging the risk of patients misusing the information to manipulate, groom, coerce, or even cause serious harm to the therapist. Many forensic patients have committed serious acts of violence and have multiple risk factors for future dangerousness. Many have serious personality pathology that is frequently misdiagnosed due to insincere self-reporting and manipulation. Many of these patients are highly skilled at getting others to cross boundaries, even using the therapist's self-disclosed information to 'prove' that they are already trusted by authority figures. Therapists must be mindful that even the most skilled clinicians can be fooled by patients who may have spent much if not most of their lives in institutions and developed more subtle and harder-to-detect strategies for achieving desired aims. Thus, it is best to exercise extreme caution when disclosing information that could be used to identify the therapist's address, family members, or other sensitive areas.

Examples of Self-Disclosure in a Forensic Setting

Example 1

A psychotherapist in a forensic hospital has been asked to meet with two sisters, identical twins who received an insanity acquittal for a serious crime of violence. The purpose of the therapy was to help understand and assess the degree to which their emotional relationship was mutually interdependent, whether one was more dependent on the other, the degree to which their crime was exclusively a function of their mental illness, and whether aspects of their mental illnesses co-varied or were shared.

Because of the sisters' shared (and individual) underlying paranoid processes, the psychotherapist, after discussing it with trusted senior peers, shared with them that she, too, was an identical twin. The reasoning behind this self-disclosure was the theory that identical twins have unique developmental experiences and are also different from single-siblings. Therefore, the very nature of the twins' emotional closeness that may have contributed to their crime might be best understood by a therapist with firsthand experience of such genetic closeness. It should be noted that the therapist in this case was a senior clinician. The therapist was elected to be the twins' therapist due to her psychodynamic training and years of experience, not merely because she too was a twin. Importantly, her disclosure was also considered appropriate and less risky because the therapist being an identical was well known to staff in the forensic hospital. Thus, the patients might have discovered this information through other means.

Following the disclosure of 'twin-ness,' the patients' progress in treatment seemed to make substantial gains. The two women at times asked appropriate questions of the psychotherapist about her twin, and when appropriate, the therapist answered honestly. When the patients asked their therapist if her twin was also a therapist, the therapist answered simply, "No . . . she chose an entirely different career path." When asked if she and her sister were close, the therapist responded, "Yes in some ways, but very separate in most ways. Not close the way you two have been." These honest answers, though limited in detail, were reassuring to the patients and seemed to help them maintain a working therapeutic relationship even during more difficult times later in the course of psychotherapy. Very often one of the patients, talking about some complicated aspect of their relationship, would simply say, "You're a twin . . . you understand," to which the psychotherapist would (if accurate) agree. It became a shorthand way of not having to go into detail about shared concepts or experiences, which furthered the therapeutic alliance. This outcome also provides an example of a point made in Chapter 2 of this text: That brief, infrequent, and relevant disclosures communicating client–therapist similarity and with focus immediately returned to the client are maximally ethical and often incrementally more helpful and effective.

Example 2

A male patient had been in the secure hospital for many years after killing his father. He was a calm, cooperative man who for many years was seen by a psychologist in group therapy. Over the years the treatment team had suggested the patient consider individual psychotherapy. Typically the patient would agree, meet once with the therapist, and then politely demur, saying, "I'm not really ready yet." When the therapist's elderly father died, he chose to share with the patients on the unit that he would be absent from work for some time due to a death in his family. Some patients overheard from staff conversations that the therapist was out specifically because of the death of his father. On their own, the patients put together a condolence card to give to the therapist upon his return.

For many patients, the opportunity to be supportive, empathic, compassionate, and in a prosocial and even healthy family kind of way is a new experience. In the prior example, the patients had not had the occasion to 'take care of' a staff person. As they later talked about in their individual and group therapies, it was reassuring for them to feel they had helped support someone rather than being the person who needed support or caused others to need support. They felt human and contributory again, stepping out of the role of patient who needed to be helped or inmate needing to be disciplined, and taking a step back into humanity and prosocial society.

For the individual patient who several times tried but quit individual psychotherapy, learning of the therapist's father's death and related occurrences in the treatment milieu had a profound impact on his course of treatment. A few weeks after the death of the therapist's father, this patient approached the therapist and asked if "maybe we could try individual therapy again." The therapist agreed, and they began to meet weekly.

Subsequently, the patient did very well and made no efforts to quit or avoid psychotherapy, a rousing success in and of itself. About six months into this course of therapy, the therapist asked the patient why—after so many years of refusal—he had changed his mind and did not terminate prematurely. The patient responded, "I always thought that talking to you about killing my father would somehow be dangerous to your father . . . after your father died, it felt safe . . . I couldn't hurt him." Although this kind of thinking was psychotic, at the same time, it was a safe way for the patient to talk about his crime, his guilt, and his wish to undo what he had done by preventing another similar crime from occurring in the future (e.g., metaphorically killing the therapist's father). Once the patient knew that the therapist's father had died, the patient had nothing to fear. He would not 'kill' anyone else, and he could then begin his own process of healing.

Conclusions

In summary, forensic patients may live in locked facilities for years and have often committed serious violent acts. In such cases, the risks and benefits of self-disclosure in different circumstances must be well understood, reflected upon, and probably consulted about prior to making decisions to disclose. A therapist who discloses to demonstrate empathy for their patient (e.g., historical disclosures as discussed in Chapter 6 on types of disclosure) can help the patient feel understood and can help foster trust in the therapeutic relationship. However, in forensic settings, patient and therapist never exist in isolation as they may in traditional clinical or private practice settings. Forensic patient and therapist are always in contact with other staff members who make up what can be thought of as a 'therapeutic triad.' All members of the triad must consider and maintain the boundaries between them in order for a therapeutic relationship to be safe, helpful to the patient, and of secondary benefit to the institution. In all cases, therapists in forensic settings must be mindful that even the most skilled clinicians can be fooled by patients, and so it is best to exercise extreme caution when disclosing information that can be used in furtherance of antisocial motivations.

References

Olarte, S. (2003). Personal disclosure revisited. *Journal of the American Academy of Psychoanalysis and Dynamic Psychiatry, 31*(4), 599–607.

Torrey, F., Kennard, A., Eslinger, D., Lamb, R., & Pavle, J. (n.d.). More mentally ill persons are in jails and prisons than hospitals: A survey of states. Retrieved from www.treatmentadvocacycenter.org/storage/documents/final_jails_v_hospitals_study.pdf.

CHAPTER 23

Clients Who Have Been Harmed by Previous Therapists

Tyson D. Bailey, PsyD

Within psychology, it is infrequent to find credible black-and-white statements about behavior. We are a field known for acknowledging the gray areas and, in many cases, actively encouraging our clients to accept and be present in the ambiguity. However, one ethical mandate is straightforward and concrete—do not have sex with your clients. Although current codes of ethics have enforceable standards associated with this type of boundary crossing (e.g., American Psychological Association, 2016), it is an unfortunate reality that many therapists continue to engage in these behaviors and harm their clients (Gottdiener, 2008; Lamb, Catanzaro, & Moorman, 2003; Pope, 1994, 2001). For instance, pooled prevalence rates from several anonymous surveys (N = 5,148) indicated 4.4% of therapists admitted to engaging in some form of sexual boundary violation with a client (Pope & Vasquez, 2016). Although the literature has discussed the deleterious impact on clients (Pope, 2001; Pope & Vetter, 1991), there continues to be a paucity of recent discussion, though comparatively less and even scant research on working with clients who have been harmed in this way. For this reason, much of the recent information in this chapter comes from this author's personal consultation and experience.

The current chapter will focus specifically on the potential benefits and pitfalls of self-disclosure while working with clients who have experienced sexual boundary violations by previous therapists. However, it is critical to note the heterogeneity and diverse needs of individuals who have been harmed by therapists, which prevents generalization. Therefore, it is critical to carefully assess what is important to each individual at the outset of treatment (Luepker, 1990a; Pope, 1994). Similar cautions are urged while working with clients who have experienced any other/somewhat lesser sort of ethical violation from a previous mental health or other trusted professional (see Pope, 1994; Luepker, 1990b for a review of how clients similarly experience sexual boundary violations in therapy and other traumas, e.g., incest and rape). Because this is not the only ethical violation that clients experience in therapy, it is important to note that much of the information in the following discussion may be informative to a conceptualization of other events a client may experience (for example, breaches in confidentiality or abandonment).

Client and Therapist Reactions

Part of this author's initial intake with therapy clients involves a discussion of previous therapeutic encounters. The purpose is to better understand some of their expectations and determine if they experienced anything that did or did not work well. It can be as early as this initial meeting that clients disclose sexual boundary violations by a previous therapist. However, Pope (1988) and (Luepker, 1990a) noted that previously violated clients often experience mistrust toward professionals, which may decrease the likelihood of discussing this information right away. When considering likely emotions that arise when working with a client who has been harmed by a prior therapist, Luepker (1990a) indicated that "most helpers are not accustomed to being (so significantly and consciously) mistrusted, and, hence, they are not prepared for the level of distrust many clients feel toward professionals" (p. 104). In addition, clients often experience marked ambivalence in regard to their feelings and potential recourses, which may include making a formal complaint, or terminating the boundary violating relationship, if violations are still occurring (Luepker, 1990a; Pope, 1988, 1994).

In addition to understanding conflicting and multi-layered client emotions, therapists working with clients with prior histories of being violated by previous therapists must have firm knowledge of reporting duties. Consistent with the transcribed experiences of Nicholson (2010), the current author has struggled with the desire to report 'the other' therapist. However, his duty to maintain confidentiality prevented him from making a formal complaint. This is likely part of the reason Brigham (1989) reported that holding knowledge of a colleague's boundary violation is akin to the stress associated with having a suicidal client. Going a step further, Luepker (1990a) highlights the importance of paying attention to whether you (a secondarily informed therapist) have a personal or professional connection with the offending therapist, as this may have a significant impact on your feelings and may require that you refer the client to another provider.

Within the literature are themes of both clients and therapists minimizing the impacts of boundary violating therapists. It is common for therapists to experience denial or suspicion in regard to client disclosures of sexual boundary violations (Nicholson, 2010; Pope, 1989, 1990, 1994). Qualitative research has suggested that therapists who engage in these violations are likely to downplay the inherent power imbalance in therapy while they are engaged in an inappropriate dual relationship, only to have problematic dynamics re-emerge and intensity if the inappropriate/sexual relationship fails (McNulty, Ogden, & Warren, 2013). As clients experience progressive shifts in the nature of the relationship, their feelings of ambivalence and confusion can increase, which, in conjunction with the shame that often arises, may lead them to minimize the impact of their therapist's violation(s) (Luepker, 1990a; Pope, 1994).

Being present with the client as they move through varying degrees of ambivalence can be extremely difficult for therapists. It is critical to keep in mind that "professionals need to work out their frustration with unethical practitioners through professional consultation, not during a client session" (Luepker, 1990a, p. 111). In order to do this effectively, one must be willing to fully acknowledge all counter-transferential dynamics, both to themselves and within their consultation/support team.

Identifying Your Personal Reactions

As is consistent with other instances wherein a therapist is making a clinical decision about whether or not to utilize self-disclosure (see Chapter 5 on decision-making), accurately identifying and being present with one's feelings is a critical component of reducing the likelihood that self-disclosing feelings/reactions (in response to a client's disclosure of prior therapist boundary violations) will become an additional rupture or violation. Imagine for a moment that you are sitting with a client who discloses a sexual boundary violation by a previous therapist. Consider your immediate thoughts and feelings as you listen to the details of this unethical (and usually illegal) behavior. Pay particular attention to your somatic cues, especially those the client might be able to see (including facial expressions). Do you, as mentioned above, have an urge to minimize the experience of the client or challenge the details? To become a detective and determine the truth of the statement? To crusade for formal action and redress? Further, what do you experience specifically in response to the violating therapist's behavior? Are you appalled, numb, or confused?

Now that you have reflected upon your personal reactions, let us take this exercise one step further—how do you choose which of these reactions to share with the client? For this, there is of course no formula or 'right' answer. The remainder of this chapter will discuss factors to consider while making decisions, regarding self-disclosure, to individuals who have experienced sexual boundary violations.

How Previous Boundary Violations Change the Landscape

Following the introductory chapter of this text, Guthiel and Gabbard (1993) expand upon the differences between boundary *crossings*, which are not inherently detrimental, and boundary *violations*—those actions that are a "harmful crossing, a transgression, of a boundary" (p. 190). While there is clarity regarding the negative effects of sexual relationships in therapy, it can be more difficult to determine the difference between a crossing and violation when considering self-disclosure practices, particularly for previously violated clients. Pope (1994) argues that historical and contextual/experiential factors, such as the client's more personal and individual experience of being harmed by a previous therapist, in turn shape a client's perspective on whether the therapist's use of self-disclosure is a crossing or violation.

Considering the impact a violation has on a client's ability to re-establish trust in therapy (Luepker, 1990a; Pope, 1990, 1994), it is imperative that therapists think carefully about how and when to utilize self-disclosure and not make the assumption it will *always* be helpful or free of the potential for harm (Pope & Keith-Spiegel, 2008). From this conceptual framework, the following section will review several specific factors to consider (see Pope [1994] and Schoener, Milgrom, Gonsiorek, Luepker, & Conroe [1990] for comprehensive discussions).

Navigating Self-Disclosure Decisions: Be Cautious, Not Frozen

Consistent with discussions on ethical issues (Pope & Keith-Spiegel, 2008), there is no 'one size fits all' process for making decisions about self-disclosure with clients who have experienced boundary violations by a previous therapist. Given the increased complexity, shaken trust, and client uncertainty, it can be argued that it is even more critical to think critically and cautiously before disclosing. G. Schoener (personal communication, July 16, 2017) indicated that a sudden switch toward using self-disclosure, if you usually do not, could indicate a potential problem. Although there are no known studies looking directly at how self-disclosure is experienced by clients with a history of boundary violations by a helping professional, clinical experience from this author and others suggests that self-disclosure can continue to be a beneficial therapeutic intervention when applied in a mindful manner (P. Barach, personal communication, May 26, 2017; G. Schoener, personal communication, May 27, 2017). Below are some principles and actions to consider when engaging in the clinical decision-making process specific to this population.

Coming from a feminist framework (Brown & Walker, 1990), judicious self-disclosure is a common tool utilized by this author. This is not to say that feminism *must* be the model used with this population, though it informs this author's thinking when considering sharing personal information with clients who have experienced previous violations. As discussed in Chapter 3 of this text (and applied in the upcoming Chapters 18, 20, and 24 on gender, sexuality, and trauma), feminist therapists utilize self-disclosure to create/maintain an egalitarian, role-modeling, and empowerment-focused relationship (Simi & Mahalik, 1997), objectives that are particularly important when clients have been harmed within a previous therapeutic relationship. The somewhat lesser theoretical emphasis on therapist expertise and power may help to instill a greater level of safety in previously violated clients.

Although in previous chapters it was mentioned that self-involving disclosures of therapists' feelings is often beneficial, self-disclosure of emotions immediately after the client reports a prior boundary violation may lead to clients overly-incorporating the current therapist's feedback, which may then interfere with clients fully integrating a complete and deeper understanding of their past and present experiences (P. Barach, personal communication,

May 26, 2017). Further, it is common for individuals who have experienced betrayal in a trusted professional relationship to become overly confused and distrust their personal reactions (Luepker, 1990a, 1990b). In turn, this may increase the likelihood of clients taking the therapist's view as 'truth,' which can prevent the rebuilding of the client's sense of personal agency as a necessary ingredient in effective treatment (Pope, 1994).

One of the common reactions for therapists working with victims of clinician boundary violations is 'intrusive advocacy,' or the tendency to push a client toward a particular solution (e.g., making a licensing board complaint [Sonne & Pope, 1991]). Providing information about potential recourses is often helpful, though must not occur in a way that explicitly or implicitly suggests that the client *must* choose a particular course of action (Luepker, 1990a; Pope, 1994; Sonne & Pope, 1991). P. Barach (personal communication, May 26, 2017), a clinical and forensic psychologist who has worked with many clients who have experienced therapeutic boundary violations, stated that his initial focus is "a combination of Rogerian-style empathic reflection and letting the client know that it took courage to bring this up and even to have started with a new therapist after the prior therapist acted inappropriately," a framework that is also consistent with this author's experience of what helps these clients begin to heal.

While therapist assumptions can be problematic in a number of areas, making assumptions about client experiences of therapist boundary violations can be particularly problematic (Luepker, 1990a; Pope, 1994). Critical to working with this population is a willingness to be fully present with the client's story and ensure that information provided is actively solicited, instead of treating therapists assuming they understand the client's experience or extent of relevant knowledge. For example, it can be shocking for previously violated clients to find out that their therapist had a longer standing history of engaging in similar unethical behavior. The client's emotions can be further complicated when the secondary/romantic relationship has continued beyond the termination of treatment (Pope, 1994). In such cases, it is critical, when applying any intervention (including but not limited to self-disclosure), for therapists to discuss with clients how they were impacted cognitively, emotionally, and physiologically. Further, it is imperative to evaluate what ways the previous therapist used self-disclosure, as it may have been among the first movement towards full breach of boundaries, in which case its continued use could be a trigger for the client (G. Schoener, personal communication, July 16, 2017).

Author's Personal Reactions

Even at this early stage in his career, the current author has worked with several clients who have been harmed by a previous therapist's unethical behavior. Although this author spends much of his clinical day working with individuals who have experienced trauma and betrayal, there is something qualitatively different about working with clients who have their trust broken in the therapy room. For a majority of the clients the current author has worked with, it has not been uncommon for other powerful figures to engage in egregious behavior. However, clients have reported a distinct set of difficulties that arose from experiencing a violation within prior therapeutic relationships. This author managing his personal reactions about violating therapists' behavior has been one of his most difficult clinical experiences, and one that put him at the most danger of not maintaining an empathic, validating, and fully present stance as the cornerstone of all helpful/appropriate therapeutic relationships (Norcross & Wampold, 2011).

This author will never forget the first time a client disclosed a sexual boundary violation in therapy, which happened just prior to pre-doctoral internship year. When the client, who was in her early forties at the time, disclosed a prior violation, the room suddenly felt to the author devoid of oxygen. The intensity of the emotional reaction (primarily anger) was staggering. The author did not disclose these feelings immediately, which was less of a conscious decision-making process than experiencing a level of affect that stalled communication.

Luckily, supervision was immediately after this experience, so that the author did not have to sit with these experiences long before getting support. As the various actions discussed above were processed in supervision, this author noticed an incredible urge to 'do something' about the other therapist's behavior, a common experience in early training, though one that put the author at particular risk of being disconnected from his client. Supervision largely focused on validating the therapist's urges, encouraging the use of emotion regulation skills, and the author being educated on the potential benefits of letting *the client* decide whether or not to make a formal report. Were it not for the consultation the author received, it is very likely he would have eventually followed his urge and pressured the client to report the violation, as a lesser though still significant form of intrusion, and instead of empowering the client to make her own decision and re-establish personal agency in the spirit of feminist therapy.

Conclusions

Although several authors have discussed the problems associated with therapists who have sex with their clients (Gabbard, 2005; Pope, 1990, 1994, 2001), there has been limited research and discussion on how and when to utilize self-disclosure when working with clients who have been harmed. Self-disclosure as a potentially problematic boundary crossing (Audet, 2011; Guthiel & Gabbard, 1993, 1998) is a consideration for clients who have experienced a clear violation by a previous therapist (Pope, 1990, 1994, 2001; Pope & Vetter, 1991), so that careful evaluation and anticipation of effects is warranted. Pope (1994) stated: "It is the therapist who *always and without exception* bears the professional responsibility to refrain from engaging in sex with a patient" (p. 59). This author extends this statement to the treatment of all clients who have been harmed by therapists, with respect to the therapist maintaining responsibility for managing the line between boundary crossing and violation, when evaluating the possibility and ramifications of sharing personal information as a therapeutic tool.

References

American Psychological Association. (2016). Ethical principles of psychologists and code of conduct with the 2016 amendment. Retrieved from www.apa.org/ethics/code.

Audet, C. (2011). Client perspectives of therapist self-disclosure: Violating boundaries or removing barriers? *Counselling Psychology Quarterly*, *24*(2), 85–100.

Brigham, R. (1989). *Psychotherapy stressors and sexual misconduct: A factor analytic study of the experience of non-offending and offending psychologists in Wisconsin* (Doctoral dissertation). Retrieved from American Psychological Association (APA) Psych Net.

Brown, L., & Walker, L. (1990). Feminist therapy perspectives on self-disclosure. In G. Stricker & M. Fisher (Eds.), *Self-disclosure in the therapeutic relationship* (pp. 135–56). New York: Springer Science and Business Media.

Gabbard, G. (2005). Patient–therapist boundary issues. *Psychiatric Times*, *22*(12). Retrieved from www.psychiatrictimes.com/display/article/10168/52646.

Gottdiener, W. (2008). Sexual boundary violations in residential drug-free therapeutic community treatment. *International Journal of Applied Psychoanalytic Studies*, *5*(4), 257–72.

Guthiel, T., & Gabbard, G. (1993). The concept of boundaries in clinical practice: Theoretical and risk-management dimensions. *American Journal of Psychiatry*, *150*(2), 188–96.

Guthiel, T., & Gabbard, G. (1998). Misuses and misunderstandings of boundary theory in clinical and regulatory settings. *American Journal of Psychiatry*, *155*(3), 409–14.

Lamb, D., Catanzaro, S., & Moorman, A. (2003). Psychologists reflect on their sexual relationships with clients, supervisees, and students: Occurrence, impact, rationales and collegial intervention. *Professional Psychology: Research and Practice*, *34*(1), 102–7.

Luepker, E. (1990a). Clinical assessment of clients who have been sexually exploited by their therapist and development of differential treatment plans. In G. Schoener, J. Milgrom, J. Gonsiorek, E. Luepker, & R. Conroe (Eds.), *Psychotherapists' sexual involvement with clients: intervention and prevention* (pp. 159–76). Minneapolis, MN: Walk-in Counseling Center.

Luepker, E. (1990b). Sexual exploitation of clients by therapists: Parallels with parent–child incest. In G. Schoener, J. Milgrom, J. Gonsiorek, E. Luepker, & R. Conroe (Eds.), *Psychotherapists' sexual involvement with clients: intervention and prevention* (pp. 73–9). Minneapolis, MN: Walk-In Counseling Center.

McNulty, N., Ogden, J., & Warren, F. (2013). 'Neutralizing the patient': Therapists' accounts of sexual boundary violations. *Clinical Psychology & Psychotherapy*, *20*(3), 189–98.

Nicholson, S. (2010). Too close to home: Countertransference dynamics in the wake of a colleague's sexual boundary violation. *Canadian Journal of Psychoanalysis*, *18*(2), 225–47.

Norcross, J., & Wampold, B. (2011). Evidence-based therapy relationships: Research conclusions and clinical practices. *Psychotherapy*, *48*(1), 98–102.

Pope, K. (1988). How clients are harmed by sexual contact with mental health professionals: The syndrome and its prevalence. *Journal of Counseling and Development*, *67*(4), 222–6.

Pope, K. (1989). Therapist–patient sex syndrome: A guide for attorneys and subsequent therapists to assessing damage. In G. Gabbard (Ed.), *Sexual exploitation in professional relationships* (pp. 39–55). Washington, DC: American Psychiatric Press.

Pope, K. (1990). Therapist–patient sex as sex abuse. *Professional Psychology: Research and Practice, 21*(4), 227–39.

Pope, K. (1994). *Sexual involvement with therapists: Patient assessment, subsequent therapy, forensics.* Washington, DC: American Psychological Association.

Pope, K. (2001). Sex between therapists and clients. In J. Worell (Ed.), *Encyclopedia of women and gender: Sex similarities and differences and the impact of society on gender* (Vol. 2, pp. 955–62). Cambridge, MA: Academic Press.

Pope, K., & Keith-Spiegel, P. (2008). A practical approach to boundaries in psychotherapy: Making decisions, bypassing blunders, and mending fences. *Journal of Clinical Psychology, 64*(5), 638–52.

Pope, K., & Vasquez, M. (2016). *Ethics in psychotherapy and counseling: A practical guide* (5th ed.). Hoboken, NJ: John Wiley & Sons.

Pope, K., & Vetter, V. (1991). Prior therapist–patient sexual involvement among patients seen by psychologists. *Psychotherapy, 28*(3), 429–38.

Schoener, G., Milgrom, J., Gonsiorek, J., Luepker, E., & Conroe, R. (1990). *Psychotherapists' sexual involvement with clients: Intervention and prevention.* Minneapolis, MN: Walk-in Counseling Center.

Simi, N., & Mahalik, J. (1997). Comparison of feminist versus psychoanalytic/dynamic and other therapists on self-disclosure. *Psychology of Women Quarterly, 21*(3), 465–83.

Sonne, J., & Pope, K. (1991). Treating victims of therapist-client sexual involvement. *Psychotherapy, 28*(1), 174–87.

CHAPTER **24**

Gender and Power Dynamics

Ryan Barbeau, PsyD

It is important for the male therapist/author to begin this chapter by acknowledging personal gender identity and intersectionality. It is essential to consider intersectionality between the author's maleness, both parties' various social identities, and the impacts of oppression, domination, and discrimination. People are wholes, not sums of parts. Moreover, people live in complicated environments, not vacuums. Thinking about how the author's self-disclosures as a male therapist may impact the client is important, though not as comprehensive as also considering intersectionality (see Chapter 18 on sexual orientation disclosures for further discussion of this point). Therefore, instead of merely thinking about male therapist self-disclosure, it is more helpful to reflect upon the impact of self-disclosure as a male, Caucasian, cisgender, heterosexual, 33-year-old, gainfully employed therapist without a disability living in the United States in 2017 while also considering how those factors intersect with *the client's* own unique set of social identity factors.

There is relatively little scholarly literature on the relationship between gender and therapeutic or more social (i.e., client to client) self-disclosure, though available research has some interesting conclusions. Henretty and Levitt (2010) qualitatively reviewed 30 studies conducted from 1974–2007 that more peripherally considered gender and converged to suggest no clear relationship between therapist/client gender and self-disclosure impacts, albeit with some (and more moderate) indications of male clients preferring self-disclosure of greater frequency, positive content, and more sexual content in a cross-gendered dyad. Consistent with Henretty and Levitt's (2010) larger gender finding, Dindia & Allen (1992) conducted a meta-analysis of studies of self-disclosure in social situations, and concluded that gender is not as predictive of amount and quality of disclosure as some theorists and researchers have suggested. Indeed, the therapist's relational style, impacts of gender role stereotypes, and traditional gender role conformity were consistently more impactful in research studies (Edwards & Murdock, 1994; Robitschek & McCarthy, 1991; Simone, McCarthy, & Skay, 1998). Along the same lines, Mattei (2008) found that research participants overwhelmingly viewed therapists positively, regardless of whether they directly/verbally disclosed to the client, and regardless of the therapist's or client's gender.

As the research does not offer a clear and certain understanding of the gender-based implications of self-disclosure in psychotherapy, beyond the numbers, a clinical commentary and exploration should be useful. Therefore, the current chapter provides fictional case examples for illustrative purposes. The reader is encouraged to use the key points in this chapter to generate hypotheses about gender intersectionality and impacts rather than making unilateral assumptions. This advisement is important because gender and other social identity factors will manifest differently in every therapeutic dyad and because psychotherapy exists within an always-evolving cultural milieu. As the zeitgeist evolves, so does the general understanding of gender, the experience and impact of both social and therapeutic self-disclosures, and the interaction between gender and self-disclosure. A more critical and multifaceted lens is key, as Western society (generally) progresses towards a less binary and more fluid understanding of gender. This progression, in turn, permits affirmation and respect for transgender and gender non-conforming individuals. Additionally, traditional, conservative, non-Western, and/or theocratic societies are increasingly faced and even confronted with such issues and controversies. Lurie's (2014) dissertation offers a compelling exploration of self-disclosure by transgender and gender non-confirming therapists.

Male Therapist Self-Disclosure in Contexts of Gender Roles

The observations and opinions offered below are idiographic in nature, limited by the author's personal perspective, and impacted by the author's conscious and unconscious responses to the social order. With these limitations in mind, the following case examples are intended to illustrate how gender roles and inequality affect self-disclosure decisions and impacts in various clinical circumstances. Please note that the cases are fictional, though are intended to provide a sense of the male author's gender-mindful clinical approach.

The setting of the author's current work is a university counseling center. This setting differs significantly from his prior practice in a correctional facility with female inmates, and with particular respect to gender dynamics. At the university, the author addresses himself by his first name and at least some amount of personal history disclosure, to clients, is the norm. In the correctional facility, the (unwritten) expectation was that the author and other professionals would be addressed by title and last name, and that staff of all gender identifications would generally refrain from sharing personal history with female inmates. As a result, any self-disclosure offered in the correctional facility (and with consideration of a male in a position of power disclosing to female inmates) was probably more potent and impactful, but probably riskier on multiple levels. Prior discussions in Chapter 2 of this text, on how self-disclosure can be negatively impactful on therapists, are highly relevant to forensic practice. In forensic settings, virtually everything is on record, confidentiality is nil, and clients may have particularly poor boundaries and personality factors to contend with.

When the author was at the correctional facility, he had worked with an older African American woman who was suffering from metastatic lung cancer. One day, she was refusing to take any medical medication and started cursing at the nurse who was trying to convince her otherwise. When the correctional officers observed this, they asked the author to coordinate with the psychiatrist (who the author was administratively in charge of) and recommend involuntary restraints and involuntary psychiatric medications. The author began the interaction with the older African American woman, unconventionally, with first name introductions. During the initial conversation, the author even more unconventionally shared information about his grandmother having recently died from metastatic lung cancer. Specifically, the client was told about how disempowered the author's grandmother felt at times, and with particular respect to medical decisions being made for her. Finally, while encouraging her to work collaboratively with the medical staff, and perhaps more openly consider the potential benefits of some of the medications that were being offered, the author assured her that she would be administered no involuntary medical/treatment procedures while she was placed on the author's unit, provided she was not an imminent danger to herself or others. In response, she somewhat begrudgingly acknowledged the author's larger points and began to communicate her positions in a more respectful/collaborative way. The initial self-disclosure not only helped establish rapport, but also sent a systemic message to correctional and medical staff in proximity about how treatment should be humanistic, and that a humanistic treatment could be put forth in a manner that supported institutional rules and boundaries. This case provides a practice example of points made in prior chapters of this text. Per Chapter 2, the author demonstrated how ethically appropriate self-disclosures (i.e., brief and relevant historical disclosures followed by quick return to a focus on the client), as well as moving up and down levels of hierarchy in a feminist-empowerment manner (as noted in Chapter 3), and self-disclosure in contexts of racial difference (as noted in Chapter 9) may be beneficial.

The reader may be wondering about the ways in which the author's maleness was relevant and impactful in the previous case. Given the culture of the correctional facility, the author would not have advised a female therapist to self-disclose in this way due to the systemic sexism that existed. The author calculated correctly that disclosing, while breaking of custom, would not have adverse blowback largely based on male privilege factors. Sadly, the author suspects and fears adverse blowback would have been more likely, at that correctional facility, if the disclosure came from a female therapist, and for the female therapist and client alike. Coming from the male author/therapist, the staff seemed to overlook the rule transgression and view the disclosure as a sign of strength. Unfortunately, a female therapist in the prior situation would have needed to base her decision on whether or not to disclose on either institutional rules or what was best for the client, and with greater possible consequences in mind. Essentially, the male author was asserting authority and communicating an expectation/direction to others. It is likely that female therapist disclosure in the prior example would have been interpreted by the staff as a sign of weakness and an indication that the therapist was 'too soft' to work in a correctional setting. In turn, her self-disclosure might have resulted in challenges to her authority, efforts to undermine her, and staff disagreements and splitting related to the older African American woman being an alleged favorite (of the disclosing female therapist). Although speculative on the part of the current author, these theories were developed from direct observations at the facility of how staff (and inmates) would acquiesce to the male author while challenging female colleagues on virtually the same issues, even though (on paper) those female colleagues had the same authority/standing as the author.

Another example from the author's work in that correctional facility involved a younger female inmate who was very sexually preoccupied, clearly suffering from psychosis and delusions, and had a history of being sexually inappropriate with male prison staff. With her, the author attempted an initial meeting. As the author entered proximity, she began to stare and display facial expressions that were highly inappropriate. This triggered jeering by the correctional officers. The author responded by immediately excusing himself from the meeting. The author also ensured that all future clinical services, for this younger female client, would be with female providers. This interaction and the prior interaction provide additional examples of how gender and oppression are impactful on outcomes, in that female sexuality is often encouraged, while female authority and direction are shunned. Upon further reflection, the author could make a theoretical argument about attempting to turn the prior interaction into a teachable moment for staff and the female inmate. However, a more humble and practical approach was preferred.

In higher risk and gender-discriminatory settings, good risk management practices are advised rather than trying to be a hero. The potential benefits of the author continuing to interact in the prior circumstance might have been marginally beneficial or corrective, though also could have escalated and led to total disintegration and ultimately a need for involuntary interventions. Thus, the less combustible idea of discontinuing the interactions and referring the female inmate to a female therapist was advantageous from both a clinical and risk management perspective.

In further illustration of that point, the author will share that when in his early twenties and working with middle and high school adolescents in an alternative school, he was much more conservative with self-disclosures when working with female clients than when working with male clients. Similarly, the author's female colleagues, also in their early twenties, reported being much more conservative with their disclosures to male clients. Given the nature of hormonal changes that occur during puberty and the still developing prefrontal cortex, adolescents may be particularly prone to misinterpreting therapeutic interactions in a manner that may be distracting and compromising of treatment.

Gender-informed therapeutic work in same-gender dyads can create particularly meaningful opportunities for self-disclosure. The author/therapist recalls a male client who was clearly in significant distress and even anguished in admitting that he was having erectile dysfunction and premature ejaculation issues due to sexual performance anxiety. The author responded by saying, "I experienced something similar when I was your age and am confident I can help you." The client's entire demeanor changed rapidly. In fact, the author has not previously seen such an affective shift from hopelessness. This interaction provides an example of the benefits of ethically appropriate, higher intimacy, and relevant personal history disclosures in terms of modeling, reciprocating, and disclosing with a clear purpose and treatment aim in mind (as discussed, in a more general way, in Chapters 3, 5, and 6 of this text). For the remainder of the therapeutic work, the male client with sexual functioning problems did not ask for, nor did the author offer any additional personal history details. Instead, the author proceeded with standard cognitive behavioral interventions, as it was apparent that the one prior disclosure was sufficient in its contribution to an empathic and validating frame for therapy.

Family-of-Origin Issues

Considering client family-of-origin can also be especially important when therapists are considering self-disclosure. Questions that come to mind include: what is the nature of the client's relationship with his/her father and mother? Do they have any brothers, and if so, what was/is the nature of their relationship(s) with them? What types of transference and countertransference may be at play in the therapeutic relationship, what enactments are likely to occur/re-occur in response to a disclosure from a similar or differently gendered therapist, and how might the enactment be reminiscent of helpful or problematic family/gender dynamics?

When the author was in his early twenties and completing his first therapy practicum, he was much younger than most of the clients at the community mental health center. Now, a decade later, at his university counseling center job, clients are usually closer in age to the author's daughter. The author has found age differences and family-of-origin factors can mediate the relationship between disclosure occurrences and impacts. When clients relate to the author as a fatherly figure instead of a brotherly figure, it may at times signify more credibility/expertness (as discussed more thoroughly in Chapter 30 on expertness), while at other times it may limit the client's ability to relate to the author in a candid way. The author may say the same words in the same way and in a roughly similar clinical scenario as he did ten years ago, but now those words may be more (or less) helpful given the nature of a different age/gender dynamic. Now, when the author perceives the client's transference as one of a fatherly role, he may shift the topic of conversation and explore the client's relationship with their father at an opportune clinical moment. The purpose is to see if there might be potential to deepen the current relationship and perhaps work towards a corrective experience. For example, if the client's father was controlling and harsh, the author may make a particular effort to respond in a more empowering and compassionate manner. If his/her father was neglectful, the author may be more directive and directly responsive.

This discussion about self-disclosure in the context of family transference brings to mind the author's work with a female engineering PhD student. She was experiencing systemic sexism in her department on campus. Specifically, her colleagues did not invite her to social gatherings where the more important work conversations happened. In addition, she never seemed to get appropriate credit for her work or fair opportunities pertaining to research funding. It happened consistently enough, per the examples she described, so that discriminatory suspicions appeared well founded. All of this made her very angry, but she internalized her anger and was suffering from significant symptoms of depression and anxiety. As she told the author about her experiences, the author too felt angry, but hesitated to fully express this to her, as the author was not sure how him getting upset would be helpful to her.

As the semester progressed, sufficient rapport did not seem to be developing and her symptoms worsened. She became frustrated and told the author she was likely going to quit both counseling and even her PhD program. Not really knowing what to do, the author apologized candidly for not being more helpful. Assuming counseling was likely to end in treatment failure, the author let his guard down and more openly (though briefly) vented about how angry the sexism in her department also made him. As this was occurring, the author remembers having the thought that verbally trashing other professors (possibly as a showing of countertransference) was not very professional and should probably stop. However, before halting, the client became tearful for the first time in her therapeutic work. She explained it was the first time she could tell that the male therapist was "not just going through the motions," but really "gave a shit" about her. Ultimately, and through her additional resources, she persisted on to earn her PhD. She eventually described in therapy more productive ways to channel her anger into advocacy, both for herself and others experiencing sexism in academia.

This interaction illustrates how non-disclosure/neutrality, particularly in contexts of oppression and forms of trauma, can be experienced as inhuman (see Chapter 8 on trauma for further discussion of this point). It is also suspected by this author that the female client may have had a rejecting father, in which case a more transparent male acknowledgment of sexism was particularly validating and empowering. The possibility of a father–daughter dynamic was considered intuitively by the author, rather than explored in that moment, because doing so could have been experienced by the client as another showing of male dismissal and superiority. Upon further reflection, the author's self-disclosure also included profanity. In retrospect, the curse words were probably a helpful way to convey genuineness, as she too demonstrated acceptance/usage of colorful language.

Conclusions

It feels appropriate for the author to conclude this chapter by self-disclosing to the reader that the last time he sought personal counseling was with a male therapist who openly and directly self-disclosed at opportune times. Specifically, the author had sought personal counseling related to his father's illness and eventual death. During bereavement, hearing the therapist disclose about his own bereavement experiences was very therapeutic, important to building and maintaining rapport, and also helped the author to take a new-found perspective on the experience, which in turn permitted coping and relief. Moreover, the author would say that the bereavement self-disclosure of his prior therapist helped the author grow in his ability to more authentically and effectively work with clients.

References

Dindia, K., & Allen, M. (1992) Sex differences in self-disclosure: A meta-analysis. *Psychological Bulletin, 112*(1), 106–24.

Edwards, C., & Murdock, N. (1994). Characteristics of therapist self-disclosure in the counseling process. *Journal of Counseling and Development, 72*(4), 384–9.

Henretty, J., & Levitt, H. (2010). The role of therapist self-disclosure in psychotherapy: A qualitative review. *Clinical Psychology Review, 30*(1), 63–77.

Lurie, S. (2014). Exploring the impacts of disclosure for the transgender and gender non-conforming therapists (Doctoral dissertation). Retrieved from Thesis, Dissertations, and Projects (No UMI no.).

Mattei, D. (2008). The effect of amount of therapist self-disclosure, gender of client and gender of therapist on perceptions of therapists' self-disclosure (Doctoral dissertation). Retrieved from ProQuest Dissertations and Theses database (UMI Number: 3318774).

Robitschek, C., & McCarthy, P. (2001). Prevalence of counselor self-reference in the therapeutic dyad. *Journal of Counseling & Development, 69*(3), 218–21.

Simone, D., McCarthy, P., & Skay, C. (1998). An investigation of client and counselor variables that influence likelihood of counselor self-disclosure. *Journal of Counseling and Development, 76*(2), 174–82.

CHAPTER 25

Suicide Risk Assessment

Asha Wilkus-Stone, PsyD

To truly accept and not reject a struggling soul who entertains ending his or her life takes a certain measure of empathic fortitude and perseverance, even courage.

(Jobes, 2000, p. 12)

Therapists often work with clients whose presentation warrants suicide risk assessment. Clients who report suicide ideation, plan, intent, previous attempts, or risk behaviors have a critical need for care and safety. In turn, therapists are challenged to provide high-quality and empathic services, while also complying with ethical guidelines to prevent harm, sometimes at the expense of client confidentiality (Sommers-Flanagan & Shaw, 2017).

The subject of death by suicide naturally evokes strong feelings, beliefs, morals, and impulses. Not immune from such emotional reality, practitioners may feel a rise in their own anxiety level, which may be as much the client's disturbance as the practitioner's own. The ethics of prioritizing clients' needs, treatment focus, and intervention-mindedness (as discussed in Chapter 2 of this text) may be helpful in containing therapist anxiety. However, in most clinical circumstances, conducting suicide risk assessment based solely on these dictates falls short of the kind of individualized care that is vital during crisis. Over-compliance with agency directives (i.e., intervening with documentation in mind) may lead to constriction in the practitioner's intervention choices, as well as rigidity paralleling the client's own cognitive constriction (Kleespies & Dettner, 2000; Richards, 2000).

This chapter will explore therapist self-disclosure (TSD) as an intervention in the context of suicide risk assessment. After a brief review of leading theoretical perspectives, including the view of suicide as stemming from protracted interpersonal distress, the chapter will move forward into a short survey of current approaches to suicide risk assessment, followed by a theory of how TSD might be incorporated into the exchange, and a case example illustrating a therapist's rationale and reflections on using TSD during risk assessment. There has been little research on the outcomes of TSD during this kind of challenging encounter. Thus, the aim of this chapter is to contextualize how certain types of TSD, specifically the self-involving type and sharing positive feelings toward the client, may be integrated into suicide risk assessment.

The Origins and Drives of Suicide

Theories about why people consider and attempt suicide include reminders that the underlying psychic structures of suicidal clients are deeply pained. Edwin Shneidman, the founder of modern suicidology, proposed three primary components. The first, *psychache*, is the core etiology for suicide ideation. Without it, death by suicide is not viable. In addition to this feeling of deep and steadfast distress, *constriction* (i.e., impaired problem solving) and *perturbability* (i.e., agitation) are facets of suicidology (Shneidman, 1993, 1998, 2001).

Thomas Joiner and colleagues (Joiner, Van Orden, Witte, & Rudd, 2009; Van Orden, Witte, Cukrowicz, Braithwaite, Selby, & Joiner, 2010) propose that the pain driving clients to conceive of and desire death by suicide stems from the presence of two interpersonal constructs, *thwarted belongingness* and *perceived burdensomeness*. Joiner, Van Orden, and colleagues conceptualize the experience of *thwarted belongingness* as dimensionally comprised of loneliness plus the absence of reciprocal care, *perceived burdensomeness* as the cognitive-affective dimensions of self-hate, and the perception of interpersonal liability (i.e., one's flawed life is inherently burdensome on others). Per this theory, a suicide attempt goes against an innate aversion to pain and death. Thus, a third factor of *acquired capability* includes an increased tolerance for pain, and a decreased fear of death (Joiner et al., 2009; Van Orden et al., 2010).

Practice Standards for Suicide Risk Assessment

The literature on suicide ideation in clinical practice includes efforts to test and document standards of care, and proposes practice guidelines for therapists to conduct thorough, timely, helpful, and ethical assessments. Standard practice of assessing for risk to self includes asking the client a number of important questions in order to guide treatment, safety planning, and management of identified risk (Bryan & Rudd, 2006). The inquiry determines the client's predisposition for suicidal behavior, precipitant stressors, symptomology, and particularly, hopelessness, which is high in attempters of suicide (Beck, Steer, Kovacs, & Garrison, 1985). The inquiry also identifies the specific nature of the suicidal thinking and related behavioral history (Bryan & Rudd, 2006).

Assessment should be culturally informed, collaborative, and include frank discussion about suicide (Granello, 2010). The collaborative approach is not only directly beneficial to clients, but may also help to contain therapists' countertransference and anxiety around the subject (Sommers-Flanagan & Shaw, 2017). Other approaches to assessment focus on safety planning to mitigate risk (Stanley & Brown, 2012), as well as addressing maladaptive coping and deficits in distress tolerance skills (Linehan, 1993, 1999). Still others treat suicidality as the presenting concern with a focus on the individual client's phenomenology of suicide ideation and behavior (Jobes, 2006).

In order to reduce the likelihood of an irreconcilable rupture in therapy, assessment should be conducted within the therapeutic frame (Fowler, 2012). When the meaning of suicide can be explored within the narrative of therapy, there is a greater likelihood that the assessment will be less stilted and hierarchal, and thus, emotionally nearer to the client's suffering. A crucial element in developing effective interventions for suicidal clients is to understand the relational function of their ideation and plan (Jobes, 2000, 2006). Interpersonal drives (i.e., affiliation, reciprocity, nurturance, and love) are vital protective factors (Joiner et al., 2009; Shneidman, 1998; Van Orden et al., 2010). Thus, exploring the client's relational world during assessment informs the therapist about the extent of a client's alienation and interpersonal dysfunction.

Theory and Impact of TSD during Suicide Risk Assessment

The therapeutic encounter with the suicidal client is an opportunity to join with another human in the throes of an agony relatively few will witness. It is a privilege that carries significant responsibility. As an application of the support in the literature for an interpersonal etiology of suicide, TSD may be a valuable intervention for clarifying and reducing risk. TSD during suicide risk assessment involves therapists confronting their own reactions, both to the client and suicide on the whole. Therapists must find the courage and compassion to validate their shared humanity. TSD in the service of the client's welfare and safety increases therapeutic efficacy (Zur, 2007).

When therapists utilize TSD in contexts of suicide assessment, they must first consider, anticipate, and conceptualize the client's likely alienation, devaluation, and maladaptive interpersonal schemas. It may be helpful to directly yet gently challenge the client's constricted cognitive patterns and limited problem solving. The intervention can address the underlying affective dysregulation and poor self-concept derived from distorted interpersonal narratives, which often compel the client to consider suicide as a viable problem-solving solution. The outcome may be that the client is more inclined to explore other aspects of misperception or misinterpretation in relationships with both self and others going forward. In effect, TSD may help to assess and moderate suicide risk.

In the following case example, the reader should consider how TSDs during the suicide risk assessment address the client's distortions and deeper sense of self-in-relationship. Additionally, the reader should reflect upon how TSD aligns with the aforementioned standards of practice in suicide risk assessment. Those standards include assessing the client's risk to self, while also providing the client with a positive and growth-inspiring therapeutic experience.

TSD as an Intervention in Suicide Risk: A Case Example

Lana is a 20-year-old, African American, queer, and female-identified second-year student at a large university within the continental United States. Lana is a biology major with intent to go to medical school. She has an outstanding

GPA, but struggles with significant stress around academic performance. She presented for services at the university counseling center reporting symptoms of depressed mood, anhedonia, irritability, poor concentration and sleep, pessimism, hopelessness regarding her potential to recover from depression, and persistent thoughts about death and suicide.

Her depressive symptoms began in elementary school. Despite periods of partial remittance, she continued to experience significant distress during adolescence and young adulthood. She reported strong identification with thoughts of death ("I don't know who I'd be without thinking of killing myself") and engaging in behaviors that reinforced her preoccupation (i.e. participation in suicide-centric online groups). Lana reported a first suicide attempt at age 11 by taking "a bottle of Tylenol" followed by four attempts in the following years. Attempts ranged from low to moderate lethality. She denied hospitalizations, but saw an individual therapist for about six months at age 16. She reported an interpersonal trauma history including molestation at age 8 by an older child, as well as childhood physical abuse by her stepfather. Her treatment plan included a referral for psychiatric medication and weekly individual therapy.

Therapy focused primarily on reducing risk for suicide. It was conducted through an integrative and relational framework, with weekly assessment for ideation and planning. Lana was consistently on time, productively engaged, and forthcoming about her hobbies and interests. She patently denied her feelings, displayed little affect, and avoided exploring the impact of her history and relationships. She endorsed suicide ideation in every session, rating her *ideation* an 8 out of 10, but rating her *intent* much lower (2 out of 10). She reported highly lethal plans (i.e., getting drunk and shooting herself in the head), but denied access to lethal means. She was openly skeptical and rejecting of the therapeutic relationship (i.e., making statements such as "You're just doing your job," and "I thought about not coming today, but didn't have anything else to do").

After six weeks, she presented much like other days, sharing academic stress and several recent drawings. In the course of the session, she reported flatly that the previous evening, while feeling "stressed, overwhelmed, and hopeless" about her progress studying, she had started to strangle herself with a computer cord. She ceased the attempt because, "I knew I had therapy today and I should have canceled the session."

The details of Lana's disclosure necessitated an assessment for imminent risk. Lana had a predisposition for suicidal behavior, previous attempts, and enduring suicidal thinking. Her symptom presentation (although moderated by medication) was severe and her coping resources limited. Despite her outward disdain for therapy, her behavior in therapy and her explanation for aborting her attempt suggested that therapy was protective. During assessment, her therapist inquired directly about this possibility. Lana responded impassively that her therapist might have felt "guilty," and "like a failure," if she had died by suicide.

Whereas an intra-psychic therapy might consider this statement reflective of a projective process warranting interpretation, from an inter-relational perspective Lana's statements seemed to be an indication of *mentalizing* about her therapist's plausible cognitions. Intervening in the direction of mentalization, Lana's therapist reflected on her countertransference, how she might feel if Lana were to have completed the suicide, and asked if she might actually like to know her feelings. Lana declined. Noting the client's resistance, the therapist instead wondered aloud how Lana imagined other people might have been impacted by her death by suicide (i.e., her roommate, professors, mother, and two younger siblings). Lana speculated their range of reactions would be somewhere between apathy and ambivalence.

Eventually, the conversation returned to whether Lana would like to know how her therapist might feel. Lana admitted she did. Sensitive to Lana's evident discomfort with the intimacy of the TSD, her therapist modulated her tone of voice and body language. She spoke tenderly and with emotion. She gently shared that feelings of guilt and thoughts about failing as a therapist did not resonate for her. Instead, had Lana died by suicide the night before, her therapist said she would have felt "extremely sad," and likely would have experienced "a great feeling of loss and sorrow." Pausing, the therapist noted Lana's vulnerability and surprise. The therapist added she might also have had "a much deeper sense of the magnitude" of Lana's suffering and felt "regret" that the depth of that suffering could not have been shared while she was alive.

In response, Lana's defensive posture returned. However, through continued dialogue, Lana rated her intent in the next day and week at a "1 or 2 out of 10," and was active in safety planning. During the course of this middle/working phase of the therapy, her therapist consulted with another psychologist, gained consent from Lana to discuss the encounter with her psychiatrist, and adjusted their weekly session time to meet sooner than usual. As the session seemed to naturally draw to a close, Lana's anxiety rose visibly. She abruptly began asking her therapist to repeat her feelings, "Really, you would have felt sad?"

Reflection on the Impact of TSD

Lana's case illustrates the benefits of TSDs of positive emotions, self-involving disclosures, and how these types of TSDs can open the door to intense and therapeutically productive *in vivo* work (as mentioned in Chapter 6 of this text on types of disclosure). Lana's suggestion that her therapist might feel "guilty" or "like a failure," was not implausible—often therapists have these feelings about chronically suicidal clients. One of the main reasons why the TSD intervention was helpful and appropriate is that it was put forth when the therapist was aware of her countertransference, had reflected upon it, and then offered an authentic response. Lana's positive response was, in turn, consistent with prior chapter discussions on authentic TSDs in cross-cultural contexts.

The therapist decided to share her feelings in the direct service of Lana's welfare. The therapist began with self-reflection and shared feelings that were client-centered and positive. Her feelings of sadness, sorrow, grief, and empathy connected with Lana's personhood. The therapist's choice to involve herself in Lana's hypothetical death by suicide, saying she might also feel "regret," effectively communicated her commitment to Lana and was intended to rouse her hope for treatment. Further, the TSD directly addressed Lana's high-risk perception that she was a burden, as well as her suspicion that her therapist was insincerely interested in helping her.

From an intra-psychic vantage point, use of TSD to re-examine Lana's projected guilt challenged her assumption that her interpersonal effect was one of liability. The therapist reinforced, through her investment in the relationship, that Lana's life (and her suffering) were valued and respected. The therapist's validation of their client–therapist connection, which had been implied via Lana's previous behavior in therapy and comment about not cancelling the session, helped to meet her immediate needs for soothing, belonging, affiliation, and reciprocity. Thus, TSD was an intervention helping to both assess and reduce her suicide risk, and was put forth in a manner aligned with empirically validated standards of practice and safety planning.

Conclusions

The serious nature of suicide risk assessment makes it challenging to balance client confidentiality with the therapist's ethical duty to warn, particularly in light of expectable and strong countertransference reactions. When the therapist weighs these mandates in session, humanistic elements of the therapeutic exchange may compete with legal mandates and at times be de-prioritized. In such cases, TSD is an intervention that can inject possibly life-saving compassion and human connection into a critical therapeutic encounter; it can serve as an antidote for the psychache, constriction, and perturbability at the core of the suicidal process (Shneidman, 1993, 1998). As Lana's case helped to illustrate, the impact of discerning and responsive TSD can effectively prioritize client welfare, convey the therapist's commitment, gently challenge negative interpersonal schemas and the intra-psychic components of suicidality, and help to meet the client's relational needs.

The future possibilities of using TSD in a context of assessment of risk to self has relevancy from both theoretical and practice-oriented perspectives. From the former vantage point, strengths, limitations, and generalizability of TSD as an intervention should continue to be researched and explored through case-by-case clinical judgment, agency procedures, and the field's ever-advancing understanding of suicidality. From the latter, the profound suffering, estrangement, and hopelessness of suicidal clients call out to be seen with eyes that surpass professional roles, making TSD a particularly powerful instrument of assessment and healing. For these most complicated and dangerous of cases, further study would be of value, while therapist patience, perseverance, and compassion is vital.

References

Beck, A., Steer, R., Kovacs, M., & Garrison, B. (1985). Hopelessness and eventual suicide: A 10-year prospective study of patients hospitalized with suicidal ideation. *American Journal of Psychiatry, 142*(5), 559–63.

Bryan, C., & Rudd, M. (2006). Advances in the assessment of suicide risk. *Journal of Clinical Psychology, 62*(2), 185–200.

Fowler, J. (2012). Suicide risk assessment in clinical practice: Pragmatic guidelines for imperfect assessments. *Psychotherapy*, *49*(1), 81–90.

Granello, D. (2010). The process of suicide risk assessment: Twelve core principles. *Journal of Counseling & Development*, *88*(3), 363–70.

Jobes, D. (2000). Collaborating to prevent suicide: A clinical-research perspective. *Suicide and Life-Threatening Behavior*, *30*(1), 8–17.

Jobes, D. (2006). *Managing suicidal risk: A collaborative approach*. New York: Guilford Press.

Joiner Jr., T., Van Orden, K., Witte, T., & Rudd, M. (2009). *The interpersonal theory of suicide: Guidance for working with suicidal clients*. Washington, DC: American Psychological Association.

Kleespies, P., & Dettner, E. (2000). The stress of patient emergencies for the clinician: Incidence, impact, and means of coping. *Journal of Clinical Psychology*, *56*(10), 1353–69.

Linehan, M. (1993). *Cognitive-behavioral treatment of borderline personality disorder*. New York: Guilford Press.

Linehan, M. (1999). Standard protocol for assessing and treating suicidal behaviors for patients in treatment. In D. Jacobs (Ed.), *The Harvard Medical School guide to suicide assessment and intervention* (pp. 146–87). San Francisco, CA: Jossey-Bass.

Richards, B. (2000). Impact upon therapy and the therapist when working with suicidal patients: Some transference and countertransference aspects. *British Journal of Guidance & Counselling*, *28*(3), 325–37.

Shneidman, E. (1993). Commentary: Suicide as psychache. *Journal of Nervous and Mental Disease*, *181*(3), 145–7.

Shneidman, E. (1998). Perspectives on suicidology: Further reflections on suicide and psychache. *Suicide and Life-Threatening Behavior*, *28*(3), 245–50.

Shneidman, E. (2001). *Comprehending suicide: Landmarks in 20th-century suicidology*. Washington, DC: American Psychological Association.

Sommers-Flanagan, J., & Shaw, S. (2017). Suicide risk assessment: What psychologists should know. *Professional Psychology: Research and Practice*, *48*(2), 98–106.

Stanley, B., & Brown, G. (2012). Safety planning intervention: A brief intervention to mitigate suicide risk. *Cognitive and Behavioral Practice*, *19*(2), 256–64.

Van Orden, K., Witte, T., Cukrowicz, K., Braithwaite, S., Selby, E., & Joiner, T. (2010). The interpersonal theory of suicide. *Psychological Review*, *117*(2), 575–600.

Zur, O. (2007). Self-disclosure. In *Boundaries in psychotherapy: Ethical and clinical explorations* (pp. 149–65). Washington, DC, US: American Psychological Association.

Part VI

Major Implications for Practitioners

Negative Consequences of Self-Disclosure: A Result of the Practitioner and Not the Technique

Cristelle Audet, PhD

Two discourses seem to have emerged in the therapist disclosure literature. First, there is an ethics discourse portraying disclosure as being in tension with boundaries that define the client and therapist roles in therapy. Second, there is a discourse that promotes therapist disclosure as a technique/ intervention. How therapists position themselves within these discourses, whether consciously or not, likely has a bearing on whether and how they disclose in sessions.

In this chapter, the author discusses therapist disclosure as social interaction versus technique, arguing that while historical/personal/extra-therapy disclosure may have a significant bearing on boundaries if delivered inappropriately, it may nevertheless have a role as an intervention that advances and deepens the therapeutic process. A review of the author's naturalistic research follows, putting into evidence a link between 'effective use' of disclosure and therapist attunement to the client. After establishing the importance of attentiveness to context, the author contends that therapist disclosure should be considered an intervention like any other and that clinical judgment in its use can and should be cultivated as a therapist competency.

Therapist Disclosure as Social Interaction or Technique?

Since 'talk' is the main mode of exchange between individuals, as a social norm, it may be challenging to discern when a therapist's disclosure is an intended part of the therapy or an unrelated social interaction. What perhaps differentiates disclosure from other in-session therapist behaviors is that it has been perceived as having a tenuous impact on therapist-client boundaries.

To follow up on points made in the Introduction and Chapter 2 of this text, ethicists have cautioned that therapist disclosure can have far-reaching effects on the therapy relationship, straining the relationship to a point of devaluing the necessary therapist-client roles (Barnett, 2011; Gutheil & Brodsky, 2008). The ethics-based discourse of boundary crossings and violations may foster practitioner hesitation or reluctance in using disclosure with clients (Peterson,

2002; Zur, 2007). This cautionary effect is reflected in therapist responses to surveys exploring the ethical use of disclosure with clients (e.g., Edwards & Murdock, 1994; Pope, Tabachnick, & Keith-Spiegel, 1987) and, possibly, its generally infrequent use. While surveys suggest the prevalence of disclosure is fairly high with at least 90% of therapists engaging in some form of disclosure (Pope et al., 1987), disclosure has been characterized as comprising an average of 3.5% of therapist behavior (Hill & Knox, 2002).

In turn, this finding on infrequency is also reflected in early analog research that attempted to isolate therapist disclosure impact on 'expertness'—perhaps a characteristic perceived as distinguishing the professional's role from the client's (Barnett, 2011; Gutheil & Brodsky, 2008). As discussed in Chapter 4 of this text, analog research has contributed to current understanding of therapist disclosure by attempting to capture the impact of frequency, intimacy, and similarity on 'ideal' therapist qualities (including expertness, warmth, attractiveness, and trustworthiness [Henretty & Levitt, 2010]).

However, within a climate of evidence-based practice, equivocal results may have dissuaded some practitioners from viewing therapist disclosure as a valid intervention. While the ethical perspective that alerts and sensitizes professionals to the pitfalls of using disclosure is important (above all, do no harm), it may also have slowed the counseling profession's exploration of disclosure as a technique. Indeed, straddling therapist disclosure as both a technique and a potential boundary crossing/violation may be a point of tension for practitioners.

It is possible that Knox and Hill's (2003; Hill & Knox, 2002) widely cited work helped shift thinking towards using disclosure as a technique. In their work, they conducted a thematic analysis of a review of research-based findings on therapist disclosure, which culminated into seven different types of disclosure: disclosures of facts, feelings, insight, strategy, reassurance/support, challenge, and immediacy. Knox and Hill (2003) explained how each type of disclosure could serve a specific therapeutic purpose, thus sensitizing practitioners to its deliberate uses. Further buttressing the idea of 'disclosure as technique' are the theoretical underpinnings that lend legitimacy and purposefulness (e.g., humanistic therapists disclose to build rapport, normalize; cognitive therapists disclose to model change strategies), as well as therapists' accounts of disclosure's potential benefits to the relationship and therapeutic process (Simi & Mahalik, 1997; Simon, 1990). Chapter 3 reviews in greater depth therapist disclosure according to theoretical orientation.

When Therapist Disclosure Does Not Work

Some generally accepted findings from analog research are that infrequent, moderate use of low intimacy disclosures of similarity should generally lead to favorable views of the therapist (Henretty & Levitt, 2010; Hill & Knox, 2002; Watkins, 1990). While this knowledge helped isolate some of the dimensions of therapist disclosure and their potential impact, examining disclosure as a single, one-time event in the early stage of therapy does not account well for the disclosure process—that is, the clinical judgment required in using disclosure within an ongoing relationship with the client. The analog findings nevertheless raised discussion about the relevance of context, citing aspects such as strength of the relationship, stage of therapy, and client expectations grounded in cultural understandings that would need to be accounted for in order to render a disclosure therapeutically useful. Indeed, the mantra to assist therapists in this decision-making process has been disclosing *what* to *whom, when, why,* and *how* (Henretty & Levitt, 2010).

Findings from naturalistic research put into evidence the importance of therapist attunement to client context and therapy needs when disclosing. What follows are examples from the author's research to illuminate this (Audet, 2011; Audet & Everall, 2003, 2010). Building on the prior discussion, these examples will illustrate some of the ways in which negatively impactful disclosures can be the result of the practitioner rather than the intervention itself.

Example of Lacking Attentiveness to Process

In one instance, a client 'Doug' described how his therapist frequently disclosed about experiences that evoked certain emotional intensity for him as the client. He described the disclosures as interfering with the therapy process in two ways. First, at times, he found himself overwhelmed by the intimate nature of the disclosure ("things would come up and I'd be like, oh this is too flowery or too touchy-feely for me . . . it almost got to be like . . . too much emotion in one day") and consequently 'shut down' in session to 'protect himself' from the emotional intensity ("after a while I'd want to run away from the intimacy of the moment; I didn't want to be in it too long and I just wanted to numb out from it"). Second, the client felt it interfered with his preferred focus in session and how the time should be spent (i.e., "sometimes I just wanted to talk, because once I'd hear myself talk I'd feel better and know the answer to my problem; but he'd always interrupt . . . and I'd be like now I gotta try and relate this to my experience"). While Doug reported an overall positive therapy experience, he sometimes disconnected from the therapy process in moments of disclosures. In these instances, the therapist's disclosure implies a certain lack of attentiveness to the client's needs in therapy, gave rise to process issues, and illustrates the ethical precautions (earlier in this text) against self-disclosures that change the focus of therapy rather than deepening the here-and-now.

Example of 'Too Frequent' Disclosure Based on Therapist Personality

It is well established that there are limits to the frequency and amount of therapist disclosure when it starts to become ineffective, usually at the expense of role-defining boundaries (Barnett 2001; Gutheil & Brodsky, 2008). In the example of 'Stan,' in Audet and Everall (2003, 2010), Stan speculated that the therapist's consistent sharing of lengthy personal anecdotes was "just the way she was." There was no introduction to the disclosive stance and its purpose in the therapy, nor any debriefing thereafter to assess its usefulness to the client. This approach suggests that disclosure may have reflected the therapist's 'way of being' rather than a purposeful technique. Regardless of the degree of intentionality behind the disclosure, a therapist's overabundance of disclosure and lack of transparency to indicate it as therapeutically relevant may leave clients attributing the disclosure to therapist personality, which may in turn impinge on client perception of the therapist's competency or expertness.

In another example in Audet and Everall (2003), the therapist seemed to justify the content of her disclosure upon noticing that the client disagreed with it. This therapist's 'defending' of her beliefs/values, as conveyed through disclosure, might also be attributable to the personhood of the therapist, thereby taking the form of unexamined countertransference. A client-focused alternative might have been to explore the client's feelings of disappointment about what the therapist had disclosed and how it might relate to the client's presenting issue. The risks of disclosure as unfiltered countertransference are well documented in the literature, particularly though not exclusively within the psychoanalytic/ psychodynamic tradition (Bridges, 2001; Goldstein, 1994; Kuchuck, 2009; Tsai, Plummer, Kanter, Newring, & Kohlenberg, 2010), and point to the importance of self-awareness in service of safe and effective use of self with clients.

Example of Disclosing for Personal Reasons

In the case of Stan and his experience of role reversal, he described the reputable yet highly disclosive therapist as though "she was getting things off her chest." He lamented having little time in session to discuss his issues and that he struggled to appreciate how her disclosures regarding social anxiety (e.g., 'butterflies' before doing a presentation) related to the agoraphobia he was experiencing. In this instance, the disclosures may have served the therapist's personal agenda. Being entrenched in her detailed anecdotes may have blinded her to the client's needs. Either way, these incongruences call into question the therapist's 'presence' in the therapy. Indeed, Stan reported that he felt "she was crazier than he was" and that it was like "she was the patient and I was the therapist." This could be considered a boundary violation whereby, unmitigated by self-awareness, therapists use the relationship to meet their own (in this case emotional) needs rather than disclosing thoughtfully and reflectively based on prioritizing anticipated benefits for the client (Smith & Fitzpatrick, 1995). In such cases, the guiding question for therapists becomes, "Who is the disclosure benefiting?"

The Importance of Attunement

What the prior three scenarios seem to have in common is that the therapists were lacking attunement. Borne out of the Rogerian concept of 'empathic responding' (Rogers, 1979), attunement has been described as "responsive communication . . . [that] relates to the therapist's desire to understand the client's immediate experience, to put the implicit aspects of the experience into words, and to communicate this understanding to the client" (Macaulay, Toukmanian, & Gordon, 2007, p. 246). In the context of disclosure, clients have described attunement as the therapist "saying the right thing at the right time" or that the disclosure was "the best thing therapist could have done at that moment." It would seem that therapists, in these instances, demonstrated awareness and receptivity by giving consideration to how disclosure might fit for the client given their identified needs in therapy, and whether the strength of the therapeutic relationship could withstand the intimacy of the disclosure.

In one example of this author's research that further illuminates attunement (Audet & Everall, 2003), 'Lisa' described how she did not appreciate her therapist's fairly non-intimate disclosure early in the therapy, as it did not align with what she expected of a therapist. The disclosure left her wondering, "Am I going to have to find myself another therapist?" Lisa speculated that because the therapist did not disclose for some time after the first disclosure, she had perhaps sensed discomfort and accordingly disclosed less. However, Lisa described subsequent disclosures once their relationship had evolved as 'synergistic.' Even though the initial disclosure was perhaps less helpful, the therapist appeared to have adjusted to therapeutic strain by refraining from disclosure until a stronger relationship and understanding of the client's needs established. In other words, the therapist was attuned in her focus on the client, intuitively addressed the rupture through restraint, and better responded to how the therapy process was unfolding.

Therapist Disclosure as a Competency

Going a step further from less effective disclosures being a result of the practitioner and not the technique, this author contends that therapist disclosure should be construed as an intervention, like any other, that requires clinical judgment and can be cultivated as a competency. Its precarious impact on boundaries and dependence on context may serve as impetus to approach it in this manner. Applying the conventionally accepted tripartite model of competency (Arthur & Collins, 2010; Sue, Arredondo, & McDavis, 1992), competency development with regard to therapist disclosure would entail (a) possessing *knowledge* in the types and uses of disclosure based on empirical research, (b) developing *skills* in its application, and (c) utilizing *awareness* (of one's values, beliefs, attitudes) reflexively and reflectively in its delivery. Construing disclosure as an intervention (rather than 'just talk') may assist therapists in sharpening their clinical judgment around its usage, as they focus on how the disclosure would best serve the moment based on the client's needs within an evolving therapy.

Advancing therapist disclosure as a competency may also heighten its ethical use and reduce negative outcomes. Practitioners' discernment process could include an exploration of underlying motivations for disclosing to minimize boundary violations, such as meeting personal needs. Doing so would be consistent with the awareness aspect of competence. Ethically, a guiding principle is also how practitioners can proceed with the intervention in service of the client (e.g., beneficence) or else without harming the client (e.g., non-maleficence).

Therapists' reasons for disclosure in practice seem to align with what has been discussed theoretically on the subject (e.g., Simi & Mahalik, 1997; Simon, 1990) in the literature and Chapter 3 of this text. Grounding the intervention in a theoretical approach may provide therapists with some guidance and confidence in its application. However, outside of self-involving disclosures, it seems the lack of focus on personal disclosure during counseling training means therapists are often left to discover—through trial and error—the therapeutic possibilities disclosure has to offer in their work with clients. Still yet, there are some indications that therapist disclosure is not always discussed openly in supervision, resulting in constricting trainees' attitudes and trainees' use of self-disclosure (Audet & Everall, 2003; Knight, 2014). This author echoes recent calls that more training programs address therapist disclosure as a clinical intervention (Henretty & Levitt, 2010; Somers, Pomerantz, Meeks, & Pawlow, 2014). Chapter 7 of this text on supervision and training, as well as the works of Somers et al. (2014) and Bottrill, Pistrang, Barker, and Worrell (2010), illuminate trainees' processes in developing competencies as evolving with the capacity to reflect as they gain knowledge, skills, and awareness surrounding its application.

Conclusions

In order to reduce less effective self-disclosure attributable to the practitioner, it would seem important to view therapist disclosure as an intervention. So doing would hopefully add deliberateness or intentionality in its use, keep at bay the undue or excess expression of therapist personality and personal needs that may compromise boundaries, and invite more ethical use of the intervention. Ironically, a preoccupation with disclosure's impact on boundaries may overshadow exploration of its potency, only to be swept under the proverbial rug. One implication is that less informed and novice practitioners may privilege a risk-management approach or even fear-based avoidance to disclosing (Peterson, 2002; Zur, 2007), a finding consistent with those from qualitative studies noted in Chapter 7 on supervision and training.

Construing disclosure as an intervention shifts our gaze to consider how it can be developed as a competency through knowledge, skills, and awareness. Enhancing therapist intentionality could reduce disclosures that reflect the therapist's way of being or personal needs that, in turn, harm clients. Of particular importance, based on naturalistic studies, is the therapist's capacity for attunement and reflexivity—a focus that training programs could serve well. Ultimately, the mantra of 'who, when, why, what, how' would seem a good place to start.

References

Arthur, N., & Collins, S. (Eds.) (2010). *Culture-infused counselling* (2nd ed.). Calgary, AB: Counselling Concepts.

Audet, C. (2011). Client perspectives of therapist self-disclosure: Violating boundaries or removing boundaries? *Counselling Psychology Quarterly, 24*(2), 85–100.

Audet, C., & Everall, R. (2003). Counsellor self-disclosure: Client-informed implications for practice. *Counselling and Psychotherapy Research, 3*(3), 223–31.

Audet, C., & Everall, R. (2010). Therapist self-disclosure and the therapeutic relationship: A phenomenological study from the client perspective. *British Journal of Guidance and Counselling, 38*(3), 327–42.

Barnett, J. (2011). Psychotherapist self-disclosure: Ethical and clinical considerations. *Psychotherapy, 48*(4), 315–21.

Bottrill, S., Pistrang, N., Barker, C., & Worrell, M. (2010). The use of therapist self-disclosure: Clinical psychology trainees' experiences. *Psychotherapy Research, 20*(2), 165–80.

Bridges, N. (2001). Therapists' self-disclosure: Expanding the comfort zone. *Psychotherapy, 38*(1), 21–30.

Edwards, C., & Murdock, N. (1994). Characteristics of therapist self-disclosure in the counseling process. *Journal of Counseling and Development, 72*, 384–9.

Goldstein, E. (1994). Self-disclosure in treatment: What therapists do and don't talk about. *Clinical Social Work Journal, 22*(4), 417–33.

Gutheil, T., & Brodsky, A. (2008). *Preventing boundary violations in clinical practice.* New York: Guilford Press.

Henretty, J., & Levitt, H. (2010). The role of therapist self-disclosure in psychotherapy: A qualitative review. *Clinical Psychology Review, 30*(1), 63–77.

Hill, C., & Knox, S. (2002). Self-disclosure. In J. Norcross (Ed.), *Psychotherapy relationships that work: Therapist contributions and responsiveness to patients* (pp. 255–65). New York: Oxford University Press.

Knox, S., & Hill, C. (2003). Therapist self-disclosure: Research-based suggestions for practitioners. *Journal of Clinical Psychology/In Session, 59*(5), 529–39.

Kuchuck, S. (2009). Do ask, do tell? Narcissistic need as a determinant of analyst self-disclosure. *Psychoanalytic Review, 96*(6), 1007–24.

Knight, Z. (2014). Students' attitudes towards and engagement in self-disclosure: Implications for supervision. *The Clinical Supervisor, 33*(2), 163–81.

Macaulay, H., Toukmanian, S., & Gordon, K. (2007). Attunement as the core of therapist-expressed empathy. *Canadian Journal of Counselling/Revue canadienne de counseling, 41*(4), 244–54.

Peterson, Z. (2002). More than a mirror: The ethics of therapist self-disclosure. *Psychotherapy: Theory, Research, Practice, Training, 39*(1), 21–31.

Pope, K., Tabachnick, B., & Keith-Spiegel, P. (1987). Ethics of practice: The beliefs and behaviors of psychologists as therapists. *American Psychologist, 42*(11), 993–1006.

Rogers, C. (1979). The foundations of the person-centered approach. *Education, 100*(2), 98–107.

Simi, N., & Mahalik, J. (1997). Comparison of feminist versus psychoanalytic/dynamic and other therapists on self-disclosure. *Psychology of Women Quarterly, 21*(3), 465–83.

Simon, J. (1990). Criteria for therapist self-disclosure. In G. Stricker & M. Fisher (Eds.), *Self-disclosure in the therapeutic relationship* (pp. 207–25). New York: Plenum Press.

Smith, D., & Fitzpatrick, M. (1995). Patient–therapist boundary issues: An integrative review of theory and practice. *Professional Psychology: Research and Practice, 26*(5), 499–506.

Somers, A., Pomerantz, A., Meeks, J., & Pawlow, L. (2014). Should psychotherapists disclose their own psychological problems? *Counselling and Psychotherapy Research, 14*(4), 249–55.

Sue, D., Arredondo, P., & McDavis, R. (1992). Multicultural counseling competencies and standards: A call to the profession. *Journal of Counseling and Development, 70*(4), 477–86.

Tsai, M., Plummer, M., Kanter, J., Newring, R., & Kohlenberg, R. (2010). Therapist grief and functional analytic psychotherapy: Strategic self-disclosure of personal loss. *Journal of Contemporary Psychotherapy, 40*(1), 1–10.

Watkins Jr., C. (1990). The effects of counselor self-disclosure: A research review. *The Counseling Psychologist, 18*(3), 477–500.

Zur, O. (2007). Self-disclosure. In *Boundaries in psychotherapy: Ethical and clinical explorations* (pp. 149–65). Washington, DC: American Psychological Association.

CHAPTER 27

There Are Risks and Benefits of Non-Disclosure

Graham S. Danzer, PsyD

While it is clear that there are risks and benefits of therapeutic self-disclosure (TSD), so are there risks and benefits of non-disclosure. This emerging theme in the TSD literature was not the primary subject of any article found through a comprehensive search of the Psych Info, Academic Premier, and Google Scholar databases. The risks and benefits of non-disclosure did, however, come up somewhat frequently in scholarly research articles on the pros, cons, and clinical considerations of TSD, as something of a secondary point of interest, and with noteworthy implications for the research-informed practitioner.

There Is No Such Thing as Complete Non-Disclosure

It is important to begin this discussion by acknowledging that a therapist can no longer reasonably expect to remain an anonymous professional (Thomas, 2008). Even in cases where a therapist may have little online presence and live as something of a recluse, much is revealed through office pictures and décor, a wedding ring, pregnancy, religious head coverings, how a therapist behaves during random/chance encounters with clients in the community, or the manner in which a therapist responds to clients suddenly asking personal questions in session (Henretty & Levitt, 2010; LaPorte, Sweifach, & Linzer, 2010). Revealing qualities or characteristics also include the therapist's gender and race (Cabaj, 1991), demeanor, body language, tone of voice, and facial expressions (Russell, 2006; Thomas, 2008; Zur, 2007), and/or the presence of LGBTQ-affirmative insignia (Daley, 2012). Intentionally or unintentionally, therapists are disclosing aspects of themselves every time they speak to clients, no matter how non-disclosive they may intend or prefer to be (Gutheil & Gabbard, 1998).

Further, a therapist who makes a fuller effort to be entirely non-disclosive is something of a rarity. Across multiple studies, 65–90% of surveyed therapists reported intentionally disclosing to clients *at least some of the time* (Audet, 2011; Audet & Everall, 2003; Henretty & Levitt, 2010; Kelly & Rodriguez, 2007;

LaPorte et al., 2010). Offering further specification, surveyed therapists in other studies reported disclosures made up between 1–13% of all of their interventions, with an average of 3.5% (Henretty & Levitt, 2010; Kelly & Rodriguez, 2007). Thus, therapists do disclose, in at least some cases *should disclose* (as discussed in prior chapters of this text), and may serve clients well by carefully considering the pros and cons *of non-disclosure* in as cautious manner as when a disclosure is decided in favor of.

Applied to Practice

The risks and benefits of non-disclosure are an important consideration for practitioners who may presume non-disclosure is usually if not always appropriate, is not likely to be harmful, and perhaps, not without reservation. Indeed, it is not unusual for a therapist who chooses not to disclose to a particular client in a particular therapeutic moment to later reflect, introspect, or consult about such scenarios and wonder what would have happened if the disclosure had occurred. In addition, it is reasonable to consider whether many therapeutic relationships that failed to develop or at some point stagnated might have developed further, or develop further in the future as a result of improved decisions related to TSD/non-disclosure.

Positions in the ethical and clinical literature that may inform a therapist's thinking about non-disclosure risks are as follows. The American Psychological Association's (APA) Code of Ethics offers no clear and explicit guidance in such scenarios, though several of its codes apply and suggest that therapists can no longer choose non-disclosure without having first considered both sides of the issue carefully (Henretty & Levitt, 2010). Therapists and conservative ethicists often worry that TSD may compromise a therapist's credibility, though common findings in client survey studies suggest therapists may anticipate more negative impact on expertness than clients experience (Audet, 2011; Henretty & Levitt, 2010; Marino, Child, & Krasinski, 2016). While TSD can be beneficial when 'delivered appropriately,' ethicists have expressed concern about its potential to compromise boundaries and suggest a lack of differentiation between the therapist's role as expert and the client's role as client (Barnett, 2011; Gutheil & Gabbard, 1998).

Therapist writers offer the perspectives that non-disclosure can alienate clients, may impact clients as much as a TSD, be less helpful than a TSD conveying client–therapist similarity, and is likely to not be significantly more or less helpful than a disclosure conveying therapist-client difference (D'Aniello & Nguyen, 2017; Hearn & West-Olatunji, 2015; Henretty & Levitt, 2010). In effect, non-disclosure cannot be assumed to be a preferred alternative to disclosure, regardless of the individual clinical circumstances at hand. Well summarized in Chapter 15 by Farber and Jackson, the challenge for the therapist is to make disclosure and non-disclosure decisions in a way that aligns with the broader goals of the helping professions, as well as the goals of the individual client's treatment.

Benefits of a Largely Non-Disclosive Stance

Fundamentally, a professional psychotherapist assumes a predominantly non-disclosive stance and manner of interacting with clients (Farber, 2006). Whereas disclosure is often intended to facilitate client–therapist rapport (Bitar, Kimball, Bermúdez, & Drew, 2014), therapist discipline and restraint (LaPorte et al., 2010) is theorized to maintain the disproportionate give-and-take of the relationship (Audet & Everall, 2003) that is central to its uniqueness (LaPorte et al., 2010). Indeed, it may be the uniqueness of the relationship that builds deeper trust and safety (Gutheil & Gabbard, 1993) and results in deeper and lasting changes (Audet & Everall, 2003).

Benefits of Non-Disclosure to the Client

Applying the prior theories to practice, a therapist's ability to practice restraint, maintain a professional stance, and essentially not encroach on the client's processing may be among the most difficult of the clinical skills to learn, maintain, and apply in key moments of therapy. In turn, and as discussed in the conceptual literature, forms of restraint and professional discipline may be *the* major determinant of clinical outcomes. Specifically, therapeutic restraint may be among the practices that help clients to feel safe in therapy, fully explore the deeper and most secret corners of their psyche, and eventually go to a far deeper level of emotion and insight than what can reasonably be expected in a dialogue where the other has and should exercise equal rights to meet his or needs in the relationship. Whereas the desire to help in a social relationship may bring the mentality 'don't just stand there, do something,' the desire to help in a psychotherapeutic relationship should bring the mentality 'don't just do something, stand there.' So doing may be what differentiates a peer and professional relationship, and one that is superficially pleasant and interesting from a relationship that is emotionally deeper and healing. Therefore, at least in some cases, and for reasons consistent with points made in Chapters 20 and 23 by Tyson Bailey, non-disclosure may be as beneficial as it is risky.

In contrast, the popularization, televised, and trending nature of therapy may give a wider impression that a psychotherapist should be a motivational speaker, actor, advice giver, and essentially a far more dynamic, entertaining, and larger presence in the room than is the client. Televised therapy frequently depicts a therapist nearly performing for a client, while the client sits and listens as if captivated, while the therapist convinces their problems to go into exile. Such efforts may be rewarded on a talk show, a popular online blog, or by boosting sales of self-help books, though would in the real world probably be grounds for licensure complaints. These impacts of therapy popularization are important for the current subject matter because they may lead clients and therapists to expect the opposite of a non-disclosive therapist, respond negatively to traditional neutrality, and in cases where neutrality may be preferred and appropriate, and results in deeper and lasting changes as mentioned earlier.

Admittedly, the desire to help by doing is at least somewhat natural, understandable, and surely among the basic reasons why anyone would want to be a therapist. It is probably a showing of caring and empathy to feel pulled to offer a suffering client an encouraging word, comfort, or an as-needed distraction. Per D'Aniello and Nguyen (2017), these are the forms of spontaneous and non-treatment focused disclosures (TSDs) that should usually be avoided.

While the majority of potential benefits of non-disclosure are not known to have been confirmed through empirical research, it is questionable that a primarily non-disclosive stance and way of relating with clients could be researched in a more standardized manner. With sufficient research controls, instructions, and formulaic delivery, the dynamic nature of therapy that drives relationship development and intervention selection and impacts would be blunted. Moreover, the prior positions on non-disclosure are generally well understood and agreed upon among professional psychotherapists, as discussed recurrently in therapist perspective articles summarized and referenced throughout this text. This is important because agreement of professional opinion is frequently regarded in clinical circles as what makes a particular intervention or style of interaction appropriate and to be used again in relevant though not necessarily replicable circumstances in the future. Thus, professional agreement on a predominantly (though not exclusively) non-disclosive stance may be a showing of wisdom from practice, which should be acknowledged as a form of evidence, no matter the inherent difficulty in quantification.

In a similar vein, research-informed practitioners are further reminded that conservative ethical positions (including but not limited to precautions against TSD) are usually generated through well-seasoned experiences with highly elusive clinical phenomena. It is not uncommon for conservative positions to advance in the aftermath of professionals making significant mistakes, with subsequent intention for the helping professions to learn from those mistakes and protect inherently vulnerable clients in similar situations in the future. Applied to the current subject matter, precautions against TSD (i.e., somewhat supporting the benefits of a non-disclosive stance) are likely to have flowed from known boundary violations. While these points should not be interpreted as indicating support for a fully non-disclosing therapist or dismissing the potential benefits of TSD outright, they do suggest that a more cautionary approach to disclosing is ethically appropriate.

Non-Disclosure in Service of Therapist Self-Care

While simultaneously benefiting the client, a primarily non-disclosive stance has additional benefits related to therapist self-care. Therapists must feel comfortable with what they reveal in order to remain authentically connected to a client (Tantillo, 2004). As discussed by Henretty and Levitt (2010), self-disclosure may have negative ramifications for the therapist. Depending in part on the client's reaction, therapists who disclose may question their clinical decision-making, judgment, and competence. As a result, future interventional strategy may be tainted and perhaps to a degree that the effort to refrain from doing harm (i.e., maleficence) interferes with the simultaneous ethical responsibility to do good (i.e., beneficence).

Discussions of non-disclosure as an issue of therapist self-care also comes up in studies of TSD in contexts of vulnerability, as discussed in prior chapters of this text. Both Adelman and Malawista (2013) and the consultation group of a dying therapist, as summarized and discussed in Alexander, Kolodziejski, Sanville, and Shaw (1989), noted that TSD of illness and mortality can be severely discomforting and even disorienting. Similarly, Pizer (2016) acknowledged that initiating uncomfortable and yet necessary discussions with clients about his blindness was exceedingly difficult, gradually became more familiar over time, and yet still led him to question his motivations for disclosing in light of strong and multi-layered client responses. In studies of TSD with mentally ill clients (Marino et al., 2016), LGBTQ therapists considering whether or not to disclose their sexual identities (Thomas, 2008), and in Chapter 22 of this text on forensic settings, TSD was discussed as a personal safety issue. Similarly, non-disclosure may be safer for eating disorder (ED) therapists in earlier stages of their career, who may find it difficult to disclose appropriately in cases where their personal history of ED may be in a less mature stage of recovery (Williams & Haverkamp, 2015). Therefore, when therapy has an additional layer or consideration of vulnerability, the previously discussed 'pros' of *non-disclosure* may deserve greater attention among therapists deciding whether or not to disclose in different clinical circumstances.

Drawbacks of Non-Disclosure

From the research it is inferred that TSD not only *does* happen, but at least a moderate and tempered extent of disclosure may be preferable to full neutrality and non-disclosure. Per D'Aniello and Nguyen (2017), the seemingly one-sided nature of therapy deviates from established social norms and may therefore be difficult for clients in need of connection to tolerate, particularly, when the extent of therapist and client disclosure is more lopsided than normal (see usual rates of TSD discussed earlier in this chapter). Thus, clients may perceive non-disclosing therapists as inaccessible or hostile (Goldstein, 1994; Henretty & Levitt, 2010). Consistent with the previously summarized therapist perspectives, surveyed clients have described therapists perceived as erring on the side of non-disclosure as overly formal, rigid, and authoritative (Audet, 2011). In response to non-disclosure, clients may become reluctant to disclose (Henretty & Levitt, 2010) and therapeutic impasses may occur (Wachtel, 1993). Whereas perfect neutrality intends to encourage and not interfere with client introspection and processing, a more fully non-disclosive stance may (in effect) have the opposite effect.

As summarized by Jennifer Henretty in Chapter 28 of this text, a randomized clinical trial was conducted by Ziv-Beiman, Keinan, Livneh, Malone, and Shahar

(2017). This clinical trial compared real clients' reactions to 'intra-therapy' disclosures (i.e., self-involving or 'here-and-now' disclosures), 'extra-therapy' disclosures (i.e., therapists' thoughts, feelings, and experiences not directly related to what is/was happening between client and therapist, including historical disclosures), and non-disclosure. Results suggested that impacts of extra and intra-therapy disclosures tended not to be significantly different, though intra-therapy TSDs tended to have a more positive effect on clients with higher levels of initial/pre-treatment symptomology. These findings were discussed as consistent with one meta-analysis (Henretty & Levitt, 2010), though not another (Henretty, Currier, Berman, & Levitt, 2014), with some indications of non-disclosure having less of a positive impact than either intra-therapy or extra-therapy TSDs. In sum, the available empirical research (while not discounting the prior positions on therapeutic ethics) suggests that, in many cases, a disclosure in either form is at least somewhat more likely than non-disclosure to be regarded more favorably by clients. At the same time, and in a more general sense, the positive reaction may be reminiscent of a short-term gain, while non-disclosure may in many cases have greater long-term benefits.

Contexts of Vulnerability, Trauma, and Oppression

At times when the therapist and client have similar or in some ways converging personal issues, non-disclosure may show boundaries while disclosure may build relationships. Of course, maintaining boundaries and building relationships are not mutually exclusive, and in fact are often synonymous in psychotherapy. The following summary of the TSD-in-vulnerability literature will be shown to highlight both possibilities. There is some extent of caution *against* non-disclosure in cases where the client will invariably know what the therapist has reservations about revealing, and encouragement (i.e., in favor) of non-disclosure with clients whose conditions presuppose problems with boundaries in relationships.

When professional helpers live and practice in communities afflicted by natural disasters or terrorism, TSD is not necessarily warranted and may be problematic when practitioners feel pulled to disclose by client suffering. However, it may be up for consideration in such circumstances where clients are particularly disconnected from humanity, may experience TSD as reconnecting, and under the purview that traditional therapeutic boundaries were not theorized/developed with the possibility of shared client–therapist traumas in mind (LaPorte et al., 2010). In such cases where the client inevitably knows that the therapist, too, has been traumatized, non-disclosure and reservation may seem outrageous and inhumane (Frawley-O'Dea, 2003; LaPorte et al., 2010; Rao & Mehra, 2015). Similar cautions against non-disclosure of the inevitable were indicated in studies of therapists who had certain visible physical health complications (Alexander et al., 1989; Pizer, 2016; Rabinor & Nye, 2003).

The prior summary in Chapter 9 of Caucasian therapists and multicultural clients did not overtly address the ramifications of non-disclosure, though has implications in this regard. Studies noted that multicultural clients tend to drop out of therapy more frequently when paired with a Caucasian therapist, and report more satisfaction with treatment including a greater extent of TSD (Chang & Berk, 2009). Benefits of TSD to cross-cultural relationships were noted in studies of Caucasian therapist perspectives, as well as African American, Latino, and Native American client perspectives (Bitar et al., 2014; Burkard, Knox, Goren, Perez, & Hess, 2006; Carlton, 1993; Cashwell, Scherbakova, & Cashwell, 2003; Chang & Berk, 2009; Lokken & Twohey, 2004). Caucasian therapist acknowledgment of racism in-session was frequently regarded as beneficial (Burkard et al., 2006; Chang & Berk, 2009). Thus, there was some extent of support for Caucasian therapists acknowledging something of a racial elephant in the living room (like prior discussions of therapist traumatization and physical illness), with a likelihood that neutrality and a sense of non-responsiveness would be damaging to the relationship. This inference from the research is presented as more of a hypothesis warranting further study and theoretical discussion.

Similar points (to those made in the previous paragraph) were made in Chapter 10 on therapist disclosure of sexuality (TSDO). Non-disclosure was a source of contention in the LGBTQ literature, as the therapist's sexuality is fundamentally concealable (unlike a therapist's physical illnesses, mortality, race, or likelihood of also being traumatized due to practicing in a disaster-afflicted community), yet cannot reasonably be considered a non-issue, may be an issue of informed consent and credibility, and particularly (though not exclusively) when the client is of an LGBTQ background (Dean, 2010; Hearn & West-Olatunji, 2015; Moore & Jenkins, 2012; Thomas, 2008). At the same time, LGBTQ therapists can reasonably expect to have unintentional encounters with clients when their communities are small, and in locations where clients may observe their therapists in scenarios, such as singles bars, which may in turn have negative implications for therapy (Goldstein & Horowitz, 2003; Satterly, 2006). Solely due to such possibilities, overt discussion and essentially revealing the therapist's sexuality may (in at least some cases) be beneficial and even necessary (Dean, 2010).

For similar reasons, and as a further showing of non-disclosure risks, non-disclosure of gay/lesbian/bisexual sexuality may implicitly give clients the impression of therapist internalized homophobia or shame (Carroll, Gauler, Relph, Hutchinson, 2011; Dean, 2010; Farber, 2006; Harris, 2015). Non-disclosure may also exacerbate LGBTQ therapist fears/anticipation of client judgment, homophobic comments, and the extent of internalized homophobia projected onto the client (Hearn & West-Olatunji, 2015). Further, it may lead therapists to feel heightened stress (Harris, 2015), a sense of misleading clients (Thomas, 2008), and loneliness, isolation, and/or inauthenticity (Carroll et al., 2011). Moreover, non-disclosure of therapist sexuality may be particularly damaging in gay male therapist-client dyads due to greater extent of discrimination against gay men (rather than lesbian women or heterosexuals [Mohr & Fassinger, 2003; Thomas, 2008]). In addition, non-disclosure was discussed in the TSDO literature as sometimes necessary to prevent loss of clients and livelihood, and (as mentioned in the self-care subsection of this chapter) for personal safety considerations (Harris, 2015; Thomas, 20008).

Like the research findings on non-disclosure in contexts of LGBTQ identification, non-disclosure in contexts of eating disorder (ED) may communicate negative messages to clients and have parallel negative impacts on therapists, with some support for such theories from limited available research. Clients with eating disorders frequently have difficulty understanding the mental states and emotions of others (Tantillo, 2004). As a result, non-disclosure may be experienced by ED clients as an indication of them having no emotional impact in relationships, in which cases non-disclosure may be abandoning, traumatizing, or a betrayal (Tantillo, 2004). Showing that Tantillo's (2004) theories apply in other contexts, therapists in research studies who had personal histories of ED often expressed reluctance to share their personal history of ED (Williams & Haverkamp, 2015), while clients in research studies reported reluctance to share a lot of information about their histories of ED to their therapists (Swan & Andrews, 2003), with a relationship in each study between non-disclosure and (therapist and client) shame and embarrassment. Thus, non-disclosure in each of the aforementioned contexts of shame, stigma, and oppression (i.e., environmental and shared traumas, physical health decline, cross-cultural pairing, LGBTQ identity, and eating disorder) may have fundamentally similar negative ramifications for the client, the therapist, and the therapeutic relationship.

Mentions of non-disclosure in studies of children, substance-abusing clients, clients with general mental illnesses, and in contexts of religiosity are summarized as follows. Studies of children and adolescents yielded mixed findings with respect to type, timing, and frequency of disclosure, with some indications of non-disclosure being preferable to over-disclosure, and non-disclosure at times associating with adolescents perceiving higher levels of therapist expertness (Capobianco & Farber, 2005; Carlton, 1993; Fotinos, 1996; Patrizio, 1990; Schimmel, 1994). Similar to the findings on non-disclosure with children, TSD of religiosity was at times well regarded (as discussed in more detail by Gerald Nissley in Chapter 16 of this text), though with indication that bannering of religious insignia (i.e., over-disclosure) is less likely to be well received (Chesner & Baumeister, 1985; Young, 2011). Reeh's (2010) dissertation involved 132 adult men in residential treatment centers who were shown hypothetical treatment scenarios of intake workers who did or did not self-disclose. Disclosure vs. non-disclosure did not predict significant differences in expressed client willingness to return for future sessions. Results from Kelly and Rodriguez' (2007) study of therapist perspectives included that therapists were frequently reluctant to disclose (i.e., preferred non-disclosure) with more mentally symptomatic clients.

Conclusions

Therapists should probably go into therapy accepting that they will inevitably reveal more about themselves than they choose to reveal overtly. Therefore, it may be advantageous to reflect upon what parts of themselves to reveal, for what clinical purposes, and with acknowledgment that forms of disclosure are often helpful, whereas non-disclosure and perfect neutrality are most likely impossible. Moreover, greater extents of non-disclosure are likely to be difficult for clients to tolerate and would probably (in many cases) be more alienating than helpful. This is particularly likely in cases where there is an issue of therapist vulnerability and/or client stigma, such as the therapist having a physical illness or practicing in a war-torn or disaster afflicted community, with suicidal clients as discussed in Chapter 25 by Asha Wilkus-Stone, with intellectually and developmentally disabled clients as discussed in Chapter 21 by Gerald Nissley, and in contexts of stigma and oppression, such as when the client and therapist are of an LGBTQ background, cross-culturally paired, or when the client *and* therapist have eating disorders. In such cases where small community factors make the client's eventual knowing inevitable, there is more research support for TSD, essentially, in the form of the therapist openly admitting what the client immediately or eventually would come to know anyway.

In addition, there is necessarily and obviously a need to balance some extent of *need to disclose* with therapeutic restraint and caution as the hallmark of professional helping. Within the vulnerability chapters of this text, there were discussions of disclosure as an integral component within the larger framework of peer-peer treatment of severe mental illness, substance abuse, and eating disorders, albeit with some indication that higher levels of TSD may lower client perception of therapist expertness. Thus, while peer-helping is frequently beneficial to client outcomes, adopting a peer stance to interactions is, by definition, at odds with professional psychotherapy. Whereas TSD may have short-term benefits related to engagement, restraint and forethinking are likely to associate with longer term, lasting, and more positive outcomes. While forms of disclosure may have immediate and positive effects on clients, a primarily non-disclosive stance is likely of benefit to the therapist's self-care. These precautions speak to the previously discussed need to modulate and temper TSDs. This is particularly advisable when the therapist is working with clients who come to therapy with substance abuse issues, severe mental illnesses, are treated in forensic settings, or demand to know the therapist's religiosity. In most if not all cases, at least some extent of TSD (i.e., *lack of* full non-disclosure) may help to maintain engagement, though may have also diminishing returns as intimacy and frequency of disclosures increase exponentially.

Just as TSD has positive and negative effects, so does non-disclosure. Therefore, non-disclosure cannot be assumed to be safer, more beneficial to clients, and thereby something of a default absent more critical reflection as is necessary in all clinical scenarios. This more mindful and less rule-bound stance was frequently discussed in the implications sections of the different vulnerability chapters in Part III of this text, as well as the clinical challenge and direct inquiry chapters by Jackson and Farber (Chapters 15 and 19), Nissley (Chapters 16 and 21), Bailey (Chapters 20 and 23), Alexander (Chapter 18), and Barbeau (Chapter 24), and as a larger showing of general therapist/researcher agreement. Concurring professional opinion is important because the lack of disclosure (i.e., a therapist's generally non-disclosive stance) would be difficult to research empirically, with such attempts most likely creating unnatural conditions that would in turn be less applicable to the less controlled and more dynamic nature of therapy in the real world. In such cases, wisdom from practice may be most appropriate to rely upon, particularly when deciding how to engage in a more controversial and potentially impactful practice such as TSD, or its absence, as has been favored historically.

References

Adelman, A., & Malawista, K. (2013). *The therapist in mourning: From the faraway nearby*. New York: Columbia University Press.

Alexander, J., Kolodziejski, K., Sanville, J., & Shaw, R. (1989). On final terminations: Consultation with a dying therapist. *Clinical Social Work Journal, 17*(4), 307–24.

Audet, C. (2011). Client perspectives of therapist self-disclosure: Violating boundaries or removing boundaries? *Counselling Psychology Quarterly, 24*(2), 85–100.

Audet, C., & Everall, R. (2003). Counsellor self-disclosure: Client-informed implications for practice. *Counselling and Psychotherapy Research, 3*(3), 223–31.

Barnett, J. (2011). Psychotherapist self-disclosure: Ethical and clinical considerations. *Psychotherapy, 48*(4), 315–21.

Bitar, G., Kimball, T., Bermúdez, J., & Drew, C. (2014). Therapist self-disclosure and culturally competent care with Mexican-American court mandated clients: A Phenomenological study. *Contemporary Family Therapy, 36*(3), 417–25.

Burkard, A., Knox, S., Goren, M., Perez, M., & Hess, S. (2006). European American therapist self-disclosure in cross-cultural counseling. *Journal of Counseling Psychology, 53*(1), 15–25.

Cabaj, R. (1991). Sexual orientation of the therapist. In R. Cabaj & S. Stein (Eds.), *Textbook of homosexuality and mental health* (pp. 513–24). Washington, DC: American Psychiatric Publishing.

Capobianco, J., & Farber, B. (2005). Therapist self-disclosure to child patients. *American Journal of Psychotherapy, 59*(3), 199–212.

Carlton, C. (1993). The effect of therapist self-disclosure and explanation of confidentiality on adolescent clients' willingness to self-disclose and therapist preference (Doctoral dissertation). Retrieved from ProQuest Dissertations and Theses database (No UMI No.).

Carroll, L., Gauler, A., Relph, J., & Hutchinson, K. (2011). Counselor self-disclosure: Does sexual orientation matter to straight clients? *International Journal for the Advancement of Counseling, 33*(2), 129–48.

Cashwell, C. S., Scherbakova, J., & Cashwell, T. (2003) Effect of client and counselor ethnicity on preference for counselor disclosure. *Journal of Counseling and Development, 81*(2), 196–201.

Chang, D., & Berk, A. (2009). Making cross-racial therapy work: A phenomenological study of clients' experiences of cross-racial therapy. *Journal of Counseling Psychology, 56*(4), 521–36.

Chesner, S., & Baumeister, R. (1985). Effect of therapists' disclosure of religious beliefs on the intimacy of client self-disclosure. *Journal of Social and Clinical Psychology, 3*(1), 97–105.

Daley, A. (2012) Becoming seen, becoming known: Lesbian women's self-disclosures of sexual orientation to mental health service providers. *Journal of Gay & Lesbian Mental Health, 16*(3), 215–34.

D'Aniello, C., & Nguyen, H. (2017). Considerations for intentional use of self-disclosure for family therapists. *Journal of Family Psychotherapy, 28*(1), 23–37.

Dean, B. (2010). Therapist self-disclosure: Heterosexual perceptions of sexual minority therapists (Doctoral dissertation). Retrieved from ProQuest Dissertations and Theses Database (UMI No. 3422542).

Farber, B. (2006). *Self-disclosure in psychotherapy*. New York: Guilford Press.

Fotinos, K. (1996). The effects of therapist self-disclosure and clients' solicitation of self-disclosure on adolescent client willingness to self-disclose and therapist preference (Doctoral dissertation). Retrieved from ProQuest Dissertations and Theses database (No UMI No.).

Frawley-O'Dea, M. (2003). When the trauma is terrorism and the therapist is traumatized too. *Psychoanalytic Perspectives, 1*(1), 67–89.

Goldstein, E. (1994). Self-disclosure in treatment: What therapists do and don't talk about. *Clinical Social Work Journal, 22*(4), 417–33.

Goldstein, E., & Horowitz, L. (2003). *Lesbian identity and contemporary psychotherapy: A framework for clinical practice*. Hillsdale, NJ: Analytic Press.

Gutheil, T., & Gabbard, G. (1993). The concept of boundaries in clinical practice: Theoretical and risk-management dimensions. *American Journal of Psychiatry, 150*(2), 188–96.

Gutheil, T., & Gabbard, G. (1998). Misuses and misunderstandings of boundary theory in clinical and regulatory settings. *American Journal of Psychiatry, 155*(3), 409–14.

Harris, A. (2015). To disclose or not to disclose? The LGBT therapist's question. (Doctoral dissertation). Retrieved from ProQuest Dissertations and Theses database (No UMI No.).

Hearn, B., & West-Olatunji, C. (2015). Deciding to disclose: The LGBTQ counselor's unique challenge. *VISTAS Online, 74*, 1–8.

Henretty, J., Currier, J., Berman, J., & Levitt, H. (2014). The impact of counselor self-disclosure on clients: A meta-analytic review of experimental and quasi-experimental research. *Journal of Counseling Psychology, 61*(2), 191–207.

Henretty, J., & Levitt, H. (2010). The role of therapist self-disclosure in psychotherapy: A qualitative review. *Clinical Psychology Review, 30*(1), 63–77.

Kelly, A., & Rodriguez, R. (2007). Do therapists self-disclose more to clients with greater symptomology? *Psychotherapy: Theory, Research, Practice, Training, 44*(4), 470–5.

LaPorte, H., Sweifach, J., & Linzer, N. (2010). Sharing the trauma: Guidelines for therapist self-disclosure following a catastrophic event. *Best Practices in Mental Health, 6*(2), 39–56.

Lokken, J., & Twohey, D. (2004). American Indian perspectives of Euro-American counseling behavior. *Journal of Multicultural Counseling and Development, 32*, 320–31.

Marino, C., Child, B., & Krasinski, V. (2016). Sharing experience learned firsthand (SELF): Self-disclosure of lived experience in mental health services and supports. *Psychiatric Rehabilitation Journal, 39*(2), 154–60.

Mohr, J., & Fassinger, R. (2003). Self-acceptance and self-disclosure of sexual orientation in lesbian, gay, and bisexual adults: An attachment perspective. *Journal of Counseling Psychology, 50*(4), 482–95.

Moore, J., & Jenkins, P. (2012). Coming out in therapy? Perceived risks and benefits of self-disclosure by gay and lesbian therapists to straight clients. *Counselling and Psychotherapy Research, 12*(4), 308–15.

Patrizio, T. (1990). Effect of self-disclosure and interpersonal touch on high school students' perceptions of a school psychologist during an initial interview (Doctoral dissertation). Retrieved from ELibrary, Hofstra University.

Pizer, A. (2016). Do I have to tell my patients I'm blind? *Psychoanalytic Perspectives*, *13*(2), 214–29.

Rabinor, J., & Nye, S. (2003). Healing through connection: Self-disclosure in psychotherapy. *Eating Disorders*, *11*(3), 235–40.

Rao, N. & Mehra, A. (2015). Hurricane sandy: Shared trauma and therapist self-disclosure. *Psychiatry*, *78*(1), 65–74.

Reeh, H. (2010). The relationships between perceived therapeutic alliance, therapist self-disclosure, and dropout expectancy among male substance abuse treatment participations (Doctoral dissertation). Retrieved from ProQuest Dissertations and Theses database (UMI No. 3433371).

Russell, G. (2006). Different ways of knowing: The complexities of therapist disclosure. *Journal of Gay and Lesbian Psychotherapy*, *10*(1), 79–94.

Satterly, B. (2006). Counselor self-disclosure from a gay male perspective. *Families in Society*, *87*(2), 240–47.

Schimmel, L. (1994). The effects of therapist verbal self-disclosure on adolescent male offenders engagement in an initial clinical interview (Doctoral dissertation). Retrieved from ProQuest Dissertations and Theses database (No UMI No.).

Swan, S., & Andrews, B. (2003). The relationship between shame, eating disorders and disclosure in treatment. *British Journal of Clinical Psychology*, *42*(4), 367–78.

Tantillo, M. (2004). The therapist's use of self-disclosure in a relational therapy approach for eating disorders. *Eating Disorders*, *12*(51), 51–73.

Thomas, M. (2008). Shades of gray: Lesbian therapists explore the complexities of self-disclosure to heterosexual clients (Doctoral dissertation). Retrieved from Smith College Theses, Dissertations, and Projects.

Wachtel, P. (1993). *Therapeutic communication: Principles and effective practice.* New York: Guilford Press.

Williams, M., & Haverkamp, B. (2015) Eating disorder therapists' personal eating disorder history and professional ethics: An interpretive description. *Eating Disorders*, *23*(5), 393–410.

Young, S. (2011). Effects of an analogue counselor's religious or financial self-disclosure and observer characteristics on therapeutic processes (Doctoral dissertation). Retrieved from Psych INFO database (UMI Number: 3473295).

Ziv-Beiman, S., Keinan, G., Livneh, E., Malone, P., & Shahar, G. (2017). Immediate therapist self-disclosure bolsters the effect of brief integrative psychotherapy on psychiatric symptoms and the perceptions of therapists: A randomized clinical trial. *Psychotherapy Research*, *27*(5), 558–70.

Zur, O. (2007). *Boundaries in psychotherapy: Ethical and clinical explorations.* Washington, DC: American Psychological Association.

CHAPTER 28

Therapist Self-Disclosure: For Better *and* For Worse?

Jennifer R. Henretty, PhD

Therapists and especially therapists-in-training would love a concrete answer to the simple question of "Is therapist self-disclosure good or bad for my client?" However, as is echoed throughout this book, there are no easy answers. Therapist self-disclosure (TSD) is a complicated, multifaceted intervention (Pinto-Coelho, Hill, & Kivlighan, 2016) with effects that are, at best, difficult to pinpoint. Furthermore, humans and human relationships are similarly complicated and multi-faceted. Thus, it is no surprise that the same TSD may have different effects depending on the therapist, the client, the therapist-client relationship, and the timing, context, and content of therapy (Knox, Hess, Petersen, & Hill, 1997; Nussbaum, 2014), (see Chapters 5 and 6 for further illustration of these points).

Although most studies and meta-analyses suggest that TSD has favorable results (e.g., Henretty, Currier, Berman, & Levitt, 2014; Henretty & Levitt, 2010; Levitt et al., 2016; Pinto-Coelho et al., 2016; Wells, 2013; Ziv-Beiman, Keinan, Livneh, Malone, & Shahar, 2017), the research often differs on the specifics of the positive results. For example, a qualitative meta-analysis (Henretty & Levitt, 2010) found that TSD had a favorable effect on the client's perception of the therapist's warmth and on client self-disclosure, but no effect on warmth or client self-disclosure was found in a TSD quantitative meta-analysis (Henretty et al., 2014). Conversely, in the quantitative meta-analysis (Henretty et al., 2014), TSD had a favorable impact on the client's perception of the therapist's level of regard for them and for the therapist's professional attractiveness, but neither of these findings were upheld in the qualitative meta-analysis (Henretty & Levitt, 2010), (these findings further illustrate previous and upcoming chapter points on how therapists and clients may experience self-disclosure occurrences and impact differently and in ways that are informative to a deeper and more reflective understanding of outcomes). The only shared findings, other than that of the overall (though slight) favorable effect of TSD, between the qualitative and quantitative meta-analyses were that TSD *did not* have a clear effect on the intimacy of client self-disclosure or on the client's perception of the therapist's trustworthiness, empathy, congruence, and unconditionality

(Henretty et al., 2014; Henretty & Levitt, 2010). However, many of the studies included in the meta-analyses (up to 94% for Henretty et al., 2014) utilized analog clients, whereas real client studies (reviewed in Chapter 4 of this text) generally purported positive findings. Therefore, could it be that the mixed and murky results in the meta-analyses were due to not using real clients?

Turning to real clients, TSD was correlated with stronger working alliances than non-disclosure (Pinto-Coelho et al., 2016) but unfortunately it was not clear in the study design if the TSD strengthened the alliance or that a strong alliance made a therapist more likely to self-disclose. Other studies of real clients, as well as the meta-analyses, examined *types* of self-disclosure (also discussed in-depth in Chapter 6 of this text)—as it has been hypothesized that different types of TSD may have differential effects that are obscured when TSD is lumped together as general TSD, which could thus account for the mixed results. Indeed, a randomized clinical trial (Ziv-Beiman et al., 2017) attempted to explore this possibility. It compared real clients' experience of (a) intra-therapy TSD (i.e., disclosures about what happens within the therapy room—that is, TSD about the therapist's thoughts and feelings about the therapy, the therapeutic relationship, and/or the client; also known as self-involving responses, 'here-and-now' disclosures, immediate disclosures, immediacy disclosures, and countertransference disclosures) versus (b) extra-therapy TSD (i.e., disclosures about what happens outside of the therapy room—that is, TSD about the therapist's thoughts, feelings, and experiences not directly related to the therapy; also known as self-disclosing responses, 'then and there' disclosures, non-immediate disclosures, and, in part, historical disclosures) versus (c) non-disclosure. Results suggested that while the effects of extra-therapy TSD and non-disclosure were not significantly different, intra-therapy TSD did have a favorable impact on client symptomology and client perceptions (of therapy and of the therapist), but only with clients with elevated pretreatment symptomology. This finding is in line with the qualitative meta-analysis (Henretty & Levitt, 2010), which also found that intra-therapy TSD had more favorable effects than extra-therapy TSD. However, this finding was in opposition to results of the quantitative meta-analysis (Henretty et al., 2014), which found that not only was the percentage of intra-therapy TSDs (out of total TSDs in a particular study) not a moderator on the effect of TSD, but, when examined separately, extra-therapy TSD actually had more detectable positive effects on clients' perception of the therapist than intra-therapy, compared to non-disclosure. A naturalistic study on the other hand, found no difference between the effects of extra-therapy and intra-therapy TSD on clients and on therapy (Levitt et al., 2016). Go figure.

To further cloud the picture, evidence suggests that researcher bias for or against TSD may have a statistically significant impact on the results: All experimental and quasi-experimental TSD studies in a meta-analysis (Henretty et al., 2014) were coded on a 5-point Likert scale—(a) researcher(s) explicitly hypothesized that TSD would have a more favorable impact than non-disclosure, (b) researcher(s) implicitly suggested a pro-TSD stance, (c) no indication of researcher bias for disclosure or non-disclosure, (d) researcher(s) implicitly suggested a pro non-disclosure stance, and (e) researcher(s) explicitly hypothesized that non-disclosure would have a more favorable impact than TSD. Findings showed that when researchers were explicitly or implicitly pro-TSD, their study yielded more favorable TSD effects. Because the vast majority of the research examining TSD (in the meta-analyses and individual studies discussed in this chapter, and in general) has been undertaken by pro-TSD researchers (Henretty et al., 2014), it is possible that unfavorable results of TSD were not as readily detected and therefore unfavorable trends that did not reach statistical significance might actually be very relevant. In support of this evidence, when qualitative interviewing methods have been used to explore TSD, clients often reported both favorable and unfavorable TSD effects (e.g., Nussbaum, 2014; Wells, 2013; detailed below). All of this—the mixed and murky conclusions, even when piecing out different types and contexts of TSD, the statistically significant favorable results paired with the unfavorable trends found by pro-TSD researchers, and the favorable and unfavorable experiences shared by clients in qualitative research interviews—just might mean that there is not only *no easy answer* as to whether TSD is either good or bad in a particular situation with any particular client or therapist. Rather, perhaps there is *NO ANSWER*.

What if Every TSD is Both Favorable and Unfavorable?

Given the mixed results within and across studies/meta-analyses (even from a mostly pro-TSD researcher base), it is plausible that every TSD has multiple effects on the client, on the client's perception of the therapist, and on the relationship. If that is indeed the case, TSD could simultaneously have both favorable and unfavorable results on the client (and on their outcome) and/or on the therapist-client relationship (e.g., on the client's perception of the therapist). Furthermore, the same TSD may have *different* positive and negative results for a different client and/or a different therapist (Knox et al., 1997; Nussbaum, 2014).

In support of the theory that many TSDs have both favorable and unfavorable effects, Nussbaum (2014), in her phenomenological study of eight real clients' 'lived experiences' of TSD in actual therapy, stated, "the results of this study contradict the opinion that TSD is generally a positive experience for clients because the data showed nearly an equal negative and positive response to disclosures" (p. 100). The researcher goes on to list the approximately equal number of favorable and unfavorable emotional responses reported by clients as they were interviewed about their experience of TSD. Favorable reactions reported included experiencing comfort, confidence, safety, and hope, and feeling cared for, protected, and supported. Unfavorable client-reported reactions to TSD included feeling anxious, awkward, disappointed, ignored, interrupted, invalidated, judged, self-conscious, uncomfortable, and unsafe. Nussbaum (2014) concluded that while TSD does have positive effects it also, at times, interferes with the therapeutic relationship, which is contradictory to the majority of research findings on TSD. Similarly, in Wells' (2013) phenomenological analysis of nine real clients' perceptions of TSD, clients described specific TSDs by their therapist as simultaneously unsettling and necessary for growth.

Especially relevant to the conversation about positive and negative effects of TSD is the human–expert continuum. By definition, experts have authoritative skills and knowledge that sets them apart and, in some respects, (arguably) even hierarchically above other humans in very specific arenas, such as therapy. However, one of the major findings of Levitt and colleagues' (2016) study of real clients, in real therapy, was that TSDs often humanize therapists (e.g., as discussed in Chapter 3 on progressive theoretical positions). Results of other studies support this finding, with TSD related to clients' having more positive perceptions of their therapist as a person (Henretty et al., 2014), of the realness of the therapist (Henretty et al., 2014), and of the realness of the relationship (Pinto-Coelho et al., 2016). Likewise, Wells (2013) found that TSD served to balance the relationship by making therapists more human, a finding that concurs with TSD research by Hill and Knox (2001) and Audet and Everall (2010). This research also relates to the findings in Chapter 9 of this text, which suggest that the efficacy of TSD is linked to authenticity and genuine interest.

However, the other side of humanizing therapists is that, for some clients at least, the therapist may simultaneously become less of the authority and expert, in ways that may not be helpful to treatment. Indeed, two meta-analyses concluded that, while the relationship between TSD and client perception of therapist expertness was unclear, trends suggested that TSD likely resulted in the therapist being perceived as less expert (Henretty et al., 2014; Henretty & Levitt, 2010). Additionally, while clients in a qualitative study of their perceptions of their therapist's TSD did not use the word 'expert,' almost 25% reported that an unfavorable effect of TSD was feeling that they needed to care for the therapist—highlighting the downside of the more balanced (i.e., more reciprocal) relationship. Thus, it is possible that many TSDs move therapists toward a more balanced/egalitarian relationship and away from a position of being the expert authority, consequently having both positive and negative effects, and accounting for some of the mixed results found within and across studies. In support of this idea, Nussbaum (2014) found that, in response to being asked about the most meaningful TSD they had experienced, clients listed TSDs related to their therapist's expertness—for example, TSDs that conferred that their therapist stayed current on the latest research, attended professional conferences, and spoke publicly in the community. These results suggest that at least some clients crave for their therapist to retain the expert role even while using TSD. A more detailed discussion of the effects of TSD on expertness can be found in Chapter 30 of this text.

Conclusions

Today's clients are sophisticated when it comes to therapy: They are much more likely than clients a few decades ago to have had the process of therapy demystified (accurately and/or inaccurately)—by television shows and other media related to therapy, by friends or family who have had therapy, and/or by past therapy experiences they have had themselves. Today's clients often have expectations of how a therapist should behave in therapy and, arguably as much as their therapist is observing them, they are observing (and evaluating) their therapist. Thus, clients may be cognizant of their therapist's TSD as a little unusual and even taboo. They may notice that, by using TSD, their therapist is taking up space or taking the focus off of them momentarily, as was found in the previously mentioned thematic analysis of real clients' interviews about their therapist's disclosures (Wells, 2013). However, these clients may also be aware that TSD leads them to feel cared for and trusted, as was also found in that thematic analysis by Wells (2013). TSD may make clients feel misunderstood (because even the best therapists miss the mark sometimes) but also simultaneously more comfortable with being vulnerable, having just witnessed their therapist modeling vulnerability via TSD (Wells, 2013). And it is possible that, as therapists self-disclose, they humanize themselves (Levitt et al., 2016) while simultaneously lessening their client's perception of them as the expert (Henretty & Levitt, 2010; Henretty et al., 2014) and creating a more balanced relationship (Well, 2013)—to all of which clients may have mixed reactions because they both crave connection with their therapist AND want their therapist to be the hierarchical expert they are paying for!

So, as therapists and therapists-to-be, rather than asking whether a particular TSD will be good *or* bad for a particular client in a particular moment, it may be more helpful to consider how a particular TSD will effect a particular client *both* positively and negatively. Furthermore, it may be especially helpful to explicitly acknowledge, reflect upon, and normalize that TSD often has both positive and negative effects before opening a dialogue with clients about how a TSD has just affected them. Lastly, it may be important to remember that just like all of the most powerful moments in therapy, it may be unhelpful and even impossible to box the moments following TSD into a good/bad, positive/negative, or favorable/unfavorable dichotomy.

References

Audet, C., & Everall, R. (2010). Therapist self-disclosure and the therapeutic relationship: A phenomenological study from the client perspective. *British Journal of Guidance & Counseling, 38*(3), 327–42.

Henretty, J., Currier, J., Berman, J., & Levitt, H. (2014). The impact of counselor self-disclosure on clients: A meta-analytic review of experimental and quasi-experimental research. *Journal of Counseling Psychology, 61*(2), 191–207.

Henretty, J., & Levitt, H. (2010). The role of therapist self-disclosure in psychotherapy: A qualitative review. *Clinical Psychology Review, 30*, 63–77.

Hill, C., & Knox, S. (2001). Self-disclosure. *Psychotherapy: Theory, Research, Practice, Training, 38*(4), 413–17.

Knox, S., Hess, S., Petersen, D., & Hill, C. (1997). A qualitative analysis of client perceptions of the effects of helpful therapist self-disclosure in long-term therapy. *Journal of Counseling Psychology, 44*(3), 274–83.

Levitt, H., Minami, T., Greenspan, S., Puckett, J., Henretty, J., Reich, C., & Berman, J. (2016). How therapist self-disclosure relates to alliance and outcomes: A naturalistic study. *Counselling Psychology Quarterly*, *29*(1), 7–28.

Nussbaum, K. (2014). Therapist self-disclosure: A phenomenological study of clients' lived experiences (Doctoral dissertation). Retrieved from ProQuest Dissertations and Theses database (UMI No. 3615061).

Pinto-Coelho, K., Hill, C., & Kivlighan Jr., D. (2016). Therapist self-disclosure in psychodynamic psychotherapy: A mixed methods investigation. *Counselling Psychology Quarterly*, *29*(1), 29–52.

Wells, H. (2013). The client's perspective of therapist self-disclosure (Doctoral dissertation). Retrieved from ProQuest Dissertations and Theses database (UMI No. 10184836).

Ziv-Beiman, S., Keinan, G., Livneh, E., Malone, P., & Shahar, G. (2017). Immediate therapist self-disclosure bolsters the effect of brief integrative psychotherapy on psychiatric symptoms and the perceptions of therapists: A randomized clinical trial. *Psychotherapy Research*, *27*(5), 558–70.

CHAPTER 29

Therapists and Clients Agree on Most Aspects of TSD, But Not All

Graham S. Danzer, PsyD

The extent to which therapeutic self-disclosure (i.e., TSD), like all other interventions, is ethically appropriate, helpful to clients, and healing is not solely tied to the perception of client *or* therapist. Rather, both experiences in the relationship are important as they naturally interplay, affect the client's experiences and emotions in therapy, and influence the therapeutic process. A better understanding of the areas in which therapist and client experiences and perceptions of TSD converge and diverge may assist with the development of an empirically informed conceptualization of multi-layered, multi-faceted clinical scenarios wherein TSD may be a possibility. As a result, clients may benefit from better informed decisions to or not to self-disclose given therapist attention to the client's individual experiences, the therapist's intuitive understanding of those experiences, and conceptualization of those experiences and in-the-moment therapeutic occurrences informed by the scholarly research. With these aims in mind, therapist and client perspectives on TSD will now be reviewed and synthesized into their main areas of convergence, divergence, and implications for practice.

Agree on the Benefits and Content of Helpful TSDs

Therapist writers, real clients in survey studies, and analog research findings consistently offer support for TSDs as enhancing perception of therapist warmth, being maximally helpful when of a particular 'structure,' and with helpful content being of therapist's positive emotions or lower intimacy content including demographic details. Therapists and clients in research studies consistently indicate that TSD often contributes to client perception of therapist warmth (Ackerman & Hilsenroth, 2003; Henretty & Levitt, 2010; Oyer, O'Halloran, & Christoe-Frazier, 2016; Stone, 2014). Therapist writers frequently suggest that ethically appropriate TSDs are relevant to the client and his or her treatment, constructively worded, infrequent, brief, and with a clear purpose or intention in mind (Audet & Everall, 2003; Bottrill, Pistrang, Barker, & Worrell, 2010; D'Aniello & Nguyen, 2017; Henretty & Levitt, 2010; Kelly & Rodriguez, 2007; LaPorte, Sweifach, & Linzer, 2010; Sturges, 2012). Studies of therapist and client perspectives frequently reported benefits associated with TSD of standard professional information (e.g., therapist's education, training, or theoretical orientation), demographic details (e.g., marital status and whether or not the therapist has children), therapist's weekend activities, and religious affiliation when similar to the client's (Audet, 2011; Audet & Everall, 2003; Bitar, Kimball, Bermúdez, & Drew, 2014; Eyrich-Garg, 2008; Simonds & Spokes, 2017; Young, 2013). In a study of 83 clients and 22 therapists, Kelly and Rodriguez (2007) found that historical content disclosures conveying client and therapist similarity often enhanced client perception of therapist likeability and treatment effect.

Types of TSD

Research studies of both therapist and client perspectives consistently support the potential benefits of therapists telling clients about their positive feelings for them (Simonds & Spokes, 2017; Vandenberghe & Silva Silvestre, 2014). So doing may be experienced by clients as therapeutically reassuring, validating, improving their self-image, and reinforcing their personal growth (Goldfried, Burckell, Eubanks-Carter, 2003; Hill & Knox, 2002; Sturges, 2012; Vandenberghe & Silva Silvestre, 2014). Consistent with research indicating greater benefit of self-involving (i.e. real-time feeling) disclosures, client survey studies have indicated that TSDs of positive feelings were *more* helpful than TSDs of theoretical orientation or training background, life experiences, acknowledging therapeutic mistakes, cultural factors, personal values, or sexuality, albeit without indication of whether the therapist and client were of similar or different sexual orientations (Henretty & Levitt, 2010; Simonds & Spokes, 2017).

Within the scholarly literature is an indication that the helpfulness and ethical appropriateness of TSD is not necessarily tied to its types (i.e., historical or self-involving). As discussed in the initial two sections of chapters in this text, there are relative advantages and disadvantages of each. In turn, the impacts necessarily and largely depend on a multitude of clinical and contextual factors (including therapeutic relational considerations, goals of treatment, and timing/decision-making).

At the same time, the following studies with greater sample sizes and empiricism suggest (while holding other clinical and contextual factors constant) that clients can be expected under many circumstances to benefit to a greater extent from TSDs of real-time feelings and reactions to therapist revelations of content from their historical pasts. Within the conceptual literature (i.e., therapist writer and researcher perspectives), self-involving disclosures are frequently mentioned as having the potential to build and repair therapeutic relationships (Sturges, 2012) and enhance client perception of therapist genuineness, likeability, and trustworthiness, and decrease client anxiety (McCarthy Veach, 2011). Self-involving disclosures may also help to model healthy communication and feedback-receiving skills (Sturges, 2012), illustrate key therapeutic points (Eifert & Forsyth, 2005), and offer therapists a more vibrant way to address lack of client motivation (Goldfried et al., 2003).

Consistent with aforementioned therapist perspective papers, multiple client survey and therapist perspective studies reported findings in favor of self-involving TSDs. Pinto-Coelho, Hill, and Kivlighan (2015) explored 185 TSD occurrences in 16 cases of psychodynamic therapy. Disclosures of feelings and insights were significantly more impactful on clinical outcomes, as opposed to historical disclosures. Self-involving disclosures also correlated with more positive client ratings of the therapeutic relationship. Historical disclosures tended to correlate with lower client ratings of alliance and outcome. Similarly, client survey studies reviewed in Henretty and Levitt's (2010) meta-analysis concluded in favor of self-involving TSDs eliciting more positive responses from clients than disclosures of factual or historical content. Applied directly to practice considerations, when therapists share their real-time feelings and reactions with a clear treatment aim, the client is afforded an opportunity to learn about how they impact the therapist as a symbolic other.

Offering further illustration, Aron's (2016) group had been meeting for over two years and included a relatively smaller number of higher functioning clients in a private practice setting. Among the members was a 40-year-old man described as having a conflicted early attachment history manifesting in an alternately charismatic and aggressive personality, as well as a tendency to be absent from group therapy approximately once per month. At one point, the group progressed into a somewhat emotionally detached discussion of grief and loss issues. Aron (2016) reflected that her initial interpretations, exploratory questions, and reflections did not appear to move group members into deeper levels of exploration and affective expression. When the 40-year-old man shared his desire to depart from the group permanently, Aron (2016) transparently shared her feelings of anger at his frequent absences, tendency to orbit the group, and avoid intimacy in a manner connected to his losses in earlier life. Group member responses and reactions varied, though were generally introspective, constructive, and contributed to a group dynamic that was clearly more productive and vibrant. This interaction demonstrates how self-involving disclosures may inspire deeper therapeutic engagement, reciprocal vulnerability and revelation, and in a manner more difficult to come by via standard therapeutic interventions or historical content disclosures.

Recurring and positive research findings encourage the research-informed practitioner to be particularly alert in session to opportunities to share their real-time feelings with clients when doing so may deepen the therapeutic process. More specifically, when therapists are considering a historical disclosure, it may be beneficial to reflect upon how the aims of the historical disclosure might be pursued through a revelation of real-time feelings. It is likely that historical TSDs are in many cases driven by the therapist's emotional states and reactions to the client. Therefore, the self-aware and well-attuned therapist considering a historical disclosure may want to first consider reflecting on his or her emotional state. Thereafter, the client may benefit from the therapist disclosing the component of his or her emotional experience driving the historical content into the therapist's conscious awareness and perhaps more relevant and reciprocal to the client's experience.

Stigma and Cultural Factors

TSD in stigma, sexual minority, and multicultural contexts was frequently well regarded by both clients and therapists in research studies. In a more general way, both therapists and clients tended to agree that TSD often helps to reduce client feelings of shame, stigmatization, and objection by appropriately conveying the therapist's humanity, vulnerability, care, and collaborative intentions (Audet, 2011; Ziv-Beiman & Shahar, 2016). Therapists and clients were also highly in agreement on the stigma-reducing benefits of gay male therapists disclosing their sexuality to gay male clients, and to a far greater extent than in other LGBTQ dyads (Cornett, 1993; Henretty and Levitt, 2010; Kronner & Northcut, 2015). Therapists and social workers in research studies practicing in disaster-afflicted communities consistently indicated benefits associated with sharing with clients that they too had been traumatized (Frawley-O'Dea, 2003; LaPorte et al., 2010; Rao & Mehra, 2015). Simulated clients, real clients, and therapists in research studies tended to agree that TSD was often helpful to establishing forms of credibility and reducing the severity of symptoms among clients in treatment for eating disorder (Oyer et al., 2016; Rabinor & Nye, 2003; Simonds & Spokes, 2017; Stone, 2014). Benefits related to stigma reduction and egalitarianism were also mentioned in Chapter 21 of this text on the benefits of disclosing to clients with intellectual and developmental disabilities (IDDs).

Studies of client and therapist perspectives frequently concluded in favor of the benefits of TSD in multi-cultural context. Within the conceptual literature, multicultural therapeutic approaches have long recognized TSD as a skill or even competency (Bitar et al., 2014; Henretty & Levitt, 2010). TSD has been discussed as an intervention that may build trust and credibility in cross-cultural contexts, impress upon the client the therapist's willingness to take risks, be experienced as gesture of openness, and encourage reciprocal client disclosure (Constantine & Kwong-Liem, 2003; Henretty & Levitt, 2010). Similar benefits of TSD were reported in survey studies of clients who were Native American adults (Lokken & Twohey, 2004), Latino youth *when* therapist disclosures were of a lower intimacy and more demographic nature (Carlton, 1993), and court-mandated Mexican American adults (Bitar et al., 2014). Chang and Berk (2009) conducted a qualitative interview study of 16 ethnic minority clients paired with Caucasian therapists and identified a significant positive association between TSD and client satisfaction with treatment. Interviewed African American and Native American providers in Marino, Child, and Krasinski's (2016) study reported TSD of their mental health history, to clients from a similar ethnic background, served a modeling function and helped clients become more open to discussion of their mental health issues in spite of culturally related stigma. Research studies of Caucasian therapists sharing with multicultural clients that they too had held racist beliefs (Burkard, Knox, Goren, Perez, & Hess, 2006) and studies of therapists sharing that they were critically ill or dying (Adelman & Malawista, 2013; Alexander, Kolodziejski, Sanville, & Shaw, 1989; Broadbent, 2013; Pizer, 2016) both indicated that such disclosures helped clients progress into addressing other important personal issues in therapy.

Offering a finding to the contrary of the prior pattern in outcomes, Wetzel and Wright-Buckley (1988) conducted a study of 33 African American women paired with either an African American or a Caucasian therapist. Wetzel and Wright-Buckley (1988) found that greater frequency of TSD predicted more reciprocal disclosure only when clients were paired with an African American therapist, though not with a Caucasian therapist. This finding is interpreted by the current author as a precaution against assuming TSDs are all one in the same, or TSD can be assumed to predict positive outcomes, regardless of the many clinical and contextual variables discussed throughout this text as essential considerations and covariates. Further exploration of how culture and gender may impact TSD decisions and impacts in different clinical scenarios, with case examples of key points, is offered in Chapters 18, 20, 23, 24, and 25 in the clinical challenge and direct inquiry sections of this text.

Agree on Some of the Cautions

In addition to agreeing on many of the benefits of TSD, therapists and clients also agree on some of the potential drawbacks or necessary precautions related to TSD. Commensurate with early psychoanalytic precautions, within the contemporary conceptual literature (i.e., the therapist perspective), it has been noted that TSD may distract from the focus of treatment (Sturges, 2012), diminish the therapist's credibility (Audet, 2011), and elevate risk management concerns (Audet, 2011). TSD may also and at times be an inappropriate shortcut to client–therapist joining, and/or may lead impressionable clients to reflect upon themselves in ways that lead them to pursue therapist-inspired, inauthentic goals (D'Aniello & Nguyen, 2017). Whereas TSD is often intended to facilitate client–therapist rapport (Bitar et al., 2014), therapist discipline and restraint (LaPorte et al., 2010) is theorized to maintain the disproportionate give-and-take of the relationship (Audet & Everall, 2003) that is considered central to its uniqueness (LaPorte et al., 2010). Indeed, it may be the uniqueness of the relationship that builds deeper trust and safety (Gutheil & Gabbard, 1993), which in turn results in deeper and lasting changes (Audet & Everall, 2003). Consistent with these precautions, interviewed clients have reported TSD made them feel burdened (Vandenberghe & Silva Silvestre, 2014) or overwhelmed (Audet & Everall, 2003). Additionally, many of the clients in Audet's (2011) interview study who reported TSDs were generally helpful *also* interpreted TSDs as an indication that the therapeutic relationship might have been becoming more personal than professional. A convergence of sources suggests therapists and clients agree that therapists should refrain from higher intimacy TSDs of sexualized content, such as erotic feelings for clients, prior sexual experiences, or personal/romantic relationship failings (Audet, 2011; Audet & Everall, 2003; Fisher, 2004).

From these findings emerges the implication that practitioners should not assume TSD will necessarily have a positive effect on therapeutic relationships. Rather, it may (1) have both positive and negative effects, and (2) have different risks and rewards depending largely on clinical and contextual factors central to the ethics and efficacy of all interventions. Both of these points are discussed further in other discussant chapters within the current section.

Perspectives on TSD Affecting Therapist as Expert

One of the key areas in which therapist and client perspectives often differ is in terms of whether or not (and if so, to what extent) TSD may affect the client's perception of the therapist as expert. This is of importance as clients should expect a certain level of expertise in professional therapy and may even take more seriously and respond more favorably to a therapist they perceive as expert. Therapists and conservative ethicists often worry TSD may compromise a therapist's credibility, though client survey data, as reported within literature reviews, suggests clients tend not to experience generally disclosing or generally non-disclosing therapists as *necessarily more or less* professional or credible (Audet, 2011; Henretty & Levitt, 2010; Marino et al., 2016). As a finding somewhat to the contrary, Stone's (2014) analogue study of 138 participants with histories of eating disorder concluded that participants tended to rate therapists who disclosed their personal histories of eating disorder recovery as significantly *more* credible, trustworthy, and putting forth an appropriate treatment. Clients in Audet and Everall's (2003) interview study rated TSD as among the most helpful interventions, while therapists rated TSD as among the least helpful. Both Carlton's (1993) dissertation research on 60 adolescents and Patrizio's (1991) dissertation research on 300 adolescents concluded in favor of non-disclosing therapists being perceived as more of an expert, albeit with some indication of comparing non-disclosing therapists to over-disclosing therapists.

Applying the prior research to practice, it is reasonable to advise that TSD should not be assumed to necessarily lower client perception of expert. However, findings also suggest a likelihood that a more moderated and relatively conservative approach to disclosing is likely to maintain an optimal balance between therapist as expert and therapist as accessible, empowering, and humanized collaborator. To this end, awareness and attunement to the client's moment-to-moment needs in-session should clue the therapist to when a client might benefit from a brief, relevant, and validating disclosure, or may benefit from the therapist exercising professional restraint and non-disclosure in service of interrupted and unshifted client processing. Maintaining this moment-to-moment balance of relationship structure and reciprocity is likely to maintain engagement and encourage deeper and more vibrant client disclosures, affective expressions, and insights. Prior findings suggest the possibility if not likelihood that TSDs are more often helpful to adults than adolescents. The potential effects of TSD on therapist expertness are more fully discussed in Chapter 30 of this text, by often-cited researcher Cristelle Audet.

Perspectives on Spontaneous TSD or Predetermined Policy

Client survey studies and therapist perspectives often conflict on the extent to which TSD policy and practice should be guided, *primarily*, by predetermined rules and boundaries, or flow primarily from spontaneous occurrences in the relationship. Surveyed clients consistently reported a desire for their therapist's decisions to (or not to) disclose to be driven by the therapist's assessment of what was happening in the relationship at the time (Audet & Everall, 2003; Bitar et al., 2014). There is also a perspective in some research studies that therapists should consider formulating a personal policy on disclosure before opportunities suddenly arise (Bottrill et al., 2010; Henretty & Levitt, 2010). Bottrill et al. (2010) noted that a therapist's personal policy should be based on the range of potentially positive and negative effects of TSD on both clients and therapists themselves. Within Henretty and Levitt's (2010) literature review, it was suggested that therapists might first orient clients to the therapist's policy and ask clients' permission to disclose when opportunities arise in session, as opposed to the therapist making an executive decision in the moment.

Further illustrating the benefits of a more predetermined approach, D'Aniello and Nguyen (2017) propose a method of differentiating TSD as an intervention from TSD of a spontaneous and potentially less appropriate nature. Disclosure as an intervention is described as having a clear purpose related to the therapeutic process, used infrequently, offering the client a unique opportunity to look into themselves, and shifting the therapeutic process without causing role reversal. In contrast, spontaneous TSDs occur when therapists are asked a question by a client and answer it almost automatically. These disclosures are suspected to occur more frequently. Although these disclosures may build rapport, they move the basis of connection into a more personal realm, away from theoretical orientation and professional experience, and in a manner that may have negative impacts on expertness as noted earlier.

Based on research reviewed in this subsection, and with potentially positive *and* negative ramifications of select TSDs in mind, practitioners are advised to formulate and then tell clients about their personal self-disclosure or non-disclosure policy. As discussed in Chapter 2 of this text, the TSD policy should incorporate client expectations for their therapy, and clarify to clients what types, content, and circumstances under which disclosure may occur. Practitioners should subsequently make decisions to or not to self-disclose based on in-session assessments of therapeutic relationship dynamics, the relative strength of the relationship, with clear purposes in mind, and in a manner reasonably consistent with the expectations set forth around the onset of treatment. This general strategy may help to optimize the balance between therapist expertness and emotional accessibility discussed in the previous subsection of this chapter, as mediating the relationship between TSD and positive therapeutic outcomes.

Perspectives on TSD to Severely Compromised Populations

Whereas therapists and clients in research studies consistently agreed on the benefits of TSD in contexts of oppression and stigma, there was a greater level of disagreement in studies where clients had severe illnesses or were involuntarily mandated to therapy. Therapists (Kelly & Rodriguez, 2007) and specifically psychologists (Doremus, 2012) in studies consistently indicated disclosing less to such populations. These findings (largely on Caucasian male and female practitioner perspectives) were somewhat in conflict with Bitar et al.'s (2014) finding from an in-depth qualitative interview study of 10 court mandated Mexican American male clients, who consistently reported favoring Caucasian therapist TSD, as well as McWilliams' (2011) recommendations regarding a higher level of disclosure often being needed to facilitate engagement with psychotic clients. Further discussion is as follows.

As court-mandated and severely ill clients (often seen involuntarily) are very difficult to engage in therapy, it would be reasonable to infer from the research that practitioners may often be reluctant to self-disclose to the degree that may be necessary to overcome engagement barriers. In many cases, this reluctance may relate to personal safety considerations, as discussed in more detail in Chapter 22 of this text. This makes for a challenge because involuntarily mandated and more severely disordered clients often do not respond favorably to traditional therapeutic neutrality. Experiencing the therapist as a real and sincerely interested person is likely to improve engagement and perhaps retention in the manner indicated in limited client survey studies. To this end, and in general, an incrementally greater frequency *of lower intimacy disclosures* may have its advantages and not necessarily elevate risk management concerns, at least in some if not many cases.

Supervisor and Trainee Perspectives on Trainee Use of TSD

Interestingly, there is considerable difference in researcher perspectives and research findings on supervisor versus trainee perceptions of the extent and quality of trainee TSD. During training, it is common for TSD to be overtly discouraged and even a *don't ask, don't tell* subject (Bottrill et al., 2010; Henretty & Levitt, 2010). Supporting this position, in Burkard and colleagues' (2006) qualitative study of 11 trainees, it was common for trainees to report having received minimal or no training in TSD during their graduate education. Given *don't ask don't tell* on the subject, trainees may require encouragement from their supervisor to candidly discuss issues pertaining to disclosure, while supervisors may in turn require similar encouragement from their parent agencies (Bottrill et al., 2010). In Bottrill et al.'s (2010) study, many of the 14 doctoral psychology trainees expressed reluctance to inquire of their supervisors about TSD, particularly with a supervisor they anticipated would be unreceptive or might evaluate them negatively. Suggestive of possible consequences associated with institutional and larger-historical discouragement, trainees in Bottrill et al.'s (2010) study were mostly of factual/historical content rather than real-time feelings discussed previously as often being more helpful to clients. Of similar concern, trainees in this study also frequently reported feeling caught off guard, flustered, and uncomfortable when clients asked them questions of a conversational nature they felt unprepared to answer, uncertain about whether TSD was appropriate (in general), and how to avoid disclosing without offending clients (Bottrill et al., 2010). Contrastingly, in Kircanski's (2015) dissertation research on five videotaped sessions with trauma survivors, trainees used more self-involving disclosures.

Expert opinions, research, and conceptual writings on the relationship between frequency of TSD and level of professional experience are also inconsistent. As noted in Henretty and Levitt (2010), experts have speculated that beginning therapists self-disclose too frequently. However, five studies conducted from 1989–2001 collectively suggested that less experienced therapists tended to disclose *less often* than more experienced therapists (Henretty & Levitt, 2010). Consistent with this last finding, Bottrill et al.'s (2010) qualitative interview study suggested trainees were quite concerned about over/inappropriate self-disclosure and demonstrated such anxiety and even reluctance about intentionally disclosing much of anything. Further, it was noted by D'Aniello and Nguyen (2017) that it is not uncommon for licensed practitioners to consult less, disclose more frequently, and disclose inappropriately as they become independent and feel relatively freer to take such liberties. However, conclusions from Doremus' (2012) dissertation study of 59 psychologists included that frequency of TSD did not significantly increase as years of experience increased.

Implications include that practitioners in a supervisory role should directly bring up TSD with trainees and not assume it has been covered sufficiently in graduate training. Further, supervisors should educate trainees about the potential benefits of self-involving disclosures, as well as timing, relevancy, and process considerations that may be beyond their immediate skill set, though helpful to learn about, reflect upon, and consider implementing as they grow in their clinical skill, experience, and competency. Frequency of trainee TSD should also be assessed, conceptualized, and discussed within supervision.

Conclusions

Similarities and differences between therapist/researcher and client perspectives on TSD are a microcosm of one of the first major points of this text. Whereas the field of psychotherapy has generally moved in a progressive direction since the 1960s, therapists may have gone a step further and clients two steps further in their desire and pursuit of even greater connectivity, reciprocity, and perhaps to a level of intimacy that has yet to be charted in the theory of the therapeutic relationship (Audet, 2011; Bottrill et al., 2010; Henretty & Levitt, 2010). In illustration of this point, prior research suggests that clients may desire more spontaneous and near-purely relationally driven disclosures, while therapists may prioritize a more well-thought-out and clinically informed decision-making process. At the same time, neither perspective appears exclusive to the other.

From this research also emerges the perspective that research-informed practitioners should consider telling clients of their approach to TSD as part of the initial orientation session. Thereafter, clients may benefit more so from a therapist who discloses briefly, infrequently, with clear purposes, and both intended and specific benefits to the relationship. Content likely to be most beneficial to the client includes the therapist's real-time feelings and reactions, positive feelings about the client, lower intimacy demographic details, and possibly higher intimacy historical content when relevant and after a therapeutic relationship has been more firmly established.

At the same time, decisions on whether or not to self-disclose, like all other clinical decisions, must be made based on therapist's intuitive and intrinsic understanding of the client's need in the moment. In turn, this conceptualization should be at least partially informed by a reflection on the scholarly literature, as is the core position of this text and *the major take-away* for the research-informed practitioner.

References

Ackerman, S., & Hilsenroth, M. (2003). A review of therapist characteristics and techniques positively impacting the therapeutic alliance. *Clinical Psychology Review*, *23*(1), 1–33.

Adelman, A., & Malawista, K. (2013). *The therapist in mourning: From the faraway nearby*. New York: Columbia University Press.

Alexander, J., Kolodziejski, K., Sanville, J., & Shaw, R. (1989). On final terminations: Consultation with a dying therapist. *Clinical Social Work Journal*, *17*(4), 307–24.

Aron, L. (2016). The conductor's self-disclosure of negative countertransference in group analytic psychotherapy. *Group Analysis*, *40*(4), 385–97.

Audet, C. (2011). Client perspectives of therapist self-disclosure: Violating boundaries or removing boundaries? *Counselling Psychology Quarterly*, *24*(2), 85–100.

Audet, C., & Everall, R. (2003). Counsellor self-disclosure: Client-informed implications for practice. *Counselling and Psychotherapy Research*, *3*(3), 223–31.

Bitar, G., Kimball, T., Bermúdez, J., & Drew, C. (2014). Therapist self-disclosure and culturally competent care with Mexican-American court mandated clients: A phenomenological study. *Contemporary Family Therapy*, *36*(3), 417–25.

Bottrill, S., Pistrang, N., Barker, C., & Worrell, M. (2010). The use of therapist self-disclosure: Clinical psychology trainees' experiences. *Psychotherapy Research*, *20*(2), 165–80.

Broadbent, J. (2013). 'The bereaved therapist speaks.' An interpretive phenomenological analysis of humanistic therapist's experiences of a significant personal bereavement and its impact upon their therapeutic practice: An exploratory study. *Counselling and Psychotherapy Research*, *13*(4), 263–71.

Burkard, A., Knox, S., Goren, M., Perez, M., & Hess, S. (2006). European American therapist self-disclosure in cross-cultural counseling. *Journal of Counseling Psychology*, *53*(1), 15–25.

Carlton, C. (1993). The effect of therapist self-disclosure and explanation of confidentiality on adolescent clients' willingness to self-disclose and therapist preference (Doctoral dissertation). Retrieved from ProQuest Dissertations and Theses database (No UMI No.).

Chang, D., & Berk, A. (2009). Making cross-racial therapy work: A phenomenological study of clients' experiences of cross-racial therapy. *Journal of Counseling Psychology*, *56*(4), 521–36.

Constantine, M., & Kwong-Liem, K. (2003). Cross-cultural considerations of therapist self-disclosure. *Journal of Clinical Psychology*, *59*(5), 581–8.

Cornett, C. (Ed.). (1993). *Affirmative dynamic psychotherapy with gay men*. Northvale, NJ: Jason Aronson.

D'Aniello, C., & Nguyen, H. (2017). Considerations for intentional use of self-disclosure for family therapists. *Journal of Family Psychotherapy*, *28*(1), 23–37.

Doremus, B. (2012). Psychologist self-disclosure with court-mandated and self-referred clients (Doctoral dissertation). Retrieved from Engaged Scholarship Archive.

Eifert, G., & Forsyth, J. (2005). *Acceptance and commitment therapy for anxiety disorders: A practitioner's treatment guide to using mindfulness, acceptance, and values-based behavior change strategies*. Oakland, CA: New Harbinger.

Eyrich-Garg, K. (2008). Strategies for engaging adolescent girls at an emergency shelter in a therapeutic relationship: Recommendations from the girls themselves. *Journal of Social Work Practice*, *22*(3), 375–88.

Fisher, C. (2004). Ethical issues in therapy: Therapist self-disclosure of sexual feelings. *Ethics & Behavior*, *14*(2), 105–21.

Frawley-O'Dea, M. (2003). When the trauma is terrorism and the therapist is traumatized too. *Psychoanalytic Perspectives*, *1*(1), 67–89.

Goldfried, M., Burckell, L., & Eubanks-Carter, C. (2003). Therapist self-disclosure in cognitive behavior therapy. *Journal of Clinical Psychology/In Session*, *59*(5), 555–68.

Gutheil, T., & Gabbard, G. (1993). The concept of boundaries in clinical practice: Theoretical and risk-management dimensions. *American Journal of Psychiatry*, *150*(2), 188–96.

Henretty, J., & Levitt, H. (2010). The role of therapist self-disclosure in psychotherapy: A qualitative review. *Clinical Psychology Review*, *30*(1), 63–77.

Hill, C., & Knox, S. (2002). Self-disclosure. In J. Norcross (Ed.), *Psychotherapy relationships that work: Therapist contributions and responsiveness to patients* (pp. 255–65). New York: Oxford University Press.

Kelly, A., & Rodriguez, R. (2007). Do therapists self-disclose more to clients with greater symptomology? *Psychotherapy: Theory, Research, Practice, Training*, *44*(4), 470–5.

Kircanski, K. (2015). Student therapists' use of self-disclosure with clients who have experienced trauma (Doctoral dissertation). Retrieved from ProQuest Dissertations and Theses database (No UMI No.).

Kronner, H. & Northcut, T. (2015) Listening to both sides of the therapeutic dyad: Self-disclosure of gay male therapists and reflections from their gay male clients. *Psychoanalytic Social Work*, *22*(2), 162–81.

LaPorte, H., Sweifach, J., & Linzer, N. (2010). Sharing the trauma: Guidelines for therapist self-disclosure following a catastrophic event. *Best Practices in Mental Health*, *6*(2), 39–56.

Lokken, J., & Twohey, D. (2004). American Indian perspectives of Euro-American counseling behavior. *Journal of Multicultural Counseling and Development*, *32*, 320–31.

Marino, C., Child, B., & Krasinski, V. (2016). Sharing experience learned firsthand (SELF): Self-disclosure of lived experience in mental health services and supports. *Psychiatric Rehabilitation Journal, 39*(2), 154–60.

McCarthy Veach, P. (2011). Reflections on the meaning of clinician self-reference: Are we speaking the same language? *Psychotherapy, 48*(4), 349–58.

McWilliams, N. (2011). *Psychoanalytic diagnosis: Understanding personality structure in the clinical process* (2nd ed.). New York: Guilford Press.

Oyer, L., O'Halloran, M., & Christoe-Frazier, L. (2016). Understanding the working alliance with clients diagnosed with anorexia nervosa. *Eating Disorders, 24*(2), 121–37.

Patrizio, T. (1991). Effect of self-disclosure and interpersonal touch on high school students' perceptions of a school psychologist during an initial interview (Doctoral dissertation). Retrieved from ProQuest Dissertations and Theses database (UMI No. 303847435).

Pinto-Coelho, K., Hill, C., & Kivlighan, D. (2015). Therapist self-disclosure in psychodynamic psychotherapy: A mixed methods investigation. *Counselling Psychology Quarterly, 29*(1), 29–52.

Pizer, A. (2016). Do I have to tell my patients I'm blind? *Psychoanalytic Perspectives, 13*(2), 214–29.

Rabinor, J., & Nye, S. (2003). Healing through connection: Self-disclosure in psychotherapy. *Eating Disorders, 11*(3), 235–40.

Rao, N. & Mehra, A. (2015). Hurricane Sandy: Shared trauma and therapist self-disclosure. *Psychiatry, 78*(1), 65–74.

Simonds, L., & Spokes, N. (2017). Therapist self-disclosure and the therapeutic alliance in the treatment of eating problems. *Eating Disorders, 25*(2), 151–64.

Stone, M. (2014). Psychotherapist self-disclosure of personal recovery in treatment of clients with eating disorders: Effects on predicted treatment outcome (Doctoral dissertation). Retrieved from ProQuest Dissertations and Theses database (UMI 3643897).

Sturges, J. (2012). Use of therapist self-disclosure and self-involving statements. *The Behavior Therapist, 35*(5), 90–3.

Vandenberghe, L., & Silva Silvestre, R. (2014). Therapists' positive emotions in- session: Why they happen and what they are good for. *Counselling and Psychotherapy Research, 14*(2), 119–27.

Wetzel, C., & Wright-Buckley, C. (1988). Reciprocity of self-disclosure: Breakdowns of trust in cross-racial dyads. *Basic and Applied Social Psychology, 9*(4), 277–88.

Young L. (2013). Characteristics and practices of sponsored members of Alcoholics Anonymous. *Journal of Groups in Addiction & Recovery, 8*(2), 149–64.

Ziv-Beiman, S., & Shahar, G. (2016). Therapeutic self-disclosure in integrative psychotherapy: When is this a clinical error? *Psychotherapy, 53*(3), 273–7.

CHAPTER 30

Disclosure May Affect (Client Perceptions of) Therapist as Expert

Cristelle Audet, PhD

Discourse on therapist self-disclosure within counseling has progressed beyond disclosure's potentially harmful effects on therapy boundaries to acknowledging ways in which it can occur in service of the client's therapeutic process (Audet & Everall, 2003, 2010; Hill & Knox, 2002; Knox & Hill, 2003). It is well documented that therapist disclosure can shape perceptions of therapist qualities, such as warmth, empathy, congruence, credibility, and trustworthiness (Audet & Everall, 2003, 2010; Hill & Knox, 2002)—qualities known to have a bearing on the therapeutic relationship which, in turn, contributes favorably to therapy outcomes (Norcross, 2011).

While therapist disclosure can be beneficial when 'delivered appropriately,' ethicists have expressed concern about its capacity to compromise boundaries that differentiate the therapist's expert role from the client's role (Barnett, 2011; Gutheil & Gabbard, 1999). To this end, focus in therapy is typically maintained on the client who does the majority of disclosing while the therapist assumes a predominantly non-disclosive stance (Farber, 2006). Understandably, when therapists start to share aspects of their private life with clients, it can be viewed as a departure from therapy norms in tension with conventional constructions of the therapist role (Barnett, 2011; Smith & Fitzpatrick, 1995). In this sense, therapist disclosure would seem inextricably intertwined with 'expertness.'

Arguably, expertness may be more affected in the case of disclosures of personal information about the therapist's private life (extra-therapy), as compared to self-involving disclosures of in-session reactions to the client (intra-therapy) (Knox & Hill, 2003; Myers & Hayes, 2006). In this chapter, the author focuses on extra-therapy disclosure given the perception that it poses greater risk to professional boundaries (Audet, 2011; Henretty & Levitt, 2010). The discussion begins with an exploration of the literature on 'therapist as expert' and ways in which expertness is encapsulated within different theoretical positions vis-à-vis therapist disclosure. After reviewing therapist disclosure research mainly from the client perspective, as it relates to therapist expertness, the author discusses expertness in the context of social constructivism to encourage an alternate view of therapist disclosure with particular implications for working within diversity.

Expertness and Theoretical Conceptualizations of Disclosure

As discussed in prior chapters of this text, theoretical conceptualizations of therapist self-disclosure vary, ranging from traditional psychoanalysts claiming that any form of therapist disclosure will contaminate the transferential process necessary for healing to take place (Goldstein, 1997), to humanists/existentialists advocating therapist transparency to generate the honest, genuine relationship necessary and sufficient for healing (Jourard, 1971). Cognitive behaviorists generally disclose to model strategies for clients to change unhelpful thoughts and behavior (Goldfried, Burckell, & Eubanks-Carter, 2003). Still yet, feminist therapists disclose to render the relationship more egalitarian and empower clients in important therapy decisions (Mahalik, Van Ormer, & Simi, 2000).

Each theoretical stance reflects a particular perspective on whether and why a therapist should disclose and illuminates a relationship between expertness and the extent to which therapists remain aligned with what their theoretical orientation 'allows for.' Theoretical examination of therapist disclosure also points to it having a place in therapy—an intervention with therapeutic purpose—and gives rise to the assumption that it will not necessarily compromise expertness providing certain adherence to theory. This is reflected in claims by Peterson (2002) and Barnett (2011) that disclosure falls within a therapist's role providing it is theoretically supported and does not violate any ethical principles.

On 'Being an Expert'

Being 'expert' can be seen as what separates the therapist from the client, and is likely a characteristic that many clients seek given the general expectation that therapist expertise is key to improving client well-being—otherwise, why bother seeing a therapist (Barnett, 2011)? Some authors have depicted the concept of expert as ambiguous and elusive, with its dynamic and fluid nature rendering it difficult to define and cultivate (e.g., Jennings, Goh, Skovholt, Hanson, & Banerjee-Stevens, 2003). In their attempt to characterize expert counseling, Jennings and colleagues (2003) identified research-informed contributions, which included "experience, personal characteristics of the counselor and therapist, cultural competence, and comfort with ambiguity" (p. 59). Other therapist writers associate expertness with possessing competencies within a specific area of practice and being grounded in the commonly accepted tripartite framework of competency, encompassing the domains of knowledge, skills, and awareness (including values and attitudes) (Arthur & Collins, 2010; Sue, Arredondo, & McDavis, 1992).

In addition to gaining knowledge and experience, expertness can include managing client perceptions by engaging in or refraining from certain behaviors related to professional expectations. One survey study showed 96% of therapist respondents overwhelmingly cited diminishing client perception of expertness as a main reason for not disclosing to clients (Edwards & Murdock, 1994)—suggesting that therapists are interested in expert appearance (Peterson, 2002).

As mentioned in Chapter 7 on training and supervision, counseling trainees initially refrain from self-disclosing to clients for reasons related to competence (Bottrill, Pistrang, Barker, & Worrell, 2010). As with most interventions, there is a developmental process involving reflection on practice to eventually gain expertise in using disclosure. Regardless of how professionals have come to understand how expertness can be accomplished, Jennings et al. (2003) emphasize an interesting distinction between *possessing expertise* and *being perceived as expert*, suggesting that expertness hinges greatly on the client's perspective—an observation that will be elaborated on later in this chapter.

Therapist Disclosure as Balancing and Blurring Boundaries

Ethicists have expressed caution about therapist disclosure's impact on the tenuous balance between personal and professional behavior, surmising that "some boundary crossings may compromise other important therapeutic factors, such as clinicians' objectivity and perceived expertise" (Smith & Fitzpatrick, 1995, p. 502). Weiner (1983) described therapist disclosure as going beyond offering professional expertise—an act of being purposely more open and genuine with the client. In either case, disclosure is seen as stepping outside the professional role.

Analogue studies looking at therapist disclosure's influence on the professional characteristic of expertness have yielded mixed findings (Henretty & Levitt, 2010). They have also been critiqued for being decontextualized given their focus on observer ratings of therapist disclosure in brief mock therapy encounters with non-clients. Oversimplifying the complexity and dynamic process of therapy may, in part, explain equivocal findings from past decades of research (Audet & Everall, 2010; Farber, 2006). Responding to calls to take disclosure research to the field (e.g., Henretty & Levitt, 2010), a growing body of qualitative research forefronting actual clients' therapy experiences challenges the idea that expertness would, unequivocally, be at stake if a therapist were to disclose. Drawing from the author's own research (Audet, 2011; Audet & Everall, 2003, 2010), some clients viewed personal disclosures as exposing the therapist's 'imperfections' and conveying certain fallibility; however, they also saw their therapist as 'more human or real.' Clients still viewed their disclosing therapist as a 'professional with expertise,' indicating that disclosure simply confirmed what they claimed to already know subconsciously—that 'even experts have problems.' In fact, it was experiencing both the therapist's competencies and personal qualities simultaneously that appeared beneficial. Similarly, the therapist's humanity conveyed through disclosure can also 'bring balance' to the therapeutic encounter by facilitating a view of the therapist as sincerely caring, and not exerting superiority over or objectifying the client—a characterization often allotted to being an expert (Audet, 2011; Levitt et al., 2016).

The dimension of similarity has received much attention and appears to shape client perceptions of the therapist possessing expertise. Some clients may appreciate the therapist's lived experience as enhancing the therapist's credibility beyond relying on "theory or a textbook" to respond to client problems

(Audet, 2011, p. 11). Indeed, and as discussed in prior chapters, shared lived experience has been cited as helpful when addressing eating disorders (e.g., Williams & Haverkamp, 2015) and substance abuse (e.g., Ham, Lemasson, & Hayes, 2013), for example, due to the perception that the therapist can 'walk the walk.' Somers, Pomerantz, Meeks, and Pawlow (2014, p. 254) best summarize these findings, stating:

> Perhaps the disclosure implies that the psychotherapist has firsthand experience that increases his or her expertise regarding the problem; that the psychotherapist will be capable of a higher degree of empathy for the client's phenomenological experience; or that the psychotherapist is 'human' or 'normal' or otherwise similar to the client rather than being far-removed.

That said, disclosure can also compromise perceived therapist expertness—bringing to fruition ethicists' concerns of blurred boundaries and, in worse cases, role reversal. Even limited, non-intimate disclosures could lead unsuspecting clients to question whether the therapist will make a habit of disclosure ("Am I going to have to look for another therapist?") and what response is expected in return ("Am I supposed to ask my therapist how that makes him feel?") (Audet & Everall, 2003). A case of what could be considered an egregious use of disclosure leading to role reversal is detailed elsewhere (Audet, 2011; Audet & Everall, 2003), demonstrating how disclosure—particularly those lacking attunement to what is therapeutically relevant or meaningful to the client—impacted perceptions of therapist credibility and competence.

De-Constructing Expertness: Implications for Therapist Disclosure within Diversity

There is growing attention on therapist disclosure in contexts of diversity and its role in "addressing cultural mistrust attitudes of clients, exhibiting a set of culturally competent skills, and establishing client perceptions of therapist expertness," (Constantine & Kwan, 2003, p. 582). Examples of navigating therapist-client difference in culturally mindful ways have begun to surface (Borden, Lopresto, Sherman, & Lyons, 2010; Burkard, Knox, Groen, Perez, & Hess, 2006). As described in Chapter 9 focusing on culture, there is also a body of literature that focuses on desirability of therapist disclosure by clients from different cultural backgrounds (e.g., African Americans, Asian Americans, Mexican Americans), which has implications for being perceived as expert (e.g., Bitar, Kimball, Bermúdez, & Drew, 2014; Cashwell, Scherbakova, & Cashwell, 2003; Cherbosque, 1987; Kim et al., 2003).

That clients from different cultural backgrounds have preferred uses for therapist disclosure highlights what Constantine and Kwan (2003) refer to as "cultural value conscriptions" (p. 585) that can shape their views of therapist expertness. In this regard, Lee (2014) advises on the importance of "clarify[ing] how [the] therapist's personal, professional, or cultural values are disclosed and used in therapy and how the client responds to the therapist's explicit and implicit self-disclosure" (p. 21). To accomplish this, Lee (2014) emphasizes the importance of drawing from epistemologies such as social constructivism that position practitioners "not as the knower or expert but as the learner or collaborator" (p. 22). A social constructivist perspective eschews the notion of 'therapist as expert' and acknowledges that it risks constricting therapeutic conversations, rather than create the necessary space for crucial client knowledge and meanings to emerge (Paré, 2013, 2014). Within this viewpoint, expertness would seem to reside not in *what* or how much a therapist knows but in *how* the therapist navigates the therapeutic conversation in consideration of the client's own interpretations.

Lee (2014) warns us how disclosures of personal, professional, or cultural beliefs will likely convey what the therapist deems "relevant or valued in therapy" (p. 22) and this may be in tension with the client's subjective experiences and therapy expectations, leading to disengagement in therapy. This possibility should be a beacon for therapists to critically monitor their disclosure, both in terms of purpose and content, to empower rather than mitigate the client's voice.

White's (2007) de-centering practices promoted within narrative approaches may prove useful here. Decentering practices aim to shift away from the therapist as expert and center of knowledge production to privileging the client's knowledge and experiences. Through the stances of a beginner's mind, 'not knowing,' and coauthoring, for example, therapists could, at a suitable point in the therapy, create space for the client to express a preferred positioning on disclosure and bring forth a mutual approach. For example, a therapist might explore the idea of disclosure with the client by asking:

- "On occasion therapists may share personal information with clients if it might help move the therapy forward, but this isn't everyone's cup of tea. I'm wondering what, if anything, you would like to tell me about therapists sharing personal aspects of themselves?"
- "What does it mean to you that a therapist shares personal information? Are there any ways you can think of, generally, where sharing might help move therapy forward? Hinder therapy?"
- "What would helpful disclosure look like for you? Unhelpful disclosure?"
- "Would you be willing to let me know if my sharing is ever uncomfortable or unhelpful?"
- [After disclosing] "Within what I have shared, what, if anything, stands out for you? What resonates the most for you? What resonates the least? How does it get you closer to/further from where you would like to be?"

Rather than uncritically apply disclosure, even if grounded within a theoretical perspective or therapeutic intentions, such questions could minimally create opportunity for the client to begin to convey more directly their cultural understandings of disclosure and expertness in a therapy context, and collaboratively create a way forward. For resources to assist therapists in developing a constructivist/poststructuralist understanding of disclosure, the author refers to the works of Kogan and Gale (1997) and Roberts (2005).

Conclusions

Taking a closer look at actual therapy events has broadened understanding in research and practice of how clients view and experience expertness in the context of therapist disclosure. Revisiting Jennings et al.'s (2003) distinction offered earlier, the literature abounds with evidence that disclosure can either hinder or enhance *being perceived as expert*, and this likely hinging on client cultural understandings of expertness. What seems to differentiate those disclosures is therapist attunement, saying 'the right thing at the right time' based on relevance to the client's needs and subjective experience. This points to the importance of clinical judgment in responding to the context in which disclosure is offered—in essence *possessing expertise* in the delivery of disclosure. This author contends that therapists' decisions to disclose should not reside within the preconceived binary of whether or not they will appear expert but in their ability to acknowledge client sociocultural understandings by exercising critical intentionality, attunement to context, and reflexivity. If agreed that expertness is a social construction, practitioners would do well to heed recent calls to develop therapist disclosure as a cultural competence (Bitar et al., 2014; Lee, 2014). Perhaps, in the end, we are not experts in content but experts in engaging clients in a process of change, however much or little therapist disclosure that may entail.

References

Arthur, N., & Collins, S. (Eds.) (2010). *Culture-infused counselling* (2nd ed.). Calgary, AB: Counselling Concepts.

Audet, C. (2011). Client perspectives of therapist self-disclosure: Violating boundaries or removing boundaries? *Counselling Psychology Quarterly*, *24*(2), 85–100.

Audet, C., & Everall, R. (2003). Counsellor self-disclosure: Client-informed implications for practice. *Counselling and Psychotherapy Research*, *3*(3), 223–31.

Audet, C., & Everall, R. (2010). Therapist self-disclosure and the therapeutic relationship: A phenomenological study from the client perspective. *British Journal of Guidance and Counselling*, *38*(3), 327–42.

Barnett, J. (2011). Psychotherapist self-disclosure: Ethical and clinical considerations. *Psychotherapy*, *48*(4), 315–21.

Bitar, G., Kimball, T., Bermúdez, J., & Drew, C. (2014). Therapist self-disclosure and culturally competent care with Mexican-American court mandated clients: A phenomenological study. *Contemporary Family Therapy*, *36*(3), 417–25.

Bottrill, S., Pistrang, N., Barker, C., & Worrell, M. (2010). The use of therapist self-disclosure: Clinical psychology trainees' experiences. *Psychotherapy Research*, *20*(2), 165–80.

Borden, L., Lopresto, C., Sherman, M., & Lyons, H. (2010). Perceptions of self-disclosing counselors among lesbian, gay, and bisexual individuals. *Journal of LGBT Issues in Counseling*, *4*(2), 54–69.

Burkard, A., Knox, S., Groen, M., Perez, M., & Hess, S. (2006). European American therapist self-disclosure in cross-cultural counseling. *Journal of Counseling Psychology*, *53*(1), 15–25.

Cashwell, C., Shcherbakova, J., & Cashwell, T. (2003). Effect of client and counselor ethnicity on preference for counselor disclosure. *Journal of Counseling & Development, 81*(2), 196–201.

Cherbosque, J. (1987). Differential effects of counselor self-disclosure statements on perception of the counselor and willingness to disclose: A cross-cultural study. *Psychotherapy, 24*(3), 434–47.

Constantine, M., & Kwong-Liem, K. (2003). Cross-cultural considerations of therapist self-disclosure. *Journal of Clinical Psychology, 59*(5), 581–8.

Edwards, C., & Murdock, N. (1994). Characteristics of therapist self-disclosure in the counseling process. *Journal of Counseling and Development, 72*(4), 384–9.

Farber, B. (2006). *Self-disclosure in psychotherapy.* New York: Guilford Press.

Goldfried, M., Burckell, L., & Eubanks-Carter, C. (2003). Therapist self-disclosure in cognitive-behavior therapy. *Journal of Clinical Psychology/In Session, 59*(5), 555–68.

Goldstein, E. (1997). To tell or not to tell: The disclosure of events in the therapist's life to the patient. *Clinical Social Work Journal, 25*(1), 41–58.

Gutheil, T., & Gabbard, G. (1999). The concept of boundaries in clinical practice: Theoretical and risk-management dimensions. In D. Bersoff (Ed.), *Ethical conflicts in psychology* (2nd ed., pp. 235–9). Washington, DC: American Psychological Association.

Ham, C., Lemasson, K., & Hayes, J. (2013). The use of self-disclosure: Lived experiences of recovering substance abuse counselors. *Alcoholism Treatment Quarterly, 31*(3), 348–74.

Henretty, J., & Levitt, H. (2010). The role of therapist self-disclosure in psychotherapy: A qualitative review. *Clinical Psychology Review, 30*(1), 63–77.

Hill, C., & Knox, S. (2002). Self-disclosure. In J. Norcross (Ed.), *Psychotherapy relationships that work: Therapist contributions and responsiveness to patients* (pp. 255–65). New York: Oxford University Press.

Jennings, L., Goh, M., Skovholt, T., Hanson, M., & Banerjee-Stevens, D. (2003). Multiple factors in the development of the expert counselor and therapist. *Journal of Career Development, 30*(1), 59–72.

Jourard, S. (Rev. ed.). (1971). *The transparent self.* Princeton, NJ: Van Nostrand.

Kim, B., Hill, C., Gelso, C., Goates, M., Asay, P., & Harbin, J. (2003). Counselor self-disclosure, East Asian American client adherence to Asian cultural values, and counseling process. *Journal of Counseling Psychology, 50*(3), 324–32.

Knox, S., & Hill, C. (2003). Therapist self-disclosure: Research-based suggestions for practitioners. *Journal of Clinical Psychology/In Session, 59*(5), 529–39.

Kogan, S., & Gale, J. (1997). Decentering therapy: Textual analysis of a narrative therapy session. *Family Process, 36*(2), 101–26.

Lee, E. (2014). A Therapist's self-disclosure and its impact on the therapy process in cross-cultural encounters: Disclosure of personal self, professional self, and/or cultural self? *Families in Society: The Journal of Contemporary Social Services, 95*(1), 15–23.

Levitt, H., Minami, T., Greenspan, S., Puckett, J., Henretty, J., Reich, C., & Berman, J. (2016). How therapist self-disclosure relates to alliance and outcomes: A naturalistic study. *Counselling Psychology Quarterly, 29*(1), 7–28.

Mahalik, J., Van Ormer, E., & Simi, N. (2000). Ethical issues in using self-disclosure in feminist therapy. In M. Brabeck (Ed.), *Practicing feminist ethics in psychology* (pp. 189–201). Washington, DC: American Psychological Association.

Myers, D., & Hayes, J. (2006). Effects of therapist general self-disclosure and countertransference disclosure on ratings of the therapist and session. *Psychotherapy: Theory, Research, Practice, Training, 43*(2), 173–85.

Norcross, J. (Ed.). (2011). *Psychotherapy relationships that work: Evidence-based responsiveness* (2nd ed.). New York: Oxford University Press.

Paré, D. (2013). *The practice of collaborative counseling and psychotherapy: Developing skills in culturally mindful helping*. Thousand Oaks, CA: Sage.

Paré, D. (2014). Social justice and the word: Keeping diversity alive in therapeutic conversations. *Canadian Journal of Counselling and Psychotherapy, 48*(3), 206–17.

Peterson, Z. (2002). More than a mirror: The ethics of therapist self-disclosure. *Psychotherapy: Theory, Research, Practice, Training, 39*(1), 21–31.

Roberts, J. (2005). Transparency and self-disclosure in family therapy: Dangers and possibilities. *Family Process, 44*(1), 45–63.

Smith, D., & Fitzpatrick, M. (1995). Patient–therapist boundary issues: An integrative review of theory and practice. *Professional Psychology: Research and Practice, 26*(5), 499–506.

Somers, A., Pomerantz, A., Meeks, J., & Pawlow, L. (2014). Should psychotherapists disclose their own psychological problems? *Counselling and Psychotherapy Research, 14*(4), 249–55.

Sue, D., Arredondo, P., & McDavis, R. (1992). Multicultural counseling competencies and standards: A call to the profession. *Journal of Counseling and Development, 70*(4), 477–86.

Weiner, M. (1983). *Therapist disclosure: The use of self in psychotherapy* (2nd ed.). Baltimore, MD: University Park Press.

White, M. (2007). *Maps of narrative practice*. New York: W.W. Norton & Co.

Williams, M., & Haverkamp, B. (2015). Eating disorder therapists' personal eating disorder history and professional ethics: An interpretive description. *Eating Disorders, 23*(5), 393–410.

Index